The Work–Family Challenge

The Work–Family Challenge

Rethinking Employment

edited by

Suzan Lewis and Jeremy Lewis

SAGE Publications
London • Thousand Oaks • New Delhi

First published 1996

SAGE Publications Ltd
6 Bonhill Street
London EC2A 4PU

SAGE Publications Inc
2455 Teller Road
Thousand Oaks, California 91320

SAGE Publications India Pvt Ltd
32, M-Block Market
Greater Kailash – I
New Delhi 110 048

British Library Cataloguing in Publication data

A catalogue record for this book is
available from the British Library

ISBN 0 8039 7468 X
ISBN 0 8039 7469 8 (pbk)

Library of Congress catalog card number 96–069551

Typeset by M Rules
Printed in Great Britain at the University Press, Cambridge

To Vi Caro and Eric Lewis

Contents

Contributors

Christine Camp has worked as Senior Manager, Equal Opportunities, at Midland Bank, UK, for the past four years. Her specific responsibilities include research, communication and policy development, particularly in the work–family area. She has written a series of research reports for the Race for Opportunity campaign, and is a founder member and chair of a working parents group. Now a mother of two small children, Christine works three days a week at Midland Bank, and is one of a small (but growing) number of managers working flexible hours.

Cary L. Cooper is currently Professor of Organizational Psychology at the Manchester School of Management, and Pro-Vice-Chancellor (External Activities) of the University of Manchester Institute of Science and Technology (UMIST), UK. He is the author of over 70 books (on occupational stress, women at work and industrial and organizational psychology), has written over 250 scholarly articles for academic journals, and is a frequent contributor to national newspapers, TV and radio. He is currently Editor-in-Chief of the *Journal of Organizational Behavior*, Co-Editor of the medical journal *Stress Medicine*, and Fellow of the British Psychological Society, the Royal Society of Arts and the Royal Society of Medicine. He was also the Founding President of the British Academy of Management.

Joyce K. Fletcher is Associate Professor of Cooperative Education at Northeastern University in Boston, USA. She is currently the Asa S. Knowles Research Fellow at Northeastern's newly established Office for the Study of Work and Learning. In her research she uses feminist theory to understand organizational issues related to gender equity, work–family integration and organizational learning.

Judith G. Gonyea is Associate Professor and Chair of the Social Research Department at the Boston University School of Social Work, USA. She also has a faculty affiliation with the Boston University Center on Work and Family. Her research interests are in ageing, family and gender studies and she has written extensively on the phenomenon of family care, the intersection of family and work roles, and the effect of social policies on women's lives. She recently co-authored *Feminist Perspectives on Family Care: Policies for Gender Justice* with Nancy Hooyman (1995). She was also the guest editor of a special issue of *Research on Aging* (March, 1994) devoted to the topic of work and eldercare. Currently, she serves on the editorial boards of the National Academy on Aging's *Public Policy* and *Aging Report*, and the journals *Research on Aging*, *Journal of Gerontological Social Work*, and *Health Care in Later Life*.

Bradley K. Googins is the Founder and Director of the Boston University Center on Work and Family, a multidisciplinary research organization, formed in 1990 under the aegis of the School of Management and the Graduate School of Social Work, Boston, USA. The Center works to bring new solutions and perspectives to family and work issues. He is also an Associate Professor at the Graduate School of Social Work at Boston University, and a recent National Kellogg Fellow (1989–92). He has published extensively on work–family issues, employee assistance programmes and workplace substance abuse. His recent publications include *Balancing Job and Homelife: Changes over Time in a Corporation* (1994), *Work/Family Conflicts: Private Lives – Public Responses* (1991), and *Linking the Worlds of Family and Work: Family Dependent Care and Workers' Performance* (1990).

Lisa Harker has worked as Research and Information Officer at the Child Poverty Action Group, in the UK, since January 1995. Formerly she worked at Daycare Trust, specializing in research into family-friendly policies. She is author of *A Secure Future? Social Security and the Family in a Changing World* (1996) and co-author of *The Family-Friendly Employer: Examples from Europe* (1992), with Christine Hogg, and *Poverty: The Facts* (1996), with Carey Oppenheim.

Helle Holt is a political scientist and researcher at the Danish National Institute of Social Research in Copenhagen, Denmark. Her research fields are: work and family life, gender segregation in the labour market and family-friendly workplaces. She is a co-coordinator of a research network on 'Workplace Contributions to Reconcile Work and Family Life', funded by the European Commission, DGV, and a co-editor of *Reconciling Work and Family Life: An International Perspective on the Role of Companies*.

Jeremy Lewis is a barrister practising at Littleton Chambers, Temple, London. He specializes in employment, discrimination, European and commercial law and is the author of a number of articles on these subjects.

Suzan Lewis is Reader in Psychology at the Manchester Metropolitan University, UK. Her major research interests are in the areas of work, family and organizational change. She has written numerous articles on these topics and is co-author (with Cary Cooper) of *Career Couples* (1989) and *The Workplace Revolution: Managing Today's Dual Career Families* (1993), and co-editor (with Dafna Izraeli and Helen Hootsmans) of *Dual Earner Families: International Perspectives* (1992). She is the founder and co-ordinator of a European roundtable of researchers on work–family policies and practices.

Peter Moss is a Senior Research Officer at the Thomas Coram Research Unit, Institute of Education, University of London, UK. Since 1986 he has also been Coordinator of the European Commission Network on Childcare and other Measures to Reconcile Employment and Family Responsibilities. His main research interests are in the fields of early childhood services, leave arrangements for parents, and the relationship between employment and family life including trends in parental employment.

Phyllis Hutton Raabe is a professor in the Sociology Department of the University of New Orleans, USA. She teaches courses and does research on work–family trends and policies and is particularly interested in viable, alternative work arrangements and career paths. Her recent research includes a study of part-time managers in the US Federal Government and a research project, 'Family-friendly Policies and Women's Employment in the Czech Republic and Slovakia: Continuity or Change?', funded by IREX (International Research and Exchanges Board, Washington, DC). A forthcoming chapter is 'Work/family policies for faculty: How "career- and family-friendly" is academe?', in *Academic Couples*, edited by Marianne Ferber and Jane Loeb.

Rhona Rapoport is Co-director of the Institute of Family and Environmental Research, London, UK. She is a consultant to the Ford Foundation on work and family issues and organizational change, to various projects on gender and organizational change at the Simmons Institute for Leadership and Change, and to the Gender Program of the Consultative Group on International Agricultural Research. She is co-author of the first publication on dual career families and of *Dual Career Families Re-examined: New Integrations of Work and Family*, *Leisure and the Family Life Cycle*, *Fathers, Mothers and Society* and *Men and Women as Equals at Work*.

Karen Taylor was previously an MMU funded research student at the Manchester Metropolitan University, UK, examining the impact of family-friendly employment policies. She is currently employed at the Vegetarian Society.

Ivan Thaulow is a senior researcher at the Danish National Institute of Social Research in Copenhagen, Denmark. He was educated in political science and his major fields of interest are the relation between work and family life, organizational change and human resource development. He is a co-coordinator of a research-network on workplace contributors to reconcile work and family life, funded by the European Commission, DGV, and a co-editor of *Reconciling Work and Family Life: An International Perspective on the Role of Companies*.

Anne Watts has over 10 years experience in equal opportunities, firstly with the National Westminster Bank and since 1988, as Equal Opportunities

Director for Midland Bank, UK. Among her many involvements she is a target team member of Employers' Forum for Childcare, Opportunity 2000 and Race for Opportunity. From 1989 to 1995 Anne was a Commissioner at the Equal Opportunities Commission and in the 1994 Honours List, Anne received an OBE for her services to equal opportunities. She currently sits on CUCO (Commission on University Career Opportunities), the Employers' Forum on Age, and the Equal Opportunities Steering Group for the Open University.

Foreword

The approach of the new millennium is a timely moment to consider the need for change, a time to rethink our attitudes to the way we organize employment to reflect the reality of life for today's workforce. Once the work–family challenge was easily solved, at least for the majority of the population. The man was the breadwinner and his domain was work; the woman was the home maker and the family was her domain – work patterns and social policy all reflected this basic assumption. Whether this stark division of responsibility was ever quite so clear cut, whether it was in fact satisfactory, is a matter of debate. What is not a matter of debate is that those days have gone.

The last decades have seen a revolution in the employment patterns in this country and in much of the developed world. There has been a change in working patterns and practices in society. We have moved away from the large monolithic organizations in which a person could look forward to a job for life. Now more and more people will experience part-time and short-term employment, with a number of job if not career changes, in their working lives.

This changing jobs market has meant that there are fewer jobs specifically geared towards the male-dominated economy and that has implications for men and women alike. Over the past 10 years in the UK approximately two million jobs in areas of traditional male full-time employment, largely in manufacturing, have been lost. The new jobs that have been created, many in the service industries, are often part time. As well as the growth in part-time work, the last decade has seen a growth in temporary and short-term contracts. This has been coupled with an increase in job insecurity and has made it difficult for men and women to plan for their careers, homes and families. This in turn has a destabilizing effect on family life and can prevent people reaching their full potential both at home and at work.

Many women choose, or have no alternative, to work and most two-parent families today are also two-earner families. As a result of the shifting balance within the traditional family unit we can no longer take any roles for granted. This means that over the past 30 or 40 years successful relationships between men and women have often had to be renegotiated to accommodate change. This has often been painful but the outcome has been, and will continue to be, a constructive new definition of roles for both sexes. We see signs of progress everywhere: more men at the school gates, pushing buggies, changing nappies. The attitude of many men to their family commitments is changing, especially in younger men. Many today want to play a greater role in their families, leading to a better balance in their lives as well as in the lives of their partners.

It is not only the care of children that places demands on today's workforce – parents or not, many people now have responsibility for elderly relatives. The care of the elderly is becoming an important issue with the growth of the number of people living into their eighties. The main burden of their care falls disproportionately on women, a whole army of women who give freely of their time, often without pay and often whilst holding down a job and other family responsibilities.

There are other demands too: those that society imposes upon its citizens to participate fully in civic society. We recognize now that a truly civilized society has links based not merely on family ties but also on communities. We come together through our churches, our schools, and our clubs and voluntary associations. All these make demands on our time. In fulfilling these demands along with those of family life we become more rounded personalities.

But what has all this to do with employers? This book shows that it has everything to do with employers. The workplace is not isolated from society. People do not leave their problems at home when they cross the threshold at work. If employees are to perform to their maximum potential for the benefit of their employers, then they have to be seen as rounded personalities, not as one-dimensional entries on a balance sheet.

For me this book has two clear and positive messages. Firstly, that 'the work–family challenge' is not a woman's issue. This is an issue of crucial importance to men. If employers recognize that men too have a legitimate wish to participate in their families and in the wider community, then organizations will really begin to change for the benefit of employers and employees alike. Once that is realized, then the second message of this book is this: these changes work! By rethinking their employment practices to reconcile work and non-work responsibilities, employers can not only achieve a better motivated workforce but a more productive one as well.

I welcome this book for its thoughtful contribution to a debate which is of crucial importance to us all. I enjoyed reading it on a number of levels: as the daughter of a working mother who still managed to give me all the love and support I needed; as a working parent myself, trying to do my best to fulfil all the roles that have come to me; as a barrister working in the field of employment law; and as an employer whose former pupil has co-edited this excellent book.

Cherie Booth QC

PART 1
THE CONTEXT FOR CHANGE

1

Rethinking Employment: An Organizational Culture Change Framework

Suzan Lewis

> Traditional assumptions about the separation of work life and personal life are no longer viable, but we have not yet created a coherent set of new values and beliefs to take their place.
>
> Rosabeth Moss Kanter, *When Giants Learn to Dance*

Most people in the industrialized world will combine employment with the care of others – children, adults or elders – at some stage in their working lives. Yet paid work is taking up ever more of people's lives, leaving little time to fit in other demands and activities (Hewitt, 1993; Schor, 1991). The question of how to bring about change in employing organizations so that people can meet the demands in the interdependent domains of work and family has been widely debated and growing numbers of employers are developing formal policies designated as 'family-friendly', (Galinsky et al., 1991; Hogg and Harker, 1992). Nevertheless, the spread of these initiatives remains limited (Brannen et al., 1994); the take-up of policies, especially by men, remains low even when they are available (Haas and Hwang, 1995); and although the management of change has become an integral part of organizational life in the 1990s, dominant organizational cultures and traditional values remain resistant to change in this respect. It is important at this stage to take stock and ask to what extent traditional assumptions about the separation of work and personal lives are being challenged by current workplace initiatives and how further progress can be encouraged.

This book explores the potential for and achievability of employment based on emergent new values, which does not discriminate against those with caring or other non-work responsibilities, and which provides opportunities for people to realize their full potential in work and non-work domains. Although this has the potential to benefit both employers and employees, the goal is often referred to as making organizations more 'family-friendly'. We consider the appropriateness and limitations of this and related terms throughout the book. The contributors explore the contexts for bringing about organizational change, examine current initiatives and processes, and discuss contemporary issues and agendas in the bid to create the new set of values to replace outmoded assumptions about the separation of work and family.

Context

The need for a new set of organizational assumptions and values in relation to work and family life stems from the profound and ongoing changes in families, in the composition of the workforce, in employing organizations and in the nature of work. Within families the once traditional pattern of breadwinner husband and homemaker wife is now a minority form and dual-earner families are increasingly the norm in two-parent families including those with young children. While a number of factors have contributed to this trend, including economic need and women's desire for independence, contemporary job uncertainties and the demise of the job for life make the reliance on one income an increasingly risky strategy for family support. At the same time, however, trends such as the ageing of the population, and public policies such as the encouragement of care in the community in the UK, which relies heavily on informal care by family members (Finch and Mason, 1993) ensure that family caring responsibilities are seldom limited to the child rearing years. Within dual-earner families partners are renegotiating traditionally gendered roles to adapt to new realities and expectations (Lewis, 1994). Although women continue to retain the majority of family caring work (Hooyman and Gonyea, 1995), there are nevertheless shifts in men's family involvement and their willingness to modify work for family, particularly among younger generations (Wilkinson, 1994; New Ways to Work, 1995). Increasingly, then, the workforce is composed of women and men with responsibilities for both the care and the economic support of families, who seek a balance between their work and private lives.

Technological development and the globalization of markets have wrought great changes in the nature of work and of employing organizations. Technology has eliminated the need for many routine jobs and blurred the boundaries between work and non-work time. It has become more feasible for employees to choose when and where they work, but technologies such as computer, e-mail and mobile telephones also make it more possible for work to spill over and intrude into family or private time. With the demise of jobs for life and widespread job insecurity many employees feel they need to be seen to be working harder and may be reluctant to make use of the potential benefits of technology.

Employing organizations are also facing new challenges within the global market place. There is a drive for greater productivity and quality and a need for a flexible workplace which can respond rapidly to new technology and changing markets. Many organizations have cut the size of their core workforce and moved towards flatter, less hierarchical structures with a parallel drive to empower individual or teams of employees to be more responsible and accountable, and to work more autonomously. Restructuring may provide opportunities for greater flexibility for employees to manage their work and non-work lives, or may be used to achieve flexibility in numbers from the employers' perspective, creating insecurity and disempowering employees in managing their personal lives.

It has been suggested that there is a now a new psychological contract between employers and employees (Herriot, 1992). Workers, it is argued, no longer expect jobs for life, but do expect opportunities for self-development. This is usually interpreted in terms of employability but, given the interdependence between work and family, also encapsulates opportunities to balance work and family in an optimal way.

As old certainties give way to dynamic new realities, traditional assumptions about the separation of work and family become more anachronistic than ever. Individuals and families may be supported to some extent by public policies which recognize the potential impact of current structural and social change. However national socio-political contexts differ in the extent to which they view the reconciliation of work and family as a public or a private concern (see Moss, Chapter 2; Gonyea and Googins, Chapter 5), and in the extent to which social policy is based on the realities of current diversity in family life. Thus the notion of the working mother informs social policy in, for example, Sweden, Denmark and France, while policy continues to be based on the outmoded ideal of the single-breadwinner family in the UK and the USA (Pascal, 1986; Lambert, 1993). However, while supportive social policies may contribute to the welfare of the contemporary workforce this does not in itself preclude the need for organizational change. Thus, for example, even in Sweden, where there has long been a political commitment to equality in the family as well as the workplace, men still tend to be reluctant to modify work substantially for family because of prevailing gendered expectations entrenched in organizational cultures (Haas and Hwang, 1995).

An Organizational Change Framework

It is clear that further progress requires fundamental organizational change, involving changes in the beliefs, values and norms that comprise organizational culture, as well as the work structures that stem from these values, to better reflect contemporary realities. The process of bringing about organizational change involves a number of stages including: clarification of terms, objectives and responsibilities, innovation and implementation, overcoming inevitable resistance to change, and evaluation. This chapter considers each of these stages in relation to work and family as a framework for the discussions in the remainder of the book.

Clarification of Terms

In an ever changing world there is a need to constantly reexamine the meanings and implications of the terms we use. 'Family-friendly' and 'traditional' employment are historical and social constructs which cannot be understood in isolation from dominant ideologies of family and work, in a particular time and place. The traditional model of work, often referred to as the male model (Pleck, 1977; Cook, 1992), embodies an expectation that the ideal employee will work full time and continuously from the end of education to retirement, making no concessions to family involvement. This model may have been family-friendly at one period in history in so far as it produced a family wage, in a society assumed to be dominated by male breadwinner families. However, it is debatable even in those circumstances whether a father's virtual absence in parent–child interactions, and women's lack of opportunities for generating income or for self-expression through paid employment, were ideal for families. The problem now is that the traditional model of work has tended to persist despite fundamental changes in the nature of families, the workforce, and indeed of work itself.

What is a *Family*?

Families come in many different forms. They include two-parent, single-parent and reconstituted families, households with young, teenaged or adult children, people in a heterosexual or gay relationship, living with friends, or in nuclear or extended families, living close together or geographically distant. Within these diverse structures men and women have a range of responsibilities determined by kinship, and to a large extent by ascribed gender roles which assume that women do not play a significant role in the labour market. To date so-called family-friendly workplace initiatives have largely tended to overlook diversity, focusing on parents of young children and, occasionally, eldercare responsibilities. This has also been reflected in discussions at national government and also European Union levels (see Moss, Chapter 2). Other relationships which make claims on employees' time are often ignored or devalued. Family has also tended to be defined as women's domain. Policies have been used primarily to enable mothers to combine employment with the care of young children. Few employers deliberate about how to become more father-friendly, even in countries subscribing to an ideology of equal parental responsibilities (Haas and Hwang, 1995). The importance of stressing that work and family is not only a women's issue is emphasized throughout the book.

Some US companies now substitute the term 'work/life policies' for work and family initiatives. Clearly this is useful in broadening the framework for consideration, and avoids judgemental attitudes about what constitutes a family. However, a danger with this and other terms which move beyond the family is that, unless they are associated with shifts in gender attitudes, pressing needs for family care and men's family roles may be totally removed from the agenda, while the importance of factors such as child welfare and the well-being of other family members may be overlooked. It may need specific efforts to change cultures to recognize that flexibility or other benefits can be legitimately used by men as well as women, for family as well as other activities.

What is *Friendly*?

The idea that employment can be friendly/responsive/supportive towards other social systems beyond work may also be open to different interpretations. This may be interpreted in the sense that employment does not conflict with family, or even supports people with family commitments to enable them to do their jobs. On the other hand it might imply that favours or benefits are provided, the implication being that this benefits employees and their families, but not organizations. Employers may thus feel justified in withholding such favours from those who have not earned them, or who are seen as dispensable by the organization. Family-friendly initiatives in this sense may be interpreted as perks, similar to recreation facilities, rather than as a basic human need and right, akin to basic health and safety provisions. This add-on approach to work and family issues can detract from the need to examine current policies and practices which can be hostile to family life, such as the requirement that employees demonstrate commitment by long hours in the office (see Lewis and Taylor, Chapter 9) or willingness to relocate at any time (see Cooper, Chapter 7).

What is a Family-Friendly *Organization*?

Organizations are often described as 'family-friendly' on the basis of the number of formal policies initiated to meet the needs of employees with family commitments. While these are important indicators of the will to change, they do not guarantee an informal culture which supports families (See Holt and Thaulow, Chapter 6; Lewis and Taylor, Chapter 9). Moreover, the idea of a family-friendly *organization* may be outliving its usefulness not least because the label implies that there is a central employing organization which has policies which affect all its workers. If, as is being predicted, companies are becoming 'organizing organizations' (Handy, 1994), wherein most people become contingent workers, it follows that few people will benefit from such policies. Already family-friendly policies are becoming increasingly irrelevant as more and more people work on temporary contracts in the periphery of organizations. This sort of employment may be family-unfriendly if it does not meet families' needs for economic support.

Lambert (1993) argues that 'family-responsive', as the term is currently used, is a misnomer, but suggests that we should be not changing the name but changing the policies so that rhetoric reflects reality. Equally, however, it may be argued that as the language we use can play a crucial role in the way we construct our own realities (Spender, 1980) it may be essential that we name the issue accurately, so that the objectives can be identified. We need to constantly reappraise the appropriateness of the terminology that we use in this debate. Another form of terminology suggested in this book, and favoured by the European Union, is the 'reconciliation' of employment and family responsibilities. Peter Moss (Chapter 2) argues that reconciliation implies a process of seeking accommodation between the needs and interests of employers, employees and those for whom they care. The goal then becomes employment which can be reconciled with family and other needs throughout the life cycle. It may not resolve the issue of how to define the family, but it has the potential to encompass the need for balance and for accommodation by all parties.

Given the lack of consensus about terminology we have not prescribed a single term for use in the book. Reliance on one term may be useful in providing a shorthand for selling the ideas, but it risks losing much of the richness and diversity of the various approaches. However, all the contributors use the terms critically. We are clear that we are addressing not narrow notions of family, or benefits, but issues of organizational change which recognize individuals' needs for balanced lives. Thus certain authors discuss family-friendly employment in terms of meeting employees' needs to provide economic support and practical and emotional care (Holt and Thaulow, Chapter 6), of meeting business and family needs (Harker, Chapter 4), or of avoiding being family-hostile or -disruptive (Cooper, Chapter 7). Others reject terms such as 'family-friendly' and focus on new ways of conceptualizing work. Whatever the preferred term it is apparent that both support for family care and modifications to work structure have a part to play in bringing about change in organizational values and behaviours.

Clarification of Objectives

This raises the need to clarify the short- and long-term objectives of organizational changes in relation to work and family. It is instructive in this respect to examine the rationales put forward for implementing work family policies and practices, and particularly to examine the assumptions, both explicit and implicit, which underpin these arguments. The main arguments that have been used are the equal opportunities, quality of life and business rationales. These are interdependent rather than mutually exclusive, based on a difference in emphasis and, to some extent, stemming from different assumptions. All have developed over time from a relatively narrow focus, to endorse broader needs for organizational change. More recently there has been a call for a synergy approach (Bailyn, 1993; Fletcher and Rapoport, this volume, Chapter 11) which emphasizes meeting the needs of all stakeholders equally.

Equal Opportunities, Diversity and Gender Equity

Proponents of change differ in the extent to which they emphasize gender equality as a primary goal. For example, Peter Moss (Chapter 2) points out that the EU goal of reconciliation of work and family life is grounded in the drive for gender equality, although economic and quality of life goals are also important considerations. Commercial organizations are more likely to emphasize the business payoffs of equality.

Equal opportunities rationales for recognizing the interdependence of work and family take a number of forms. At its most basic, the equal opportunities objective seeks *to give women and men equal access to paid work.* Given women's greater traditional involvement in family care, this can be addressed by providing support for childcare or other care, and time and flexibility to fit in family demands. Historically this stems from debates about the rights of women with family responsibilities to take up paid work. Some, particularly Marxists, assumed that women's presence in the labour market would in itself bring about equality in the workplace and beyond. However, experience tells us otherwise. Women's employment guarantees neither equality in achievement and opportunities at work, nor a redistribution of unpaid work within families.

A more developed objective is *to achieve equal representation of women and men at all levels of organizations.* Work and family policies or practices are often conceived as removing barriers to women's achievement at work. However, the glass ceiling usually remains intact even in organizations with formal equal opportunities or family-responsive policies and practices. This is hardly surprising as women's greater family responsibility is only one, albeit a very important, factor contributing to gender inequality. Other factors such as the sex segregation of the labour market, undervaluing of the work women do, stereotyping, discrimination, women's exclusion from formal and informal networks of power and decision making and many others help to maintain the status quo and perpetuate inequalities. Moreover, some initiatives designed to be family-friendly, such as part-time work or career breaks, without concomitant changes in other aspects of organizational cultures, can actually perpetuate and exacerbate gender inequalities in all spheres, by creating 'mommy tracks'.

The problem with this approach is that it attempts to remove barriers to promotion within current systems, rather than questioning the appropriateness of these systems and structures. This overlooks the male bias in organizational cultures, which are based around traditional male lifestyles. Initiatives such as childcare assistance enable women to act and succeed as surrogate men, putting in long hours of work and acting as though they have no primary responsibilities for family. This does not challenge beliefs and values about traditional ways of working and about the interdependence of work and personal lives.

Consequently equal opportunities arguments are moving away from an emphasis on sameness to take account of the differences between women and men, whether biologically, historically or culturally determined (Abdela, 1995; Cockburn, 1991). It is increasingly recognized that women and men have different needs, and bring different attributes to the workplace. Too often, however, the focus is on the different needs rather than on valuing the different attributes. Initiatives such as career breaks enable women to follow a different career path to those without family responsibilities, but if different is interpreted as deviant (from the accepted norm of continuous careers), and if this difference is not valued equally, such well-meaning initiatives may contribute to the perpetuation of women's second-class status in the labour market and society in general. The diversity approach goes a step further by highlighting the different contributions diverse groups can make to organizations. It argues for culture change such that diversity is valued rather than assimilated and stresses the business advantages of such an approach (Herriot and Pemberton, 1995). Relating this to work and family, the objective becomes *to enhance opportunities for men and women to adapt work for family reasons, with the diverse work patterns that emerge from these adjustments being as equally valued as traditional patterns of work.* Phyllis Raabe (Chapter 10) points out some of the assumptions about standard and non-standard forms of work which mitigate against the valuing of diversity in current contexts.

The diversity approach can encompass employees' diverse work family situations, but is nevertheless limited by its focus on the workplace. A gender equity approach (Rapoport and Rapoport, 1975; Bailyn, 1993; see Fletcher and Rapoport, Chapter 11) extends this argument by emphasizing equity and fairness of rewards and constraints at the workplace and beyond. For gender equity to occur it has to be taken for granted that men and women are equally responsible for generating family income and for family care giving. Within the workplace this requires not just recognition of diverse constraints on people's working lives imposed by family commitments, but also a reevaluation of organizational practices which render it difficult to achieve work and family goals. The objective of the gender equity case can thus be expressed as *to challenge and modify all organizational practices based on an assumed separation between work and family lives so as to empower men and women to make optimum contributions in both spheres.*

This implies a need to address not only work structures but also the ways in which gender is socially constructed and reproduced within organizations and families. Women's family roles, especially as mothers, tend to be highly visible in organizations, but they are frequently played out in a context where the dominant social constructions of the ideal mother and the ideal worker are mutually exclusive (Lewis, 1991). Men's parenting and other family roles are much less visible than their provider roles, in the workplace and sometimes even in the family. Another goal is therefore *to make women's and men's family and work roles equally visible, legitimate and valued.* This involves a commitment to encouraging an equitable division of labour in the home, which is explicit in the European Commission's agenda on reconciliation (see Moss, Chapter 2), but is not always implied or intended in workplace change objectives.

The Quality of Life Rationale: Stress and Well-Being

The quality of life argument for family-friendly employment rests on the case that multiple roles in work and family have the potential to create stress. It is based on a growing literature which examines the relationships between work, family and well-being. This includes the long tradition of examining the impact of maternal employment on women's well-being, as well as the impacts on other family members (Repetti et al., 1989; Barling, 1994; Barnett et al., 1992; Noor, 1994; Warr and Parry, 1982). Other research stems from the exposure of the 'myth of separate worlds' of work and family (Kanter, 1977) and subsequent recognition and examination of work and family linkages for men as well as women (Zedeck, 1992; Zedeck and Mosier, 1990; Bolger et al., 1989; Jones and Fletcher, 1993). The quality of life approach recognizes that multiple roles can be sources of satisfaction (Baruch and Barnett, 1986; Crosby, 1987; Kagan and Lewis, 1993) and even protect against stress in some circumstances. However, it is argued that multiple roles can also be a source of role strain, particularly role conflict and overload, which in turn are associated with stress, job dissatisfaction, burnout and other negative consequences for individuals, families and, by implication, organizations (Lewis and Cooper, 1988). It is argued that role strain is due to the failure of organizations to adapt to demographic and social changes, rather than to any inherent conflict between the two domains (Lewis and Cooper, 1987; 1988; Cooper and Lewis, 1993).The psychosocial rationale is linked to the business argument in that a stressed workforce has costs for organizations, and is supported by evidence that family-oriented policies, especially flexibility and supervisor supportiveness, are associated with enhanced perceived control over work and family and decreases in work family conflict (Thomas and Ganster, 1995).

The basic objective of this approach therefore is *to adapt organizational policies and structures to enable people to manage multiple demands in work and family with maximum satisfaction and minimum stress.*

Clearly some feelings of control over where and when work is performed are necessary to avoid strain in work and family management. Are they also sufficient? One implicit assumption underpinning the quality of life approach is that time spent in work, rather than the nature of work itself, is the source of conflict, overload and stress. For example, Barling (1994) argues that the implementation of flexible or reduced hours schedules is based on the assumption that work exerts a negative effect on families only to the extent that it keeps people away from their families. Atypical work schedules, career breaks, and even on-site childcare, it can be argued, all give people the opportunity for more time with family members. However, Barling argues that the quality of the work, rather than the amount or timing of the work, is critical to an understanding of the balance between work and family. This is because stress from the workplace spills over to affect family interactions and experiences (MacEwen and Barling, 1991), which in turn spill back into the workplace (Barnett, 1994). A further assumption which could be implicit in the stress rationale, then, is that organizations need to examine all their practices, concerning both work time and other conditions of work, to determine their impacts on work and family stress.

Following this argument we can identify a broader objective which is implied by the quality of life argument. This is *to reduce stress at work and minimize the potential negative impact of work on families and vice versa.* This implies that employers may have a responsibility not only to their employees, but also to their employees' families. Concern for child welfare, for example, would be a legitimate organizational concern, both in its own right, and because of the importance for employees' own well-being. This points to the need for organizations to examine their overall practices and to identify systemic stressors and ways of reducing these to ensure the well-being of employees and their families. It is worth noting, however, that organizations implementing stress reduction initiatives tend to be more willing to consider ways of enabling people to adapt to the stress of current systems than to focus on ways of changing the nature of those systems (Burke, 1993). It is not surprising therefore if the response to the quality of life argument tends to be to add policies to existing cultures, rather than to change fundamental organizational structures.

A further assumption of the quality of life rationale is that it is objective rather than subjective demands of work and family roles which have the potential for conflict, overload and energy depletion. A contrasting argument is that it is the subjective appraisal of the demands that determine the outcomes. For example Marks (1977; 1994) argues that time and energy expand to meet the demands of roles to which we are highly committed, and that a balanced set of commitments is less stressful than over- or under-commitment to one role. Commitment to a role is related to the extent to which it is central to a person's identity, with the demands of roles with which we are closely identified being viewed most positively (Burke and Reitzes, 1991). Marks (1994) argues that cultural systems differ in the extent to which they encourage balanced commitments. Those cultures which encourage equally positive commitments to all roles and activities generate low strain and high energy. In contrast, those which consider some roles and activities as more legitimate than others generate high levels of strain, anxiety, preoccupation and feelings of scarce energy and time (Marks, 1994). There is some debate about whether a balance is needed between all roles or just core roles, and whether a balanced set of commitments will be consistent with high levels of well-being in all circumstances (O'Neil and Greenberger, 1994). Nevertheless, this approach does suggest that social systems which acknowledge family and other commitments to be equally legitimate to occupational demands and activities, may create less stress. Family-friendly policies which provide greater control over time or place of work may thus not be sufficient if the non-occupational uses to which time is put are not valued and if parental and other family roles are considered less important than occupational roles.

A further objective then would be *to develop organizational cultures which respect people's overall identities and encourage balanced commitments.*

In this respect organizations cannot be considered in isolation from the social contexts in which they operate. Wider social norms and practices which reinforce a view that, for example, family roles are more important than occupational roles for women, and occupational roles are more important than family roles for men, do not encourage balanced commitments and may therefore increase stress. Social policies such as parental leave and paternity leave can help to encourage greater balance, and interact with workplace policies to acknowledge employees' full needs and identities.

While overlapping in some respects with both the equal opportunities and economic arguments, the psychosocial approach helps to focus on conditions of work and on well-being of families. It also points to the need to regard employees as whole people with integrated identities.

The Business Case

The business argument draws on both the psychosocial and equal opportunities arguments but stresses bottom line advantages of adapting to change. It moves away from the view that change is a luxury or a moral imperative towards a view that recognizing the connectedness of people's work and personal lives is a strategic business adaptation. Any successful organizational change requires that all those involved are convinced of its value. This involves communication in language which people understand, and appealing to and building upon existing value and cognitive frameworks. This is the strength of the business argument. It also has the potential to move responsibility for change from the province of personnel or human resource departments to that of line management as it addresses a central business concern. It is clear from the contributions to this book that this is the most widely used and potentially useful rationale for bringing about change.

The business case like other rationales has developed from a relatively narrow to a broader argument. It has often stemmed from a concern about the cost of losing highly trained (usually women) employees after they have children. This concern has been strongest in sectors such as the financial sector which rely heavily on internal sources of labour. More recently it has been broadened to take account of other contemporary business concerns, and Gonyea and Googins (Chapter 5) argue that work and family balance should now be regarded as a key business concern and strategic tool.

At its most basic, the major objective of the business rationale can thus be expressed as *to reduce stress, and strengthen equal opportunities in so far as this will enhance the performance of the organization.* This implies that business needs are paramount. In practice most proponents of family-friendly employment draw on multiple and related arguments, although they are not always viewed as compatible. It can be argued that the psychosocial argument prioritizes the needs of workers, and the equal opportunities case emphasizes a particular set of human values. As long as these are viewed as compatible with business needs there is no problem. However, to the extent that they are not seen as compatible, family-friendly initiatives will be relegated to the margins. It is increasingly being argued that the goals can be compatible, and that we should be adopting a *synergy* approach: that is, looking for solutions which will benefit employers, workers and families and the wider society

(Bailyn, 1993; Cooper and Lewis, 1995). Joyce Fletcher and Rhona Rapoport (Chapter 11) illustrate the processes which might be involved in seeking such solutions within the workplace. The broader, long-term objective of this approach can therefore be summarized as *to work towards solutions to work and family issues which are mutually beneficial to all stakeholders.* Unlike other approaches this explicitly regards different stakeholders as equally important. The aim here is for systemic change, including shifts in fundamental ways of working, and in the distribution of power. This reflects calls by business leaders and managers to develop ways of working which will benefit all stakeholders, rather than the traditional narrow focus on single stakeholder groups such as shareholders or clients (RSA, 1994), and is also reflected in the European Union's goal of reconciliation (see Moss, Chapter 2).

It can be argued that this requires organizations to develop a sense of social responsibility for the broader community in which they operate. Many current organizational trends are contradictory in this sense. For example, a period of downsizing may be followed by the development of work–family and other policies for the core workforce. This is double edged: work–family balance may be achieved for the minority at the expense of the majority. To what extent can solutions be found which meet all needs? This question is debated at various levels within the book.

Delineation of Responsibilities

The effective management of change requires a third form of clarity: that of relative responsibilities. Within organizations responsibility for change may lie with senior management, human resource professionals, line managers and/or work groups. Lisa Harker (Chapter 4) also points to the role of trade unions and Fletcher and Rapoport (Chapter 11) point to a possible role for researchers or consultants as outsiders working collaboratively with those in the workplace. However, organizations do not exist in a vacuum. The interrelated systems of work and family also interact with wider social contexts which they influence and are influenced by. It is also necessary to consider the role and responsibilities of different levels of government, and individuals. Countries differ, for example, in the extent to which family care is considered to be primarily the responsibility of government or individual families, or can become the responsibility of employers. The latter view assumes that care is the responsibility of families, and that employers who take people away from their caring responsibilities have an obligation or a choice to replace that care. Where there is an infrastructure of quality public provision of care, employers may bear less responsibility, while the absence of such an infrastructure requires employers to consider such provisions (see Harker, Chapter 4). Other responsibilities, such as the provision of adequate working conditions and flexibility at work, are clearly more within the domain of organizational responsibility. Nevertheless, states legislate on health and safety at work, and clearly could do so on other conditions of work were this to be considered appropriate (see Lewis, Chapter 3). The clarification of the objectives of family-friendly employment thus needs to include debating where various responsibilities lie for the reconciliation of work and family. What is the role of legislation and social policy? Do they for example, create conditions for change, legitimate changes already occurring, or remove the need for employers to consider change?

Bringing about Change

Organizational culture change depends on a focus on process rather than outcomes. This process requires actions appropriate to context, including both broad social, political and economic context, and local context at the organizational or even departmental level. It is therefore not possible to prescribe detailed and widely applicable strategies, only to explore useful processes. Within this framework a number of questions need to be considered for working towards a change in assumptions about the connectedness of work and family. These are debated throughout the book.

First, what are the conditions for different forms of change to occur? The conditions which will enable men to be involved in family life may be different from, and not just a development of, conditions to enhance women's balance of work and family life.

Secondly, what are the crucial components of the change process?

Thirdly, what are appropriate models of change? The change process may involve incremental change, full scale innovation or a combination of both over time. Incremental change involves minimal disruption and therefore may encounter less resistance. An example of incremental change would be the introduction of policies such as family leave. This raises the issue on the agenda and makes the work–family interface visible. If it can be shown that this is beneficial and does not cause the disruption that some may fear, it paves the way for the introduction of other policies or practices. It can be argued that this approach creates the conditions for more fundamental change and can gradually work towards, for example, securing the acceptance of more flexibility for men as well as women. This model, which is illustrated in the case studies in Chapter 8 and Chapter 9, is the one most frequently adopted, often with a considerable degree of success. It has not yet led to widespread acceptance of men's family roles, although this may be because the change process remains at a relatively early stage. Alternatively it may be argued that a focus on marginal policies detracts from the central issues.

More abrupt change or innovation requires major adjustments. The process of innovation is illustrated by Fletcher and Rapoport in Chapter 11. Successful change is likely to involve engagement with topical concerns and perspectives and hence innovation can occur in association with other changes. For example rigid boundaries between departments are increasingly viewed as malfunctional as it is recognized that cross-disciplinary project teams develop more creative and productive ways of working. In this context it may be easier to see the concomitant need to reduce the rigidity of work and family boundaries. Innovation, however, requires a willingness to try new ways of doing things and may involve more risk taking and hence meet more resistance than incremental change.

Fourthly, how can resistance to change be overcome? Both incremental and innovative change are likely to meet with some initial resistance. There will always be those who argue that 'this is the way we have always done things', or 'call me old fashioned, but I think if people can't give total dedication they should not be working'. Clearly these are not functional attitudes in today's ever changing workplaces. Nevertheless it is important to acknowledge that these views exist and to deal with the anxieties which underpin them. Other attitudes which can block change include feelings of resentment by those who believe that colleagues with family commitments are being treated more favourably than others. This implies that people should be treated equally, that is the same regardless of their needs and constraints, rather than equitably to enable them to do their jobs (Bailyn, 1993), and this assumption must also be addressed.

Evaluation

Once changes have been implemented there remains a need to ensure that they are effective. Most research evaluating work–family initiatives has examined cost effectiveness (Truman, 1986; Holterman, 1995). This is necessary to convince management of its value as well as to persuade other organizations of the benefits involved. The examination of cost effectiveness is important in evaluating success in terms of the business case. However, a synergy approach also implies the need to examine quality of life and gender equity outcomes. Furthermore there are both narrow, short-term and broader, long-term objectives which can be addressed by organizational change initiatives to recognize the interdependence of work and family. It is important at the evaluation stage to identify facilitators of change and barriers to achieving particular objectives, to keep in mind intended outcomes and to deal with unexpected consequences. The identification of barriers will often necessitate a reexamination of the objectives of change and the criteria for success, and will certainly require a rethinking of strategies for implementation, thus reactivating the dynamic process of change.

Overview of the Book

Organizational change takes place within specific global, international and national socio-political, legislative and economic contexts which influence needs for, processes of and barriers to change. The first part of this book examines aspects of these contexts which are potentially significant for the development of workplace changes to support work and family, with a focus on Europe. Peter Moss in Chapter 2 discusses the current and potential future roles of the European Union, an international body with a concern to enhance the reconciliation of employment and family life. He examines the usefulness of the term 'reconciliation', the reasons for the EU's concerns in this area, the steps that have been taken to date, as well as future agendas and possibilities. The question of the relative responsibilities for developing and implementing new approaches to reconciliation, including those of international, national and local governments, employers, employee groups and individuals, is also raised and taken up in later chapters.

Workplace policies are viewed as one strategy within a partnership approach. In Chapter 3 Jeremy Lewis explores the role of the law within this partnership. He argues that in the past the law has encouraged traditional models of work. However, with reconciliation of work and family clearly on the EU agenda, he demonstrates how English and European law, particularly discrimination and health and safety law, can be and is being used to discourage the perception of non-standard forms of work as peripheral to mainstream organizational interests, and to bring about wider organizational change by challenging the ways in which work is organized. Nevertheless, he argues that the efforts of the law are currently indirect and their impact is limited, and he considers conditions under which the role of the law in promoting individual life choices for reconciling work and family may be enhanced. Although the discussion is based on English and European law, the processes considered have implications for other legal contexts.

Part Two of the book examines current organizational policies and practices. In Chapter 4 Lisa Harker examines formal policies on flexible working, leaves, and childcare and eldercare services across European Union states, and considers the extent to which they may be considered to be family-friendly according to four key criteria. She considers the interplay between social policy and employer provisions.

While the book begins with a focus on European perspectives it is also useful to draw on the US experience in this field. In Chapter 5 Judith Gonyea and Bradley Googins discuss aspects of the contemporary US socio-political context, and its significance for work and family issues. They argue that within a context which creates considerable burdens for families, work–family benefits are becoming increasingly commonplace. However, they point out that there is a pressing need to make the transition from regarding work and family as a corporate welfare issue, marginal to the real purpose of organizations, to defining work–family balance as a central business concern which is a strategic tool for corporate effectiveness. They explore a range of strategies for making this leap and suggest the concept of mutual flexibility as the basis of new employer–employee contracts, based on dialogue and real mutual recognition of needs and a willingness to look for ways of meeting these. While they do not overlook the challenges involved in reaching this stage, they do present the current context as a window of opportunity for working towards more fundamental changes.

Moving on to look at aspects of organizational culture, Helle Holt and Ivan Thaulow in Chapter 6 examine both formal and informal aspects of workplace flexibility and latitude. Drawing on Danish research they highlight the nature and significance of informal flexibility, and show how, for example, informal flexibility differs in male- and female-dominated organizations. They argue that an analysis of informal culture is essential for a full understanding of how workplaces facilitate and constrain the reconciliation of work and family.

If organizations are to change to accommodate the interrelatedness between work and family they need to examine all their existing policies and practices as well as develop new ones. One organizational practice which can be highly disruptive to families is relocation. In Chapter 7 Cary Cooper describes the problems that relocation can create, particularly for members of dual-career couples, and considers how employers can modify their relocation policies to benefit employees, families and organizations. He draws primarily on the quality of life and business arguments for organizational change, but also points to the importance for gender equality.

Part Two ends with a case study of one UK organization, Midland Bank, in Chapter 8. This focuses on the processes of development and implementation of the bank's work and family policies. It illustrates the strategic use of evolving business arguments together with consultation, communication and support, the engagement of resistance, and evaluation. Work and family issues are still regarded primarily as women's issues at the Midland, but issues concerning men's roles in the organization and the family are increasingly on the agenda, and some discernible shifts in behaviour and attitudes are beginning to emerge.

The contributors to the final part build on earlier discussions of the limitations of a focus on specific policies and practices and reiterate the need for a transition from that focus towards the search for more systemic organizational changes. The family-friendly and systemic change approaches are not necessarily mutually exclusive but may be complementary or represent different stages in the overall search for work structures reflecting contemporary realities. In Chapter 9 Suzan Lewis and Karen Taylor present a case study evaluating the formal policies for employees with family commitments in one organization. They show that the policies do meet some short-term goals but that barriers to more fundamental change include both formal ones such as management discretion and informal ones including narrow and gendered constructions of family commitments and a dominant discourse of time as a commodity representing productivity and commitment. Some pockets of awareness of the counterproductive nature of these assumptions are beginning to emerge, offering the possibility of challenges to organizational culture in the long term, but again the process is slow.

In Chapter 10 Phyllis Raabe argues that resistance to a 'pluralistic' model of work, which incorporates the equivalence of diverse work arrangements, is a major barrier to the rethinking of employment to meet the needs of employers and employees. She examines the assumptions underpinning the 'standard' model of work and argues that a pluralistic model better fits the needs of contemporary organizations and their workforces. She provides some evidence from European and North American research that reduced work time and other pluralistic practices can work successfully and argues that the challenge for organizations is to become family- and career-friendly by altering work structures and norms to better fit the needs of the contemporary workforce and post-industrial work.

In the penultimate chapter Joyce Fletcher and Rhona Rapoport reiterate the implications and limitations of the benefits approach to work and family needs and the importance of systemic change. They illustrate ways in which these concerns can be converted to action via a case study of action research in which work–family issues are used as a catalyst for change to enhance business effectiveness and meet the broader needs of the workforce. The case study demonstrates the importance of collaboration, partnership, and mutual problem solving, of considering local needs and of emphasizing the process of change rather than outcomes, which will vary across contexts. It sets out a model of considerable potential for bringing about systemic change in organizations, by focusing on processes within the workplace rather than individual work–family needs.

Finally, Chapter 12 draws on the preceding chapters to argue for the importance of a contextual approach, in which partnership and collaboration at all levels play a crucial role in rethinking employment to meet the contemporary work–family challenge. It considers some of the directions in which future research and practice can develop to facilitate these changes.

References

Abdela, L. (1995) *Walk the Talk.* Solihull: Metra.

Bailyn, L. (1993) *Breaking the Mold: Women, Men and Time in the New Corporate World.* New York: Free Press.

Barling, J. (1994) 'Work and family: In search of more effective workplace interventions', in C. Cooper and D. Rousseau (eds), *Trends in Organizational Behaviour.* Chichester: Wiley.

Barnett, R.C. (1994) 'Home to work spillover revisited: A study of full time employed women in dual earner couples', *Journal of Marriage and the Family*, 56: 647–56.

Barnett, R.C., Marshall, N.L. and Singer, J.D. (1992) 'Job experience over time multiple roles and women's mental health: A longitudinal study', *Journal of Personality and Social Psychology*, 62: 634–44.

Baruch, G.K. and Barnett, R.C. (1986) 'Role quality, multiple role involvement and psychological well being in mid life women', *Journal of Psychology and Social Psychology*, 51: 578–85.

Bolger, N., Delongis, A., Kessler, R.C. and Wethington, E. (1989) 'The contagion of distress across multiple roles', *Journal of Marriage and the Family*, 51: 175–83.

Brannen, J., Meszaros, G., Moss, P. and Poland, G. (1994) *Employment and Family Life: A Review of Research in the UK (1980-1994).* Sheffield: Employment Department.

Burke, R.J. (1993) 'Organisational level intervention to reduce occupational stressors', *Work and Stress,* 1: 77–87.

Burke, R.J. and Reitzes, S. (1991) 'An identity theory approach to commitment', *Social Psychology Quarterly*, 54: 239–51.

Cockburn, C. (1991) *In the Way of Women: Men's Resistance to Sex Equality in the Workplace.* London: Macmillan.

Cook, A. (1992) 'Can work requirements change to accommodate the needs of dual-earner families?', in S. Lewis, D. Izraeli and H. Hootsmans (eds), *Dual-Earner Families: International Perspectives*. London: Sage.

Cooper, C.L. and Lewis, S. (1993) *The Workplace Revolution: Managing Today's Dual Career Couples.* London: Kogan Page.

Cooper, C.L. and Lewis, S. (1995) *Beyond Family Friendly Organisations.* London: Demos.

Crosby, F.J. (1987) *Spouse, Parent, Worker: On Gender and Multiple Roles.* New Haven, CT: Yale University Press.

Finch, J. and Mason, J. (1993) *Negotiating Family Responsibilities.* London: Routledge.

Galinsky, E., Friedman, D. and Hernandez, C.A. (1991) *The Corporate Reference Guide to Work Family Programmes.* New York: Families and Work Institute.

Haas, L. and Hwang, P. (1995) 'Company culture and men's usage of family leaves in Sweden', *Family Relations,* 44: 28–36.

Handy, C. (1994) *The Empty Raincoat*. London: Hutchinson.

Herriot, P. (1992) *The Career Management Challenge*. London: Sage.

Herriot, P. and Pemberton, C. (1995) *Competitive Advantage through Diversity.* London: Sage.

Hewitt, P. (1993) *About Time: The Revolution in Work and Family Life.* London: IPPR/ Rivers Oram Press.

Hogg, C. and Harker, L. (1992) *The Family Friendly Employer: Examples from Europe.* London: Daycare Trust.

Holterman, S. (1995) 'The costs and benefits to British employers of measures for equality of opportunity', *Gender, Work and Organisation*, 2: 102–12.

Hooyman, N. and Gonyea, J. (1995) *Feminist Perspectives on Family Care: Policies for Gender Justice.* Newbury Park, CA: Sage.

Jones, F. and Fletcher, B. (1993) 'An empirical study of occupational stress in working couples', *Human Relations*, 46: 881–903.

Kagan, C. and Lewis, S. (1993) 'Social change and the family: Accounts of women with multiple commitments', Manchester: IOD Occasional Paper, Manchester Metropolitan University.

Kanter, R. (1977) *Men and Women of the Corporation*. New York: Basic Books.

Kanter, R. (1989) *When Giants Learn to Dance: Mastering the Challenge of Strategy, Management and Careers in the 1990s.* New York: Routledge.

Lambert, S. (1993) 'Workplace policies as social policy', *Social Service Review*, 237–60.

Lewis, S. (1991) 'Motherhood and/or employment', in A Phoenix, A. Woollett and E. Lloyd (eds), *Motherhood: Meanings, Practices and Ideologies.* London: Sage.

Lewis, S. (1994) 'Role tensions in dual career couples', in M. Davidson and R. Burke (eds), *Women in Management: Current Research Issues.* London: Paul Chapman.

Lewis, S. and Cooper, C.L. (1987) 'Stress in two earner couples and stage in the life cycle', *Journal of Occupational Psychology*, 60: 289–303.

Lewis, S. and Cooper, C.L. (1988) 'Stress in dual earner families', in B.A. Gutek, A.H. Stromberg and L. Larwood (eds), *Women and Work: An Annual Review*, vol. 3. Beverly Hills, CA: Sage.

MacEwen, K. and Barling, J. (1991) 'Effects of maternal employment experiences on children's behaviour, mood, cognitive difficulties and parenting behaviour', *Journal of Marriage and the Family*, 53: 635–44.

Marks, S. (1977) 'Multiple roles and role strain: Some notes on human energy, time and commitment', *American Sociological Review*, 42: 921–36.

Marks, S. (1994) 'What is a pattern of commitments?', *Journal of Marriage and the Family*, 56: 112–15.

New Ways to Work (1995) *Balanced Lives: Changing Work Patterns for Men.* London: New Ways to Work.

Noor, N.M. (1994) 'Children and well being: A comparison of employed and non employed women', *Work and Stress*, 8: 36–46.

O'Neil, R. and Greenberger, E. (1994) 'Patterns of commitment to work and parenting', *Journal of Marriage and the Family*, 56: 101–12.

Pascal, G. (1986) *Social Policy: A Feminist Perspective.* London: Tavistock.

Pleck, J. (1977) 'The work family role system', *Social Problems*, 24: 417–27.

Rapoport, R. and Rapoport, R.N. (1975) 'Men, women and equity', *The Family Co-ordinator*, 421–32.

Repetti, R.L., Matthews, K. and Waldron, I. (1989) 'Employment and women's health: Effects of paid employment on women's mental health', *American Psychologist*, 44: 1394–401.

RSA (1994) *Tomorrow's Company: The Case for the Inclusive Approach.* Interim report. London: Royal Society of Arts.

Schor, L. (1991) *The Overworked American.* New York: Basic Books.

Spender, D. (1980) *Man Made Language*. London: Routledge.

Thomas, L. T. and Ganster, D.C. (1995) 'Impact of family supportive work variables on work family conflict and strain: A control perspective', *Journal of Applied Psychology*, 80: 6–15.

Truman, C. (1986) *Overcoming the Career Break: A Positive Approach.* Sheffield: Training Agency.

Warr, T. and Parry, G. (1982) 'Paid employment and women's psychological well being', *Psychological Bulletin*, 91: 498–516.

Wilkinson, H. (1994) *No Turning Back: Generations and the Genderquake.* London: Demos.

Zedeck, S. (1992) 'Exploring the domain of work and family concerns', in S. Zedeck (ed.), *Work, Family and Organizations*. San Francisco: Jossey-Bass.

Zedeck, S. and Mosier, K.L. (1990) 'Work in the family and employing organization', *American Psychologist*, 45: 240–51.

2

Reconciling Employment and Family Responsibilities: A European Perspective

Peter Moss

This chapter is concerned with the long-standing interest and increasing involvement of the European Union (EU) in the relationship between paid work on the one hand and the responsibilities and unpaid work arising from providing care on the other. The Eurospeak shorthand that will appear frequently is 'the reconciliation of employment and family responsibilities', and I shall discuss the meaning of this term, comparing it with the term 'family-friendly'. The chapter considers why the EU has an interest in reconciliation, how it is actively seeking to promote reconciliation, the role of the EU in developing reconciliation in relation to the other parties involved, and the future European agenda.

The EU is not unique among international bodies in paying attention to this issue of reconciliation. Over the last 20 years or so, the issue has been addressed by the United Nations (1979 UN Convention on the Elimination of All Forms of Discrimination against Women; the Forward-Looking Strategies for the Advancement of Women, adopted for the 1985 Nairobi Conference to review the UN Decade of Women; the Action Programme for the 1994 UN Conference in Cairo on Population and Development); the International Labour Organization (Convention 156 concerning equal opportunities and treatment between workers with family responsibilities, 1981); the Council of Europe (resolution on policies to accelerate the achievement of equality between men and women, 1989); and the OECD (in a report entitled *Conducting Structural Change: The Role of Women*, 1991). These reports share a broad approach to family responsibilities, covering not only children but other family members who need care and support; propose a wide range of measures and conditions to enable and support reconciliation, including terms and conditions of employment, working hours, tax and social security, leave arrangements and childcare services; and in most cases recognize the need for family responsibilities to be shared more equally between men and women (for example, the preamble to the 1979 UN Convention refers to 'a change in the traditional role of men as well as the role of women in society and in the family [being] needed to achieve full equality between men and women', paragraph 14).

As with the EU, the interest of these other international bodies in the area of reconciliation owes much to concerns about equal opportunities and improving the position of women in the economy and society. But where the EU differs is in its nature as an international organization, in the powers it has to take forward its objectives and in its permanent institutions to determine the exercise of those powers. While it may have no more moral force than the UN, ILO or Council of Europe, the EU has far greater potential for initiating cross-national and political action.

Why is Reconciliation on the EU's Agenda?

It is important to answer this question first, to appreciate both the current potential and the limitations of a European perspective in this field. The starting point is to emphasize that the EU cannot take on issues at will. To adopt major initiatives on a subject, there needs to be legal competence based in the treaties of the Union, in other words an authority for the Union to become involved on a significant scale in that subject.

The major competence for the EU's active involvement in promoting reconciliation between employment and family responsibilities arises from the Union's commitment to the objective of gender equality in the labour market. The legal basis for this objective, and for EU action to promote and enforce this objective, comes from Article 119 of the Treaty of Rome, which deals with the principle of equal pay, and the five subsequent Directives relating to equality of treatment between women and men. EU statements and initiatives on reconciliation are mainly grounded in this objective of gender equality, for reconciliation is viewed primarily, in the European perspective, as one of the conditions needed to attain genuine equality of opportunity in the labour market.

But there are other factors which increase the EU's involvement with reconciliation. The EU has an interest, although no specific legal competence, in the field of family policy. In the conclusions of a meeting held in September 1989, ministers with responsibility for family affairs agreed that there should be 'a regular exchange of information and views at Community level on major themes of common interest as regards family policy . . . [including] measures making it possible to implement policies on equal opportunities for men and women, in particular access for women to the labour market' (89/C277/02). In 1994, the Commission's Family Policy Unit established a Families and Work Network, focusing on innovative practice in the workplace. A Directive (92/85/EEC) adopted in October 1992, which set minimum standards for maternity leave in the Union, was proposed and adopted as a health and safety at work measure.

A new perspective emerges in the European Commission's (1994a) White Paper on *Growth, Competitiveness, Employment*. This document recognizes the importance of childcare services in the context of a discussion about the sources of new jobs. The White Paper proposes that 3 million out of a target of 15 million new jobs by the year 2000 could come from expanded employment in a range of services 'dealing with new needs . . . [arising from] changes in lifestyles, the transformation of family structures, the increase in the number of working women and the new aspirations of the elderly and very old people' (1994a: 19); these services include childcare services and domiciliary services for elderly and handicapped people. The theme is pursued in the Commission's White Paper on *European Social Policy* which commits the Commission to 'undertake an economic assessment both of the job-creation and reflationary potential of child and dependant-care infrastructures and services' (1994b: 43). In short, reconciliation is beginning to be seen not only as a condition of employment, but also as a generator of new employment.

But underlying the European-level involvement in reconciliation, as in other areas of social policy, is the debate about the nature of the Union, and in particular how far it has a social as well as an economic purpose. Reconciliation measures can be argued for in economic terms, for their contribution to making best use of human resources and supporting the free movement of labour within the Union. However, they can also be argued for in terms of the benefits they bring to individual workers and families. Article 2 of the Maastricht Treaty on European Union gives the EU certain social as well as economic goals:

> The Community shall have as its task . . . to promote throughout the Community a harmonious and balanced development of economic activities, sustainable and non-inflationary growth respecting the environment, a high degree of convergence of economic performance, a high level of employment and of *social protection, the raising of the standard of living and quality of life, and economic and social cohesion and solidarity among Member States.* (my emphasis)

The European Commission itself has argued that 'economic and social progress should go hand in hand' (1993: 6), that 'competitiveness and solidarity have both to be taken into account in building a successful Europe for the future' and that 'the development of European social policy cannot be based on the idea that social progress must go into retreat in order for economic competitiveness to recover' (1993: 7). Reconciliation policy, where the economic and social so clearly intersect, provides one of the clearest indicators of the health of social Europe and of the Commission's search for a Europe in which the social and economic dimensions are complementary rather than mutually exclusive.

Reconciliation or Family-Friendly

Before it is considered what the EU has actually done to promote reconciliation, the term 'reconciliation' itself requires closer scrutiny. The term has been the subject of some criticism on the grounds that it implies the restoration of a harmonious relationship between employment and family responsibilities which once existed and has subsequently been lost – by implication, as a result of women entering the labour market. Hence, it has been argued, 'reconciliation' contains an implicit criticism of women, particularly those with children. In fact, the European Commission is quite clear that the term, at least in the English language, does not imply restoration; there is no assumption of a lost 'golden age'. Instead, it implies an attempt to harmonize or bring together different activities or interests so that they can be conducted with as little friction, stress and disadvantage as possible.

But is 'reconciliation' synonymous with 'family-friendly'? Here there is no guidance from the Commission, so the view is personal. The term 'reconciliation' implies the need to seek accommodation between various needs and interests – of employers, but also children, other 'cared for' groups, women, men and society – and as such indicates a more differentiated and interactional approach than 'family-friendly'. It accommodates the possibility of potential or actual conflicts of interest, in a way that 'family' and 'family-friendly' cannot do with their implicit assumption that all individual needs and interests can be subsumed within the family unit. In practice, the needs and interests of individual family members may not be equally served by particular measures: for example, a measure such as part-time employment taken up by a mother, while her partner continues to work long full-time hours, may be supportive of one strategy for managing employment and family life, but it may have differential short term and long-term consequences for different family members.

If 'reconciliation' has a weakness it is the implication that may be read into it that perfect balance can be found between all the different interest groups. Perhaps more realistically, reconciliation should be viewed as a dynamic process, in which an equilibrium that equally meets the needs and interests of all parties is unobtainable yet constantly sought through a process of debate, review, negotiation and conflict. Viewed in this light, 'family-friendly' may appear bland and static, geared more to the world of marketing than a world of inequalities, change and conflicting interests.

The European Union and Reconciliation: a Short History

As far back as 1974, the Social Action Programme of the (then) Community called for 'action for the purpose of achieving equality between men and women as regards access to employment and vocational training and advancement and as regards working conditions including pay . . . [and] to ensure that the family responsibilities of all concerned may be reconciled with their job aspirations'. Since then, commitment to the need for reconciliation has been frequently expressed by the main institutions of the Union – the Commission, the Parliament and the Council – and most recently in the Commission's White Paper on *European Social Policy*: 'the growing participation by women in the economy has been one of the most striking features of recent decades, suggesting that there is now an urgent need, in the interests of society as a whole, for working life and family life to be mutually reinforcing' (1994b: 42–3).

These expressions of concern have been accompanied by a number of initiatives. One aim of the First Action Programme on the Promotion of Equal Opportunities for Women (1982–5) was 'extending parental leave and leave for family reasons' and to this end the Commission put forward a draft Directive on Parental Leave and Leave for Family Reasons in 1983 (COM(83) 686, 24 November 1983). A second aim was 'building up the network of public [childcare] facilities and services'. This resulted in a report on services for children under three (Piachault, 1984), followed, under the Second Equal Opportunities Action Programme (1986–90), by the Commission establishing a Childcare Network in 1986; the network has continued through the Third Equal Opportunities Action Programme (1991–5), renamed in 1991 the European Commission Network on Childcare and Other Measures to Reconcile the Employment and Family Responsibilities of Men and Women. This network consists of an expert from each member state, with a coordinator, and is one of a number of 'equality' networks established by the Equal Opportunities Unit within the Commission's Directorate-General V (Employment, Industrial Relations and Social Affairs). With a remit to monitor developments, evaluate policy options and collect and disseminate information, the network has conducted a wide range of work covering childcare services, leave arrangements and promoting increased participation by men in the care of children (for further details of this work, see European Commission Childcare Network 1995).

Two significant developments took place under the Third Equal Opportunities Action Programme. First, as part of a Community Initiative Programme – New Opportunities for Women (NOW) – money was specifically set aside to support the development of 'childcare' services and training for workers in these services. Although a few isolated instances already existed of such services receiving funding from the main Structural Funds of the EU, the NOW Programme was the first instance of EU money being specifically allocated to support the development of 'reconciliation' measures.

Second, the Council of Ministers adopted a Recommendation on Child Care in March 1992 (92/241/EEC). The objective of the Recommendation is 'to encourage initiatives to enable women and men to reconcile their occupational, family and upbringing responsibilities arising from the care of children' (Article 1). The Recommendation was adopted as part of the Action Programme to implement the Community Charter of the Fundamental Social Rights of Workers, in particular point 16: 'measures should also be developed to enable men and women to reconcile their occupational and family obligations'.

The Recommendation provides the clearest statement yet of how policy on reconciliation is developing at a European level. Three points are particularly important. First, as yet the policy is confined to reconciling employment with one aspect of family responsibilities – those arising from the upbringing of children. More specifically, initiatives taken by the Commission have so far concentrated on families with younger children, notably 'childcare services' and parental leave, although the preamble to the Recommendation acknowledges that 'responsibilities arising from the care and upbringing of children continue up to and throughout the period of children's schooling'.

Second, reconciliation is envisaged to require a broad approach in policy terms. The Recommendation proposes that initiatives are needed in four areas: childcare services (Article 3); leave for employed parents (Article 4); the workplace, to make 'the environment, structure and organisation of work . . . responsive to the needs of workers with children' (Article 5); and measures to 'promote and encourage, with due respect for freedom of the individual, increased participation by men [in the care and upbringing of children], in order to achieve a more equal sharing of parental responsibilities between men and women and to enable women to have a more effective role in the labour market' (Article 6).

This last area is particularly striking. It places a clear commitment on member states to address the current unequal division of care and other family responsibilities. This emphasis on 'more equal sharing of family responsibilities' has been a persistent feature of EU statements on reconciliation (see the explanatory memorandum to the draft Directive on Parental Leave; the 1984 Council Recommendation on Positive Action; the Green Paper on *European Social Policy*). Most recently the theme recurs in the White Paper on *European Social Policy*:

> Progress towards new ways of perceiving family responsibilities may slowly relieve the burden on women and allow men to play a more fulfilling role in society. However greater solidarity between men and women is needed if men are to take on greater responsibility for the caring roles in our society and if flexibility in employment is not to lead to new pressures on women. (European Commission 1994b: 43)

Such statements have not led so far to widespread initiatives at European, national, local or workplace levels to recognize and support men's role as carers (for a fuller discussion of this issue, including examples of initiatives that have been taken, see European Commission Childcare Network, 1994a). However, it is significant that the issue of the domestic division of labour and men's roles as carers has received formal recognition by the Union and member states and that the issue is clearly on the Union's public agenda.

Finally, within some of the four areas, the Recommendation also begins to identify key objectives and principles, albeit with some ambiguity and notable omissions (for example, there is no reference to 'quality' in Article 3 on childcare services). Childcare services should be affordable, flexible, diverse and coherent; combine care and a pedagogical approach; be equally available in all areas including rural areas; be accessible to children with special needs; work closely with local communities and be responsive to parental needs; and provide basic and continuous training for workers in these services that is 'appropriate to the importance and the social and educative value of their work'. Leave arrangements should provide 'some flexibility as to how leave may be taken'.

Respective Responsibilities for Reconciliations

The Recommendation assumes a broad responsibility for promoting reconciliation. In several parts, the Recommendation refers to 'the respective responsibilities of national, regional and local authorities, management and labour, other relevant organisations and private individuals' (Articles 2, 3, 4, 5). However, having identified these various responsible partners, the Recommendation has nothing to say about how the 'partners' might be enabled to work together (in contrast, the European Parliament in its opinion on the Recommendation (22 November 1991) proposes 'the establishment of a framework for promoting the development of close partnership between governments, local authorities, organisations and social partners'). Even more important, the Recommendation offers no guidance about what might be the 'respective responsibility' of each 'partner'.

My own view, discussed in greater detail elsewhere (Moss, 1993), is that government has a major responsibility for the achievement of effective reconciliation for three reasons: because parenthood and other forms of caring are a socially important role; to reduce the risk of replicating in work–family relationships the inequalities that permeate the labour market; and to ensure that the needs of all interest groups are recognized and met. This central role should involve developing a policy on reconciliation, which includes defining the responsibilities of the different partners; creating a framework to promote partnership; and taking action to implement those measures defined as government's responsibility. Finally, taking the four areas of the Recommendation on Child Care, government should take the lead role and responsibility in developing services for children and ensuring a basic range of leave entitlements for employed parents, leaving social partners to take the lead role in the workplace.

However, this proposed division of responsibility does not mean exclusive areas of interest. While it may be inappropriate for individual employers to become involved in the funding or provision of services for children (Moss, 1992), employers' (and trade union) views should be considered in planning services. Employers and trades unions can encourage and support workers wishing to use their leave entitlements as well as supplementing these entitlements (European Commission Childcare Network, 1994b). Government, in turn, can provide a range of support and encouragement to employers and trade unions who wish to develop workplaces responsive to the needs of workers with children. Last but not least, government and social partners have a shared responsibility for measures to promote more participation by men in the care of children.

Of the member states, Denmark comes closest to this division of responsibility (see Holt and Thaulow, Chapter 6). The provision of childcare services is a public responsibility; the Government has set a target of providing a publicly funded place for all children over 12 months by 1996 (although it looks doubtful that this target will be met, considerable progress has been made, so that in 1995 two-thirds of local authorities were offering some sort of place guarantee and waiting-lists nationally had fallen to 12,500 from 35,000 in 1992 (EC Childcare Network, 1996)). There is a statutory right to partially paid maternity leave, paternity leave and parental leave. However, for many workers these statutory leave entitlements are supplemented by collective agreements, for example in the public sector where statutory benefit from public funds paid to workers taking leave is made up to full replacement of earnings. At the same time, there is increasing awareness of the significance of the individual workplace for achieving reconciliation, with for example a publicly supported initiative to encourage employers to develop work practices and policies that are supportive of working parents.

At the other extreme, UK policy assumes that reconciliation is essentially a private matter to be resolved by parents, for example by purchasing private services or using informal social networks, with the support of individual employers where they consider such support in their interest. The only exceptions are an entitlement to maternity leave, a measure tolerated with great reluctance by successive Conservative governments who have extended coverage to all women only when forced to do so as the result of an EU directive, and small amounts of public support for childcare services (for example, a short-term programme to stimulate school-age childcare and a disregard of childcare costs for Family Credit claimants), introduced in a piecemeal way.

In between these two extremes, most other member states recognize a public interest in and responsibility for reconciliation, expressed in some provision of publicly funded childcare services for children of employed parents and statutory parental leave arrangements, even if they have not developed public policies to the extent of Denmark (with the possible exception of Sweden and Finland).

The EU Role

The missing partner in this equation is the European Union itself. What responsibilities does it have? What tasks can be best done at European level? The White Paper on *European Social Policy* suggests two key roles. First, 'the convergence of goals and policies over a period of time by fixing common objectives . . . [respecting] Member States' choices about how to achieve their goals' (European Commission, 1994b: 12, 13). The Council Recommendation can be viewed as a first step in this direction for reconciliation, although it is not clear how effective this non-legally binding measure has so far been in actually influencing national policy; this will become clearer when the Commission completes its review on implementation, which it is required to do under Article 7 of the Recommendation, on the basis of a questionnaire completed in spring 1995 by each member state.

The second role is 'the establishment of a framework of basic minimum standards . . . [as] a bulwark against using low social standards as an instrument of unfair economic competition and protection against reducing social standards to gain competitiveness . . . [and also as] an expression of the political will to maintain the momentum of social progress' (1994b: 12). The proposed parental leave Directive, and the adopted Directive covering maternity leave, are two examples of attempts to establish minimum standards through conferring rights upon individual workers. In other cases relevant to reconciliation, in particular concerning the development of childcare and other services, any attempt to establish minimum standards would most probably need to involve placing obligations on governments but leaving a wide choice in method of implementation. The balance between these two approaches is not discussed in the White Paper.

The concept of basic minimum standards raises other questions. On what basis should a 'basic minimum standard' be defined, if it is to be more than simply the lowest common denominator? How should standards be set that accommodate the very differing resources and conditions of diverse countries? The White Paper wants to see standards that do not 'over-stretch the economically weaker Member States' yet do 'not prevent the more developed Member States from implementing higher standards', a difficult balancing act to achieve. Will such standards remain unchanged or evolve over time? The White Paper proposes that 'the continuing aim should be to develop and improve standards for *all* the Members of the Union' (1994b: 12). What will be the respective roles of Union legislation and Union-level collective agreements? The White Paper suggests that legislation will be used sparingly – 'the Commission considers that there is not a need for a wide-ranging programme of new [legislation] . . . [which] will be considered only when strictly necessary to achieve the objectives of the Union' – with more emphasis placed on agreement between social partners. This in turn raises questions about 'respective responsibilities' and the position of the increasing proportion of the workforce not covered by collective agreements.

Finally, the EU provides opportunities for cross-national exchange and collaboration, opportunities which are increasingly exploited in the area of reconciliation through Community initiatives such as networks and cross-national components in the NOW Programme, as well as through less formal initiatives (for example, the growing number of visits by practitioners, politicians and others to see services in other countries and the development of exchange programmes). Much still remains to be done, for example through developing systems of cross-national monitoring of policies, cross-national evaluations of policies (e.g. of the operation of different parental leave measures) and through funding collaborative research and development projects (e.g. to develop workplace practice and policy and measures to encourage men's involvement in the care of children). Apart from the benefits to knowledge, increased cross-national exchange, collaboration and comparison may have a cumulatively powerful effect by raising expectations (already seen in the media's growing use of European 'league tables' in a wide range of areas from water quality to childcare services) and speeding the dissemination of new ideas, policies and practices.

In this outline of the potential role of the EU, as well as from the short history of earlier initiatives, it can be seen that the Union has begun to deploy, on behalf of promoting reconciliation, most of what the Green Paper on *European Social Policy* refers to as 'the tools at the disposal of Community social policy' (European Commission, 1993: 9). Directives and Recommendations come under the heading of 'legal provisions', the NOW Programme is an example of 'financial support', while networks exemplify 'cooperation, mobilization and exchange'. The main tool not deployed until recently has been the 'social dialogue': this omission is now being made good as I shall describe in the final section.

Areas for Future Development

The EU's intervention in reconciliation continues to evolve. A second NOW initiative will provide more funding for childcare services. The European Commission will be reviewing implementation of the Council Recommendation on Child Care, as well as producing its own guide to supplement the Recommendation. Most significant, however, is the implementation of that part of the White Paper on *European Social Policy* in which the Commission commits itself 'to examine the possibility of a framework directive covering the issues of reconciling professional and family life . . . [which] would set minimum standards within a framework designed to encourage competitive solutions in a changing world' (1994b: 31). The Commission has begun this examination, having accepted that the original proposal for a parental leave Directive is now dead mainly due to the continued opposition of the UK government. It is following the procedure laid down by the Social Protocol for the adoption of measures in the social policy area; in the first place this involves resort to the Social Dialogue, described in the Green Paper on *European Social Policy* as:

> a key feature of the Commission's method of work in bringing forward proposals in the social field [involving] extensive consultation of the social partners [employers and trade unions] at various stages in both the conception of initiatives and the detailed writing of texts . . . [and taking place] principally via the network of tripartite consultative committees which exist in all the main areas of policy, such as health and safety and equal opportunities. (1993: 12)

In February 1995, the Commission invited the social partners to give their views on reconciliation of employment and family life, embracing not just parental leave but also the issue of training leave and other areas identified in the Council Recommendation on Child Care. In December 1995, the social partners (represented on the employer's side by UNICE and CEEP and on the trade union side by ETUC) reached a framework agreement on parental leave. This agreement provided for at least three months leave for each parent, which in principle should be non-transferable (i.e. if a mother or father choose not to use their right, they cannot transfer their leave to their partner). Under Article 4 of the Social Protocol, the signatories passed their agreement to the Commission requesting it be submitted to the Council of Ministers for approval. The Commission decided to do this in the form of a proposal for a

Directive, and this Directive was duly adopted by the Council of Ministers on 3 June 1996. It will apply to all member states except the UK, and must be implemented within two years.

This measure is not the end of the issue. At the time of writing, the Commission is still considering possible further action on reconciliation. In the Fourth Medium-Term Community Action Programme on Equal Opportunities for Women and Men (1996–2000), the Commission says that it 'will propose measures aiming at setting higher standards for the care of children and other dependants possibly within a framework directive'.

The evolution of EU policy is also likely to be affected by the accession of three new member states – Austria, Finland and Sweden – at the beginning of 1995. Finland and Sweden in particular have highly developed social policies in the area of reconciliation. All three countries might be expected to support the development of European objectives and standards in the area of reconciliation.

Although a European perspective on employment and family responsibilities is emerging gradually, there are a number of issues, relevant to national as well as European-level policies, that need to be addressed, and for which the EU provides a valuable framework for exchange, debate and collaboration. The first of these concerns the development of a comprehensive approach to reconciliation. There is a wide range of groups with an interest in reconciliation, ranging from children to society, and from employers to families. A major challenge involves identifying these groups; defining their needs and what objectives a reconciliation policy should seek to achieve for each group; and seeking to develop reconciliation policies that encompass all these groups, needs and interests. Reconciliation is a labour force issue, but also an issue for child welfare, gender equality and family policy; employers' needs must be taken fully into account, but so too must those of children, parents and the society as a whole.

At the level of European policy, this is currently made difficult because of the limits of the EU's legal competence. In particular, there is no competence either to take major initiatives to promote the well-being of children (or indeed other citizens not in the labour market, such as elderly people or non-employed carers) or indeed to take their needs and interests into account in EU policies. In many respects, children and other groups not in the labour market have a marginal or even invisible place in the Union; the Commission's (1993) Green Paper on *European Social Policy*, for example, makes no mention of children in its 108 pages.

Extending the Union's competence to cover child welfare and well-being might well run foul of national concerns about subsidiarity. A solution which would avoid this trap would be to require all EU measures, including Directives and Recommendations, to take account of their impact on children, ensure they are consistent with the rights of children and promote their quality of life; the approach could be extended to other groups who are also not active in the labour force. One consequence of this would be to require the Union to develop a position on the rights of children and children's quality of life. Such an approach would be compatible with a proposal in a report on *The Problems of Children in the European Community* (1991), prepared by the European Parliament Committee on Youth, Culture and Education, which called for the 'creation of a legal basis in the European treaties to enable a Community policy on children to be formulated, respecting the principle of subsidiarity'.

This issue of reconciling different needs and interests leads directly to the issue of defining 'respective responsibilities'. As already noted, the Council Recommendation on Child Care acknowledges the responsibility of different levels of government, social partners and other organizations, as well as private individuals, for promoting reconciliation – but draws back from defining what responsibility each 'partner' has. Clarifying this issue requires not only clarification of principles, objectives and interests, but also some further research on a number of specific questions. Do strong public policies on reconciliation provide a firm foundation on which employers and trade unions are encouraged to build or do they discourage social partners from playing an active role? What are the costs and what are the benefits, and to whom, of public and workplace policies?

A final, and in many ways most demanding, challenge concerns the nature of reconciliation. At present EU policy on reconciliation in practice focuses on helping parents with young children to combine employment with the care and upbringing of these children. In effect, the task is to help men and women manage one defined period of the life course. This limited focus is not unique to the Union; it is replicated, in most cases, at national and workplace level.

There is however no intrinsic reason for maintaining this narrow perspective. The term 'family responsibilities' can be broadly interpreted. The framework Directive that the Commission raises in its White Paper on *European Social Policy* refers to the 'reconciliation of professional and family life'; it is not simply about the care of children. The White Paper also recognizes other care needs: 'changing demographic trends mean that the responsibility for elderly dependants is moving up the social agenda, although childcare is still the major problem' (1994b: 43). The proposed economic assessment of the job creation and reflationary potential of infrastructures and services, that the Commission commits itself to undertake, covers 'child and dependant care'.

The challenge facing the Union, as well as member states and social partners, is to move to an approach to reconciliation that starts from the premise that both men and women are likely to have caring responsibilities throughout all or much of their working lives; and further to redefine caring responsibilities as including not only dependent relatives but the maintenance of a range of personal relationships which involve elements of reciprocity and caring – relationships with partners, relatives, friends, community. Going even further, it might be argued that there is a need to reconcile employment not only with relationships and responsibilities to others, but also with personal time, development and well-being.

Key concepts here are a life-course approach, as opposed to a focus on a particular transition or stage in life, and the reallocation of time and work. The issue of time is particularly important in the light of a structural change that is at once self-evident and yet rarely fully appreciated. Current trends are leading to an increasing compression of work – paid and unpaid – within the 25–49 age group. The European Commission (1992: 10, 11) itself has noted how this age group's share of the labour market has increased from 51 per cent in 1960 to 62 per cent in 1990, with further increases projected as men's employment in this age group has remained high while women's employment (mainly among women with children) has increased steadily and continues to do so. At the same time, the average age for women to have a first child has moved upwards into this age group, currently standing at 27 years.

As a consequence of this trend, the European Union and member states face three overlapping challenges in relation to time and its distribution. These are, first, to spread time spent on work, whether paid or unpaid, more evenly over the life course; second, to redistribute the use of time between men and women, so that men spend less time overall in paid work and more on unpaid care, and women vice versa; and finally, to reallocate time spent working between employed and unemployed men and women, to increase employment overall at the same time as relieving some of the acute time pressures on men and women in the 25–49 year work compression zone.

One key building block in a life-course, time-focused approach to reconciliation could be the development of a 'time account' or lifetime 'career break' system. This system would give workers entitlements to a time allocation, to be drawn on as they chose throughout their working life in the form of leave or reduced working hours, with a job guarantee and some income replacement. Early forms of this approach have already been introduced in Belgium and Denmark, while Norway outside the EU has recently introduced a 'time account' scheme tied exclusively to early parenthood but claiming to offer parents wide choice in how they use their allocation of leave time (European Commission Childcare Network, 1994b).

Much further work remains to be done on such time account schemes, to monitor and evaluate their operation for individual men and women as well as for their workplaces. Attention will need to be paid to whether and how men's take-up can be increased – so that we move to new and more varied lifetime employment patterns for men as well as women, and avoid 'time account' schemes perpetuating gender inequalities. There are many issues too about the relevance and application of such schemes to the increasing number of workers who are not permanent employees – the growing army of casual and temporary workers and self-employed.

The EU can provide a framework, as well as the means, to explore new and radical approaches to reconciliation. This should be one of a number of items on a research and development agenda that the EU could support. Some other items for this agenda have already been mentioned: the respective roles of public policy and action by social partners; the costs and benefits of different public and workplace policies; action research on initiatives to encourage more equal sharing of family responsibilities between men and women. A final item for the agenda is to explore the implications for reconciling employment and family life of the economic, technological, demographic and social changes that are sweeping through all European countries. The debate on reconciliation within the EU urgently needs to be informed by an understanding of the opportunities and constraints that these changes bring with them.

References

European Commission (1992) *Employment in Europe 1992.* Luxembourg: Office for Official Publications of the European Communities.

European Commission (1993) *European Social Policy: Options for the Future (Green Paper).* Luxembourg: Office for Official Publications of the European Communities.

European Commission (1994a) *Growth, Competitiveness, Employment: The Challenges and Ways Forward into the 21st Century (White Paper).* Luxembourg: Office for Official Publications of the European Communities.

European Commission (1994b) *European Social Policy: A Way Forward for the Union (White Paper).* Luxembourg: Office for Official Publications of the European Communities.

European Commission Childcare Network (1994a) *Men as Carers: Towards a Culture of Responsibility, Sharing and Reciprocity between Women and Men in the Care and Upbringing of Children.* Brussels: European Commission Equal Opportunities Unit (DGV).

European Commission Childcare Network (1994b) *Leave Arrangements for Workers with Children.* Brussels: European Commission Equal Opportunities Unit (DGV).

European Commission Childcare Network (1995) *Annual Report 1994.* Brussels: European Commission Equal Opportunities Unit (DGV).

European Commission Childcare Network (1996) *A Review of Services for Young Children in the European Union 1990–95.* Brussels: European Commission Equal Opportunities Unit (DGV).

European Parliament (1991) *Report of the Committee on Youth, Culture, Education, the Media and Sport on the Problems of Children in the European Community.* Brussels: European Parliament.

Moss, P. (1992) 'Employer childcare – or services for children, carers and employers', *Employee Relations*, 14, 20–32.

OECD (Organization for Economic Co-operation and Development) (1991) *Conducting Structural Change: The Role of Women.* Paris: OECD.

Moss, P. (1993) 'EC perspectives', in C. Hogg and L. Harker (eds), *The Family Friendly Employer: Examples from Europe.* London: Daycare Trust.

Piachault, C. (1984) *Day Care Facilities and Services for Children under 3 in the European Community.* Brussels: European Commission Equal Opportunities Unit (DGV).

3

Work–Family Reconciliation and the Law: Intrusion or Empowerment?

Jeremy Lewis

The use of governmental social policy to engineer change in working practices is controversial in the United Kingdom. While the aspiration of achieving work–family reconciliation is firmly on the agenda in the European Union, the United Kingdom has chosen to opt out of the Social Chapter and has vetoed successive family-friendly initiatives such as the proposed introduction of parental leave. The gist of the objections put forward by the current Conservative government has been that it is wrong to interfere with business, firstly because this constitutes an interference with management autonomy and secondly because this would increase costs, thereby reducing competitiveness and causing job losses. However, it will be argued in this chapter that the law, rather than adopting a neutral stance, has in the past encouraged a perception of atypical forms of work as peripheral to employing organizations and thereby suitable for low pay, low benefit and low status, perpetuating traditional models of work. I use the term 'atypical' to refer to part-time work, home working, temporary work, etc., albeit that it may be increasingly inaccurate to refer to these forms of work as atypical. Further, the law has a well-established role in limiting the parameters within which business autonomy and competition are to be permitted and encouraged.

To what extent can the law be used to challenge the primacy of traditional forms of work and to facilitate the reconciliation of work and family? Based on the UK experience this chapter first explores the potential role of discrimination law in discouraging employers from regarding non-standard workers as peripheral to the organization and then considers its further potential in challenging the way work is organized. Consideration is then given to the strengths and also the problems of using discrimination law as a vehicle for change and to a further approach based on safeguarding health and safety at work, which may focus less on traditional gender roles. It will be argued that having accepted a role for the law in limiting the parameters of business freedom in order to promote *equality* of opportunity, the next challenge is to focus on promotion of full and diverse opportunities, thereby fostering an environment in which individuals are empowered with employment options conducive to reconciliation of work and family.

Discrimination Law and Work–Family Reconciliation: The Legislation

The matrix of relevant rights in the field of discrimination law in the UK is a product of both European and domestic law. Under the European Communities Act 1972 provisions of domestic law must comply with relevant European law provisions. Among the principal relevant measures at the European level in the field of discrimination law are Article 119 of the Treaty of Rome (which sets out the principle of equal pay for equal work), the Equal Treatment Directive (ETD) (requiring equal treatment in regard to working conditions) and the Equal Pay Directive (EPD).

Domestic legislation also differentiates between discrimination in relation to contractual terms, which are covered by the Equal Pay Act 1970 (EqPA), and other forms of discrimination, which are covered by the Sex Discrimination Act 1975 (SDA). The EqPA states that a woman's terms of employment must be equal to those of a man in the same employment provided that the man is employed on like work or work rated as equivalent (i.e. after a study has been undertaken) or work of equal value. (The same principle applies vice versa where a man claims he has been paid less than a woman.) The SDA provides that it is unlawful for an employer in Great Britain to discriminate against a person in relation to recruitment (including the terms upon which employment is offered), dismissal or access to opportunities for promotion, transfer, training or any other benefits, facilities or services. *Discrimination* is defined as less favourable treatment on the grounds of sex. In addition, *indirect discrimination* is defined as the application of a requirement or condition, applying equally to men and women but with which fewer women than men (or vice versa) can comply, which cannot be shown to be justifiable on grounds other than sex, and which is detrimental to the person who cannot comply.[1]

The application of these provisions in relation to issues of work–family reconciliation is considered below. A distinction may be drawn between the impact of discrimination law in improving the quality of existing alternatives to traditional full-time work (which I refer to as 'the Job Enhancement Role'), and its role in engineering wider organizational change (which will be referred to as 'the organizational challenge role').

The Job Enhancement Role of Discrimination Law

Challenge to Exclusion from Employment Protection

For many years the legal framework in the United Kingdom has encouraged the perception of part-time workers, and others working in 'atypical' ways, as peripheral to the workforce. By denying employment rights available to other employees (such as the right to claim unfair dismissal) employers were encouraged to view part-time workers as valuable principally because of the ease with which they could be hired and fired. This clearly restricts the choices open to family members for managing career and family roles, and it has generally been women who have made the necessary accommodations at the expense of their careers or job security. One of the most high-profile contributions of discrimination law in recent times has been to challenge the exclusion of those in atypical forms of work from employment rights. Most notably in what has become known as the '*EOC* case'[2] the House of Lords held that the requirement for there to be a 16 hour working week in order to qualify for unfair dismissal and redundancy pay after two years was indirectly discriminatory and had not been shown to be objectively justified. The thresholds were therefore declared incompatible with Article 119 and the ETD and EPD. As a result the statutory provisions imposing different qualifying periods for employment rights for part-time workers have now been removed.[3] Similarly in the '*Perez* case'[4] the Court of Appeal granted a declaration to the effect that, at least at the time of the complaint, the two-year qualifying period for unfair dismissal claims was incompatible with the ETD.[5]

Equal Pay

While exclusion from employment protection facilitates the treatment of atypical forms of work as peripheral, for much part-time work low pay has been as great a problem as lack of job security. There is no national minimum wage legislation in the United Kingdom, but equal pay legislation provides some protection against lower pay for those in part-time work (being predominantly women). The effect of this legislation is limited by the need to find a comparator of the opposite sex in the same employment carrying out like work or work rated as equivalent or of equal value. Nevertheless, once it is shown that a female employee is not accorded equal treatment – because she is paid less than a man doing work rated as equivalent – the onus is then on the employer to show that the difference in pay could be due to a difference other than sex. The result in cases where the employing organization contains non-part-time workers, even though they may be engaged on different jobs, may be to prevent employers simply assuming that it is permissible to pay lower rates to those in jobs predominantly characterized by part-time work.

Justification: Considering the Business Case

In relation to all claims of indirect discrimination, whether on grounds of pay or otherwise, employers can argue that the discrimination is objectively justified other than on grounds of sex. It is in this context that employers may raise arguments such as the detrimental effect of the legislation upon business opportunities. *Justification* must then satisfy three criteria; it must be shown that the discrimination is in the pursuance of a *necessary aim,* that the means chosen are *suitable* for attaining this aim, and that it is *requisite* for achieving this aim.

Necessary Aim In relation to national measures, the *EOC* case affirmed that a policy regarded by the government as a beneficial social policy aim (in that case increasing the availability of part-time work) could qualify as a necessary aim. Beyond this a range of social, economic and political circumstances may be considered as justification for different treatment. For example, the European Court of Justice (ECJ) has held that measures could be taken in order to avoid imposing administrative, financial and legal constraints upon small businesses of such a nature as to hold back their creation and development.[6] Where the indirect discrimination is other than in relation to national policy, justification will normally be on economic or administrative grounds. However, it is necessary to provide a justification for the discrimination rather than merely an explanation of how it arose. For example, where there is prima facie discrimination between two groups of workers, the fact that the rates of pay are determined by separate collective bargaining processes cannot constitute objective justification even if there is no discrimination within either of the bargaining processes.[7] In any event, however, the justification must be 'gender neutral'.[8]

Suitable Once it is shown that a necessary aim is being pursued, the means chosen must be shown to be suitable for attaining that aim. In the *EOC* case the UK government argued that the qualifying periods for claiming unfair dismissal furthered the aim of reducing unemployment by reducing the indirect labour costs of employing part timers. The UK government's resistance to implementation of EU social policy was thereby brought into conflict with the non-discrimination principle. The conflict was encapsulated in the speech of Lord Keith who noted in the *EOC* case that while the government's stated aim of increasing the availability of part-time work was to be regarded as a beneficial social aim, the policy of furthering that aim by seeking to reduce indirect costs could not be distinguished from a policy of seeking to do so by reducing direct costs by allowing part-time workers to be paid a lesser rate. According to Lord Keith such an obvious breach of the principle of equal pay clearly could not be a suitable means of furthering the aim in question. Therefore the House of Lords held that there were some means of pursuing a beneficial social aim that could not be pursued because of the conflict with the non-discrimination norm.

In the *Perez* case the Court of Appeal accepted, by way of refinement of this observation, that regard should be had to the degree of discrimination that needs to be justified and that it was only if the degree of discrimination was disproportionate to the good sought to be achieved by the discriminatory measure that the court would interfere. It remains to be seen how this will be applied in practice since in *Perez* the Court of Appeal was not satisfied that any good would follow from the policy in question (the two-year qualifying period for bringing an unfair dismissal claim) since the studies relied upon did not support the government's assertion that the policy increased employment opportunities.

In any event the essence of Lord Keith's observation in the *EOC* case was to recognize the paucity of any argument which proceeds simply on the assumption that avoiding an increase in employment costs is a complete answer to a proposed social measure. While the importance of competitiveness is not to be overlooked, the same arguments about increases in employment costs might equally be raised against most elements of employment protection including prohibition on direct discrimination and essential health and safety measures. Once it is accepted that there is a need to regulate employment and thereby to limit acceptable forms of competition, objections as to additional costs become issues of degree (as emphasized in *Perez*) to be considered in the particular employment context and/or in relation to the importance of the aim being pursued.

Requisite Even if the policy or practice to be justified is a suitable means of achieving a necessary aim it must also be shown to be requisite for attaining that aim. In both *EOC* and *Perez* the courts were not convinced by the government, on the basis of the evidence presented, that it was possible to draw any inference of a connection between the policy in question and the aim to be pursued (increasing the availability of part-time work in the *EOC* case and preserving job opportunities in the *Perez* case). In the *EOC* case for example a comparison was drawn with other EU countries. In particular it was noted that in France in the period since 1982 when part-time employees were given the same protection as full timers the rate of part-time employment has increased to a greater extent than in the UK.

Challenging Assumptions While the approach in the *EOC* and *Perez* cases illustrates the ability to scrutinize the business case put forward at a national level, the justification test has also facilitated a challenge to various assumptions which have contributed to the treatment of atypical forms of work as being peripheral. Generalized assumptions in relation to atypical forms of work will not be sufficient either at national level or at individual employment level to provide objective justification for prima facie discriminatory practices. For example, the ECJ has held that it was insufficient to assert that workers who work less than 10 hours a week or 45 hours a month are not integrated in and connected with the undertaking in a way comparable to that of other workers.[9] Similarly the ECJ has held that generalizations to the effect that full-time workers would acquire skills and experience more quickly would be insufficient. It is necessary to establish a connection in the particular circumstances of the case between the nature of the duties performed and the experience afforded by the performance of those duties.[10] The ECJ has also emphasized that adaptability to variable work schedules and places of work may be justification for differential treatment, but only if it is demonstrated that such adaptability is important for the performance of specific duties entrusted to the worker.[11] Thus, at least where workers are already engaged in atypical forms of work, the business case for preferring flexible ways of work can be pursued without being held back by stereotypical assumptions as to the role of non-paradigm workers.

The Job Expansion Role: Challenge to Organizational Structures

While some provisions contribute towards improving the quality of work by securing basic employment rights and preventing discrimination in pay and in other benefits, a more radical approach might involve inducing or requiring employers to adapt ways of working which are sympathetic to those with family (or other dependency) commitments by transcending assumptions as to the ways work should be organized. Developments in the case law of indirect discrimination suggest that this may become a powerful tool at least to require employers to face up to those assumptions and perhaps also to challenge them.

Requirement or Condition

In the context of indirect discrimination case law, one obstacle to challenging the way work is organized has been the need to show that the refusal to offer an alternative to full-time work or to offer flexibility constitutes a 'requirement' or 'condition' within the meaning of the SDA. One line of authority suggests that there is no 'requirement' or 'condition' and no 'detriment' where the failure to offer a benefit, or the imposition of a detriment, is just part and parcel of the job. In *Clymo* v. *Wandsworth London Borough Council* (1989)[12] Ms Clymo, a branch librarian, asked her employers if she could carry out her duties part time after the birth of her child and share her job with her husband who was also a librarian. The employers refused, asserting that the managerial aspects of the job made it unsuitable for sharing. Ms Clymo then resigned and claimed that her employers had indirectly discriminated against her in that they had applied a requirement of full-time work which was such that the proportion of female librarians with dependent children who could comply with it was smaller than the number of male librarians with dependent children who could comply. In rejecting the application, the Employment Appeal Tribunal (EAT) held that rather than there being any requirement to work part time this was just part of the job, and that the decision as to what was part of the job was one for management provided that the decision was made on adequate grounds bearing in mind the need to avoid discrimination.

The effect of this decision was to relieve the management of the stricter requirements of justifying the refusal to offer the opportunity to job share. However, the contrary view was advanced by the EAT in *Home Office* v. *Holmes* (1984).[13] In that case Ms Holmes had requested that she be permitted to return to work part time after the birth of her two children. Her request was refused and it was argued that there was no requirement or condition applied, and therefore no breach of the discrimination legislation, in that the obligation to work full time was fundamental to her contract. This was rejected by the EAT on the basis that the words 'requirement' and 'condition' are fully capable of including any obligation of service, whether for full- or part-time work. The reasoning in *Holmes* has subsequently been preferred to that in *Clymo* by the Northern Ireland Court of Appeal (*Briggs* v. *North Eastern Education and Library Board* 1990).[14] As such it seems that this obstacle to the potential of the indirect discrimination legislation to challenge ingrained attitudes as to the proper organization of work may have been removed, although the same issues will arise in relation to whether the denial of flexible working patterns can be justified.

A further argument upheld in *Clymo* and rejected in *Briggs* was that a requirement and condition must be specifically 'applied' to the applicant and that in merely refusing to offer an advantage (in that case job sharing) no requirement or condition had been applied. Subsequently, the Court of Appeal has rejected this argument (*Meade Hill and National Union of Civil and Public Servants* v. *The British Council*).[15] It was argued that a mobility clause in the applicant's contract of employment constituted a requirement that the applicant must work in whatever location in the United Kingdom her employers might direct. The judge commented that the employers would be able to justify the term if they could show that they had a need to be in a position, if the circumstances so required, to direct the employee to work anywhere in the UK irrespective of whether she could in practice comply with such a direction. Alternatively the mobility clause could be modified so that an employee who was not in practice able to relocate would not be required to do so. With this caveat, the effect of the decision is that while a genuine need for the employer to demand mobility will be respected, merely demanding mobility as a basis of displaying commitment or from outmoded assumptions as to the way employment should be organized (see Cooper, Chapter 7) will be open to challenge.

Can Comply

Once a requirement or condition is identified, the next issue is whether the proportion of women who can comply with it is considerably smaller than the proportion of men who can comply. If a narrow view was taken of this it would to a large extent neutralize the potential of the legislation to promote opportunities for those who have chosen to take on family or other caring commitments outside work. However, from a relatively early stage it has been recognized that it cannot be said that a person 'can comply' merely because she can physically comply. The relevant question is whether she can in practice comply according to the 'current usual behaviour of women . . . as observed in practice'.[16] For example, on that basis fewer women than men can comply with a condition stated in an advertised post that they should be aged between 17 and 28 as more women than men will be returning to full-time work at a later age.[17]

Justifiability

The above developments offer the prospect that where a disparate impact can be established both employers and the government will be required to justify practices and policies which have a detrimentally adverse impact on women.

While it remains open for an employer to show that the indirect discrimination is justified, mere generalized assumptions will not be sufficient. There is a degree of uncertainty as to the extent to which marginal savings in efficiency or costs will justify indirect discrimination. In one case the EAT upheld the Industrial Tribunal's finding that if there was indirect discrimination in a collective agreement for part-time workers to be selected for redundancy this was objectively justified on the basis of marginal advantages of part-time working. These marginal advantages consisted of a reduction in record keeping and administration reflecting the reduced number of full-time employees employed to do the work, a reduction in laundering requirements for employees' overalls and the elimination of a 'mild degree' of disruption which occurred with more frequent shift changes where part-time workers were employed. The EAT considered that the Industrial Tribunal's finding reflected a realistic recognition that in a highly competitive industry small advantages can cumulatively be crucial in the success or failure of business.

While it is unlikely that an appeal tribunal would today interfere with such a finding of fact,[18] recent cases, not only in relation to national legislation but also in relation to individual employment decisions, suggest that there may be less willingness to accept that marginal efficiency advantages will suffice. In *London Underground Limited* v. *Edwards* (1995)[19] the applicant had been employed as a train operator working a shift system which she was able to organize so as to fit in with her responsibilities as a single mother. London Underground then introduced a new rostering system which would have involved her working excessively long hours in order to work only during the day. She therefore resigned and brought a sex discrimination claim. The Industrial Tribunal held that there was indirect discrimination and that this had not been justified. In particular the Tribunal found that it was feasible to cater for single parents or those with primary care of children who were only able to work social hours without significant detriment to the savings which London Underground were seeking to make by introducing the new rostering system. No doubt it would have been cheaper to have a uniform approach applicable to all but that was not sufficient to justify the failure of London Underground to avoid discrimination by addressing the need to reconcile work and dependent childcare commitments.

In any event once the justification test is reached the need arises to focus on the merits of the working practice in question. It may well be that this will provide a stimulus for employers to reconsider the way work is organized since the business case for allowing such changes may have to be fought out in litigation. Certainly the focus on justification emphasizes the important role for research in addressing business fears and demonstrating that policies designed to contribute to the reconciliation of work and family are compatible with a healthy economy and with business productivity.

Implications Concerning Discrimination Law

It will be apparent from the above that the indirect discrimination legislation holds enormous potential from the perspective of encouraging policies conducive to work–family reconciliation. It has been possible to challenge both legislative and firm-specific measures which have had the effect of encouraging a perception of atypical work as being peripheral. Indeed, in respect of national legislation, in the *Perez* case Lord Justice Neill suggested that in future:

> any proposed legislation, particularly in the social field, *which may* have a disparate impact between the sexes will have to be examined before it is introduced to see whether any consequential disparity can be objectively justified. (my emphasis)

Beyond this, as illustrated by *Holmes* and *London Underground Limited* v. *Edwards* (relating to hours of work for those with primary childcare responsibilities) and *Meade Hill* (in relation to job mobility), indirect discrimination provisions have the potential not only to shift away from the perception of part-time workers as peripheral but also to offer the prospect of challenging the very way that work is organized.

Nevertheless, from the point of view of a political culture which traditionally concentrates on conferring rights upon individuals rather than groups it may appear strange that legislation has been adopted which rests upon establishing a disparate impact upon a group (usually women). Nor can the legislation be easily explained on the basis of a redistributive policy redressing the balance between a traditionally advantaged group (men) and a traditionally disadvantaged group (women). Were this to be the case then the form of the legislation which (with a few exceptions) requires equal treatment and thereby prohibits positive discrimination would be difficult to explain.

The most obvious explanation for the legislation is therefore that it promotes equality of opportunity for individuals. One aspect of this is to seek to provide a mechanism for identifying circumstances in which those who take on the primary burden of unpaid work (in the home) tend to lose out in the sphere of paid work. Indeed an appreciation of this appears to be reflected in the wide interpretation of whether a claimant 'can comply' with a requirement or condition.

This approach also explains the role of national and international policy in fostering change. On one view reliance might be placed on the individual market place to lead to an environment in which there are a range of realistic options as to how to reconcile work and family. In reality abstention from conferring benefits upon certain types of workers while other traditional forms of work are given employment protection, rather than being a neutral approach, encourages the exploitation of atypical workers and a perception that they are peripheral. Beyond this, the state can play a role in fostering an environment conducive to equality of opportunity by defining illegitimate forms of competition so as to reduce the prospect of those who adopt high employment standards being undercut by more unscrupulous rivals. Indeed it was this rationale that originally provided the impetus for much of the EC social agenda. Once discrimination law is viewed, like the imposition of minimum health standards, as defining the legitimate boundaries of competition it follows that, the fact that labour costs, whether direct or indirect, can be reduced by discriminating should not necessarily be regarded as constituting objective justification.

Further, once it is accepted that the law plays a role in fostering equality of opportunity it is only a short step to recognize that it has an important role in empowering individuals by fostering an environment in which there is a rich choice of valuable life options. Given the centrality of work and family to many people's lives, an important element of any such society must be the provision of a range of options as to how to reconcile work and family.

From this wider perspective some of the inadequacies of discrimination legislation become apparent. In particular, from the perspective of encouraging family-friendly employment, the reliance on anti-discrimination law raises the difficulty that, rather than focusing directly on the needs of those with dependency responsibilities outside work, it is necessary to focus instead on the disparate impact between men and women so as to address the aim of compensating women as a disadvantaged group. Indeed, paradoxically, in so far as anti-discrimination provisions are to retain their teeth as a means of engineering change in working patterns so as to facilitate reconciliation of work and family, they require a perpetuation of the gender inequity in relation to caring responsibilities that leads to findings of disparate impact. This may have the effect of insulating some employers from the legislation on the basis of numerical accident. In one case, for example, a part-time worker complained against the decision to offer a promotion only to those holding full-time posts on the basis that more women than men were part timers.[20] The EAT held that the Industrial Tribunal was entitled to find that the relevant pool for comparison was those men and women with the appropriate qualifications for the job. On that basis no evidence of a disproportionate impact had been shown. No issue as to discrimination against part-time workers could therefore be pursued.

Even if a disparate impact can be shown, the anti-discrimination approach underscores the treatment of issues of reconciliation as women's issues. No doubt if the facility of job sharing is made available to women on the basis that to do otherwise would be indirectly discriminatory, it would then also be possible for a male employee in the same employment who chose to undertake primary care needs to claim this opportunity on the basis that there would otherwise be direct discrimination (less favourable treatment on grounds of sex). However, the very fact that it is the need to ensure equal treatment for women that is the primary impetus to change would appear to reinforce cultural assumptions (reflecting usual practice) that such facilities are principally to be made available for use by women. As such it would appear that the very instrument for producing change also risks encouraging the marginalization of policies for reconciliation and fails to address the need to value reconciliation not solely as a concession to demands by women but as fostering opportunities for a healthy work/life balance.

Alternative (or Complementary) Approaches: Health and Safety Provisions

In the light of these potential shortcomings of the anti-discrimination approach, an alternative (or more realistically an additional) approach to fostering reconciliation of work–family is to treat this as a health and safety issue. Article 118A of the Treaty of Rome provides that member states are to pay particular attention to encouraging improvements, especially in the work environment, as regards the health and safety of workers. The adoption of this Article in 1978 prompted a dramatic increase in the scale of EC Directive activity so that the EC is now the main source of new UK health and safety law. Over 20 Directives have been adopted under Article 118A and most of these have been transposed into UK law. From the perspective of the implementation of reform at a European level, this has the advantage that whereas the United Kingdom is entitled to exercise a veto over Directives and measures introduced under Article 119 of the Treaty, measures introduced under Article 118A (the health and safety provision) can be introduced by qualified majority voting.

The range of measures introduced as health and safety measures suggests a potential to address a fairly wide range of issues relevant to work–family issues. Indeed the division between what constitutes a health and safety issue and what is a broader social or equal opportunity issue is far from clear. For example, it is now established that to treat a woman less favourably on grounds of pregnancy constitutes less favourable treatment on grounds of sex and is therefore direct discrimination.[21] However, the Pregnant Workers Directive[22] which came into effect on 16 October 1994 was introduced pursuant to Article 118A as a health and safety measure. This has caused sweeping reforms in domestic legislation including a right not to be unreasonably refused paid time off to attend ante natal care appointments during working hours,[23] a right irrespective of length of service not to be dismissed for a reason connected with pregnancy[24] and an entitlement to 14 weeks' statutory maternity leave irrespective of length of employment and hours worked.[25] Additionally if a woman has been employed for two years at the beginning of the eleventh week before the expected week of childbirth then (subject to satisfying various notification requirements) she will be entitled to extended maternity leave whereby she can return at any time up to 29 weeks after the beginning of the week in which childbirth occurred.[26]

Whilst the Pregnant Workers Directive illustrates the potential of health and safety measures to be used to provide important rights in order to combine family commitments with existing patterns of work, it may also be that, as with discrimination legislation, there is potential to challenge those traditional patterns. Most controversially, the Working Time Directive[27] provides, with certain exceptions, that member states are to enact measures to ensure that the average working time for each seven-day period, including overtime, does not exceed 48 hours. Other provisions relate to minimum rest breaks, minimum weekly rest periods and minimum annual leave. Various derogations from these provisions are permitted. In particular most of the obligations do not apply to those, such as managing executives, whose working time is not measured or predetermined or who can determine for themselves when they will work.

Even aside from the European dimension there have been common law developments suggesting a potential for addressing some of the health and safety concerns identified at Community level. In particular, in *Walker* v. *Northumberland County Council* (1995)[28] the duty upon the employer to provide a safe system of work and to take reasonable steps to protect the employee from reasonably foreseeable risks was applied so as to find an employer liable for mental injury to the employee. It was held that Northumberland County Council was in breach of the duty of care owed to its employee in respect of a second mental breakdown which he suffered as a result of stress and anxiety occasioned by his job as Area Social Service Officer responsible for an area with a very heavy workload. The court explained that an employer owed a duty to its employees not to cause them psychiatric damage by the volume or character of the work which they were required to perform. The standard of care to be expected of the employer would depend upon the nature of the relationship with the employee, the magnitude of the risk of injury which was reasonably foreseeable, the seriousness of the consequences to the person to whom the duty was owed of the risk eventuating, and the cost and practicability of preventing the risk (taking into account the resources and facilities at the disposal of the person or body who owed the duty of care, and the purpose of the activity which had given rise to the risk of injury). It may be therefore that some of the protection which the Working Time Directive is designed to confer could be provided in response to common law development of the guidelines set out in this case. Perhaps more significantly, the potential for such claims may stimulate reconsideration by employers of the traditional association of long hours with commitment to the employing organization.

Towards Reconciliation

Notwithstanding these developments, English law as it stands falls far short of providing a basis for a fundamental reassessment of working conditions. Indeed *Walker* was to some extent an extreme case, the employer having ignored the plaintiff's difficulties even though he had already suffered a mental breakdown. It is at least open to doubt whether the health and safety rationale will be capable of providing a basis for challenging deep-seated assumptions as to the way work should be organized. In any event to the extent that reconciliation of work–family is an issue of fostering opportunity/empowerment, it is unfortunate that the issue should be clouded by having to be cast in terms of non-discrimination or health and safety. Nevertheless, having introduced the issue of reconciliation onto the agenda, albeit indirectly, the argument for considering the issue directly is stronger than ever, especially considering the high profile now being given to the issue by the EU (see Peter Moss, Chapter 2).

Implications for Research

The focus upon justification of discrimination emphasizes the important role for research in addressing business fears and demonstrating that policies designed to reconcile work and family are compatible with a healthy economy and with business productivity. Further, while the law may provide an environment which is conducive to the encouragement of work–family reconciliation, it is only one of a number of influences for change. Other influences include worker representatives, resources of the employing organization and the influence of multinational companies (see Harker, Chapter 4). Research is required as to the relationship between these various influences. However the law has the potential to require employers at least to consider whether flexibility should be offered. It may also be, as suggested by Lisa Harker, that legal developments will constitute a floor of rights and a bargaining chip which can be used to negotiate both for greater benefits and as to the means of implementation. In any event, as Joyce Fletcher and Rhona Rapoport demonstrate in Chapter 11, implementation of relevant policies will have to be sensitive to the needs of individual employment and may be more successful if the policy is developed as a result of participation at all levels. Further, as noted by Gonyea and Googins (Chapter 5), much may depend on whether issues of work–family reconciliation are regarded as a corporate strategy for furthering business interests rather than as a benefit for individual employees. If so it may be important that debate focuses squarely on the merits of policies to encourage work–family reconciliation rather than furthering those policies indirectly under the cloak of anti-discrimination or health and safety initiatives.

Notes

1 Sex Discrimination Act 1975, Section 1(1). The legislation provides that it is also unlawful to discriminate on the grounds of marital status.

2 *R.* v. *Secretary of State for Employment ex parte EOC* [1994] ICR 317 (House of Lords).

3 Employment Protection (Part Time Employees) Regulations 1995 (SI 1995/31).

4 *R.* v. *Secretary of State for Employment ex parte Seymour-Smith and Perez* [1995] ICR 889 (Court of Appeal).

5 At the time of writing this decision is subject to an appeal to the House of Lords.

6 *HarkerKirshammer-Hack* v. *Sidal* [1994] IRLR 185 (ECJ).

7 *Enderby* v. *Frenchay Health Authority* Case C-127/92 [1994] ICR 112 (ECJ).

8 *British Coal Corporation* v. *Smith* [1994] IRLR 342 (Court of Appeal).

9 *Rinner-Kuhn* v. *FWW Spezial-Gebaudereinigigung GmbH & Co KG* [1989] IRLR 49 (ECJ).

10 *Nimz* v. *Freie Und Hansestadt Hamburg* Case C-184/89 [1991] IRLR 222 (ECJ).

11 *Handels-og Kontorfunktionaererernes Forbund I Danmark* v. *Dansk Arbejdsgiverforening (acting for Danfoss)* Case 109/88 [1989] IRLR 532; [1991] ICR 74 (ECJ).

12 *Clymo* v. *Wandsworth London Borough Council* [1989] ICR 250 (EAT).

13 *Home Office* v. *Holmes* [1984] IRLR 299 (EAT).

14 *Briggs* v. *North Eastern Education and Library Board* [1990] IRLR 181 (Northern Ireland Court of Appeal).

15 *Meade Hill and National Union of Civil and Public Servants* v. *The British Council* [1995] ICR 847 (Court of Appeal).

16 *Price* v. *Civil Service Commission* [1978] ICR 27 (EAT).

17 *Kidd* v. *DRG (UK) Limited* [1985] ICR 405.

18 The EAT can only hear appeals on points of law and, provided that the correct test was applied, it would have to be shown that the decision of the Industrial Tribunal was perverse in the sense of being one which no reasonable tribunal, properly directed, could reach.

19 *London Underground Limited* v. *Edwards* [1995] ICR 574 (EAT).

20 *Pearse* v. *City of Bradford Metropolitan Council* [1988] IRLR 379 (EAT).

21 *Webb* v. *EMO* [1993] ICR 175 (House of Lords); [1994] ICR 770 (ECJ).

22 The Pregnant Workers Directive: Council Directive 92/85/EEC on the introduction of measures to encourage improvements in the health at work of pregnant workers and workers who have recently given birth or are breastfeeding.

23 Section 31A of the Trade Union Reform and Employment Rights Act 1993 (TURERA).

24 EPCA (Employment Protection (Consolidation) Act 1978), Section 60.

25 EPCA, Sections 33–38A.

26 EPCA, Sections 39–44.

27 Council Directive 93/104/EC Concerning Certain Aspects of the Organization of Working Time. The UK government has argued that the Directive is an attempt to regulate conditions of employment so that it can only be passed by a unanimous vote and has therefore lodged legal proceedings to challenge the treaty base for the Directive. The Advocate General has given an opinion against the UK's objections but at the time of going to press the decision of the European Court of Justice is still pending.

28 *Walker* v. *Northumberland County Council* [1995] IRLR 35.

PART 2
POLICY AND PRACTICE

4

The Family-Friendly Employer in Europe

Lisa Harker

This chapter considers 'family-friendly' workplace policies in the various European[1] social contexts and examines key issues relating to these policies. A brief survey of family-friendly policies[2] across the European Union is presented and the factors influencing the development of such practices are discussed. Finally, lessons to be learnt and questions for the future are considered.

Key Objectives

Little consensus about the definition of 'family-friendly' currently exists and establishing a working definition is difficult, particularly when a European perspective is taken. Nevertheless it is possible to identify key objectives which policies must address if they are to be considered 'family-friendly':

1. At their most basic, policies must enable people to fulfil family as well as work demands.
2. In order to enable all employees to do so, policies should be based on the promotion of gender equality and the sharing of family responsibilities between men and women.
3. Policies must also be non-discriminatory, employee-friendly and accompanied by acceptable working conditions.
4. Overall, no family-friendly policy is successful unless a balance is established between the needs of the employees and the employer. This balance has been variously referred to as the 'invisible' contract or 'trust' relationship between an employer and an employee, or synergy.

Family-Friendly Working Practices: A European View

No European-wide audit of 'family-friendly' policies exists. It is, however, possible to identify a range of initiatives which have been adopted by employers and highlight examples of such initiatives from countries throughout the European Union. This section outlines some employer initiatives on flexible working practices, leave arrangements, childcare schemes and eldercare policies.

Family-friendly policies have not developed in a uniform way throughout Europe. For example, flexible working practices are more common in Denmark, Germany and the Netherlands than in France and Ireland; job sharing is more widespread in the UK, Germany and the Netherlands than elsewhere in the European Union.

Flexible Working Arrangements

The traditional working day is becoming a rarity in some parts of Europe. Table 4.1 shows that in some European countries 'atypical' work is common. New forms of working, such as short-term contract work, annual hours,[3] job sharing and teleworking have developed alongside significant levels of part-time work. According to an Equal Opportunities Commission (EOC) survey undertaken in 1991, only one in three employees in the UK work a traditional 9 to 5 working week (Hewitt, 1993). Similarly in the Netherlands, one-quarter of employees work part time (FNV, 1994).

Table 4.1 *Short and long working hours in the European Union, 1990*

	% women employed 0–19 hours a week	% men employed 0–39 hours a week	% women employed 40+ hours a week	% men employed 50+ hours a week
Belgium	15	57	16	13
Denmark	4	66	9	17
Germany	27	47	18	13
Greece	3	21	59	21
Spain	7	9	64	15
France	7	51	15	12
Ireland	14	16	36	27
Italy	8	26	43	12
Luxembourg	13	3	53	10
Netherlands	65	57	7	11
Portugal	4	13	65	15
UK	41	18	15	36

Source: Commission of the European Communities, 1993a

In other parts of Europe the traditional working week has persisted but is under threat. There is a European-wide growth in short-term contract and casual employment with a corresponding declining level of participation in permanent, full-time work. Policies which have been seen to largely benefit those with family responsibilities (as well as those undertaking study or leisure pursuits) have developed alongside flexible working practices which do not fulfil the objectives set out above: they are accompanied by lower pay, instability of employment and a lack of employment rights. This has led some to question the motives behind the introduction of family-friendly working practices (Simkin and Hillage, 1992). Many forms of flexible work do not meet the objective of enhancing gender equality because of different patterns of take-up. The differences in take-up of part-time work amongst mothers and fathers is particularly striking across all members of the European Union, with the rate of part-time work amongst mothers 13 times that of fathers (Commission of the European Communities, 1993b). Such work is often poorly paid, contributing to the gender wages gap in Europe.

Nevertheless, flexible working practices which achieve a balance between the needs of the employer and those of employees have been successfully introduced in some cases. For example, Ludwig Beck, a German retail company specializing in fashion, adopted a flexible working policy as long ago as 1976 after undertaking a survey of staff needs. The 'individual work hours' scheme is open to all employees and currently applies to about 85 per cent of the company's workforce. Each worker decides how many hours to work each month, within a minimum of 60 hours and a maximum of 163 hours. After discussion with the department head, working hours are agreed and an individual contract of employment is drawn up. Each department then draws up provisional monthly plans and detailed weekly plans for organizing work. Employees are allowed to renegotiate their contract of work at any time. Company surveys of employees' and management's views of the scheme suggest that it is extremely popular amongst the staff and many working parents have benefited from the scheme (Hogg and Harker, 1992).

Leave Arrangements

The most commonly adopted form of support for working parents is leave arrangements. In all European countries women have the right to a period of leave after the time of the birth and some employers offer enhanced maternity conditions in addition to the statutory provisions, in the form of extended leave or additional maternity pay. For the employer this measure involves limited additional cost and can bring benefits in terms of the retention of skilled personnel. Leave for fathers is also extremely important if the objective of the equal sharing of family responsibilities between men and women is to be achieved. Statutory paternity leave is available in four member states. Statutory parental leave, which normally follows on from maternity leave and can be taken by the mother or the father, is available in 12 member states, varying in length from three months for each parent (Greece) to up to three years in total (Germany).

Although the full extent of employers' enhancement of leave policies relating to the birth of a child through collective agreement is not known, widespread practice has been noted in almost all member states (Commission of the European Communities, 1994). It is occasionally offered by companies in countries where there is no statutory leave for fathers. At Littlewoods, the UK retail company, for example, new fathers are offered 10 days' paid leave. Some employers in the UK also offer employment breaks which allow employees to take time off to look after their children or elderly relatives, travel or study and have a guaranteed job when they return.

Other leave arrangements policies are also the subject of collective agreements and have been documented by the European Commission Childcare Network.[4] In Denmark all workers in the public sector and about 95 per cent of those in the private sector have the right to take paid leave on the first day of a child's illness. In France all women in the public sector, and some men and women in the private sector, are entitled to take 12 days' leave a year to look after a sick child and in Ireland civil servants can take five days' paid leave in such circumstances. A limited number of workers in Italy are entitled to take a few days' leave to spend time at a nursery when a child first starts to attend (Commission of the European Communities, 1994).

Some employers have automatically associated the right to family leave with mothers and have limited such schemes to their use. Such an approach, although helping parents with their family responsibilities, contributes towards the persisting gender division of paid and unpaid work. But even when policies are offered equally to men and women, this may not automatically result in a greater sharing of the family responsibilities. Statutory parental leave schemes throughout Europe are more often taken up by women only, even when both parents are entitled to such measures. The experience of Scandinavian countries suggests that offering non-transferable rights to mothers and fathers to take parental leave encourages a higher rate of take-up amongst men (Commission of the European Communities, 1994).

Childcare

Differences in the level of publicly funded childcare provision have had an impact on the extent to which employers offer such support to parents. In countries with substantial public provision, employer-sponsored childcare provision is scarce. On the other hand childcare is more likely to be on the agendas of companies in the UK, where statutory childcare provision is comparatively low: there are approximately 500 employer-sponsored nurseries in the UK (Working for Childcare, 1994).

In recent years childcare partnership schemes have been particularly popular, offering a more cost effective option for employers and other partners, such as local authorities. Since 1990 a Dutch government scheme has increased the number of childcare places, partly financed by national government and partly financed by employers. The scheme has resulted in a decrease in workplace provision and an increase in the number of employer-subsidized places (Hogg and Harker, 1992). This option is also often favoured by employees who may prefer to use childcare nearer to home rather than workplace provision.

In the region of Emilia-Romagna in Italy, an initiative was set up in 1990 to coordinate planning for the opening hours of a range of services such as childcare, health and education facilities, in an attempt to meet the needs of users and take account of caring responsibilities. The regional government, the municipalities and districts of cities involved in the project, community associations and organizations have worked in partnership to meet these ends. The scheme has led to the establishment of more flexible childcare services including enabling access to services for parents with reduced working hours (Commission of the European Communities, 1993c).

Flexibility in childcare can be achieved by other schemes such as childcare vouchers or allowances, although such schemes are not common in countries other than the UK. Recognizing that employees face particular difficulties finding childcare provision, other employers offer or buy into a resource and referral scheme. In Germany, for example, BMW, the car manufacturing company, set up a childcare information and referral service for their employees in 1992, using the services of a specialist agency *Kinderburo*. Employees can obtain information, either by telephone or in person, about childcare facilities in the area. Specialist advice on arranging and selecting daycare, emergency care and babysitting is also offered (Harker and Brinkhoff, 1993).

Eldercare

Eldercare has received limited attention from employers to date, despite growing recognition throughout Europe that increasing numbers of employees will be responsible for caring for adult dependants. Initiatives undertaken by employers to date have been varied. Some are aimed at the carers, such as offering flexible working practices, financial assistance, adult daycare services or counselling. For example, in 1991 Barclays Bank PLC introduced 'responsibility breaks' for all employees with a minimum of two years' service, enabling them to take a complete break or work part time for up to six months, in order to care for an elderly dependant. Pilkington Glass, a UK-based company provides respite care and various welfare services for its retirees, through a charitable trust set up by its founders, and these facilities are also available for some elderly relatives of current employees.

Factors Influencing the Development of Family-Friendly Practices in Europe

Family-friendly employment practices are not a new concept for the 1990s. Employers throughout Europe have intermittently contemplated the family responsibilities of their workforce. During the First World War, for example, workplace crèches were set up by UK governmental agencies in response to the need for mothers to work to meet labour shortages. In France, at the end of the First World War when the labour market contracted, officials instructed employers to retain married women in preference to single women on the assumption that the former had family responsibilities and hence some claim to work (Pedersen, 1993). Similarly, in Slovenia firms are currently required by law to take into account family obligations in making decisions about redundancies (Nevenka Cernigoj Sadar, personal communication, October 1994). Short-term measures such as these have done little to sustain the development of family-friendly policies because they have tended to pursue one of the key objectives outlined above at the expense of the others.

Systematic research has yet to be undertaken as to the impetus for the development of family-friendly policies, but the introduction of initiatives by employers is likely to be a combination of international, national and local influences.

International Level

At an international level some family-friendly policies have spread from outside the European Union, especially via multinational companies whose staff seek benefits equal to their international counterparts. For example, the initiative for, and elements of, the equal opportunities programme set up by the head office of Levi Strauss (Europe) came from the parent company in the USA and was subsequently adapted to meet conditions in Europe; the equal opportunities policy which was implemented in the UK IKEA department stores originated from the Swedish parent company; and pressure for Eisai, a Japanese company, to introduce family-friendly policies in the research and development branch which the company has opened in the UK came from the staff, who had experienced such benefits when working for the company in Japan (Erler et al., 1994; Hogg and Harker, 1992). Research is needed to determine the conditions necessary for the spread of family-friendly policies within multinational companies. It is possible, for example, that where family-friendly policies in multinational firms have struck a balance between the needs of the employer and those of employees they have been more likely to be taken up across the whole company.

The global economy has undoubtedly had an impact on the development of work-family policies in Europe. The relationship between a country's (or, indeed, company's) prosperity and the likelihood of family-friendly policies being implemented is not a straightforward one, however. In a recession companies value skilled staff as much as ever and are particularly reluctant to lose the investment that they have made in their expertise. Even in periods of high unemployment, employers have been found to introduce policies to retain staff with specialist skills (Rajan and van Eupen, 1989). However, when a company is experiencing financial difficulties it will often be cautious about introducing too much change, despite evidence of the cost effectiveness of such measures.

Cultural differences have also had a significant impact on the development of family-friendly policies in Europe. Differences in attitudes to employment, the value placed on family life and individuals' sense of entitlement (see

Lewis and Taylor, Chapter 9), and therefore the demands of working parents, are all likely to be important factors. Differences in levels and type of employment amongst working women reflect national attitudes about the roles and responsibilities of parenthood. Table 4.2 shows that in the Netherlands and the UK levels of part-time work amongst working women are high. Here, opposition to mothers going out to work when their children are young is more likely to be heard than in countries such as Denmark and France, where the employment of mothers is more accepted. Interestingly one of the few persistent trends in Europe is the level of full-time employment amongst fathers, which remains consistently high (Commission of the European Communities, 1993b).

Table 4.2 *Parental employment and unemployment in the European Union, 1991*

	% employed (part time)		
	Women with child aged 0–9	Men with child aged 0–9	Women aged 20–39, no child
Belgium	60 (22)	94 (1)	81 (14)
Denmark	75 (28)	92 (2)	77 (15)
Germany	55 (24)	94 (1)	84 (10)
Greece	41 (3)	96 (1)	57 (3)
Spain	33 (4)	91 (7)	65 (4)
France	59 (16)	92 (1)	76 (10)
Ireland	30 (9)	81 (2)	77 (3)
Italy	42 (5)	95 (2)	57 (5)
Luxembourg	40 (13)	97 (-)	85 (4)
Netherlands	40 (35)	92 (8)	79 (29)
Portugal	69 (6)	96 (1)	79 (3)
UK	51 (35)	88 (1)	87 (8)
All	51 (20)	92 (2)	76 (9)

Source: Commission of the European Communities, 1993a

National Social Policies

National policies interact with the practices of employers. In countries where statutory social policies are advanced employers are not required to offer duplicate services. Levels of statutory childcare provision, for example, vary considerably throughout the European Union. The actions of employers vary accordingly: in Denmark, for example, childcare provision is largely organized by local authorities and is available for the majority of preschool children. Consequently the principal role of employers, with regard to family-friendly policies, is, to a large extent, to provide alternative support (such as flexible working hours). In 1989 Danish State Railways, the Danish national railway company, obtained government funding to campaign to lengthen the opening hours of local childcare facilities to meet the working hours' needs of their employees better (Hogg and Harker, 1992). In this case it was seen to be more appropriate for the employer to play an advocacy role on behalf of its employees than to provide the facilities directly.

Statutory leave arrangements also vary across Europe and affect employer responses. Parental leave is available in nine, and paternity leave in six, of the current member states. Although there is no comprehensive source of data on the extent of collective or company agreements which supplement statutory leave policies, such agreements are known to make a significant contribution (Commission of the European Communities, 1994). Where statutory leave provision is generous, companies are often willing to supplement arrangements: in Germany, for example, where three years' statutory parental leave is offered, an estimated 14 per cent of companies offered employees a longer period of parental leave in 1991 (Commission of the European Communities, 1994). Where statutory provision is low, employers may play a different role by offering substitute arrangements. In Luxembourg, for example, public sector workers are entitled to one year's unpaid leave or to work part time until a child reaches the age of four, and in the UK an estimated 15 per cent of employers offer career breaks, where workers can take a period of leave (normally unpaid) to care for their children (Commission of the European Communities, 1994).

There is no evidence to date of whether policies are more effective if initiated primarily by the state or by employers. However, as argued by Peter Moss in Chapter 2, the role of the state would seem to be most central to the development of comprehensive and gender equitable policies on family care. However, the role of employer in implementing policies and responding to local demands and needs would seem to be vital, if secondary to that of the state.

Encouragement of employer schemes by governments is more direct when they are in the form of tax reliefs or subsidies. In Belgium some workplace childcare services receive subsidies from one of the statutory welfare agencies in each of the French, Flemish and German communities, respectively. Similarly between 1990 and 1994 employers in the Netherlands were able to receive subsidies for workplace childcare provision, as well as partial tax relief on their childcare costs. In Germany, childcare allowances have been tax deductible since 1992. All these measures have been claimed to have had some impact on the development of employer provision, and assessment of the relative effectiveness of their impact is a challenge for future research. In France, on the other hand, employers are required to pay high levels of social insurance contributions which help fund the statutory childcare system. As a result few employers invest in childcare facilities themselves.

A key influence on the development of policies at a national level is the role and attitudes of trade unions and other employee representatives. The level of involvement of trade unions and other bodies such as workers' councils varies throughout Europe. Trade unions throughout Europe have traditionally opposed 'atypical'[5] employment patterns – despite their potential for being family-friendly – because of the lack of pro rata benefits. Nevertheless, in some countries their influence on family-friendly policies can be noted. In Germany action has been taken by the Union of Public Services, Transport and Communication Workers (ÖTV) to draft a collective agreement for part-time workers ensuring: the right to return to a full-time job; the right to establish one's working hours; the right to take part in training courses and to have the opportunity of advancing professionally; and a condition to ensure that the volume of work must be reduced to correspond with the reduction in working hours (Harker and Brinkhoff, 1993). Similarly Dutch unions have been pressing for rights to part-time work and part-time leave, with these issues dominating collective agreements (*FNV News*, 1993).

In Germany trade unions favour public childcare rather than employer-sponsored childcare. German trade unions frequently oppose family daycare (childminding) on the grounds of the unstable work situation of the care giver and the lack of 'professionalism' of some carers (Hogg and Harker, 1992). Partnership schemes to set up childcare and flexible working practices undertaken by employers are more likely to be welcomed by the trade unions. In Ireland trade unions have been influential in the development of workplace childcare and their role is becoming increasingly important in negotiations. The workplace nursery at Radio Telefis Éireann (RTE), the national broadcasting organization, was set up by a trade union in 1987, for example, and continues to be managed by it.

Trade unions and workers' councils can enable employees to have a fuller involvement in the planning and implementing of family-friendly policies and therefore help meet the key objective of balancing the needs of employees with those of employers. What method of consultation – through collective bargaining, workers' groups or forums, for example – is most effective may be specific to the sector or workplace. Nevertheless, useful research could be undertaken to establish effective strategies for employee consultation (see e.g. Fletcher, and Rapoport, Chapter 11).

Local Influences

Limited research has been undertaken to establish why employers choose to adopt family-friendly policies. Employers have offered a variety of reasons such as the reduction of absenteeism, the retention and recruitment of staff and public relations, and response to employees' demands (Hogg and Harker, 1992). Schemes often originate from a suggestion from an employee, or from a recognition by management that productivity is being threatened by a failure to meet employees' needs. One example is the childcare scheme adopted at Casterman, a Belgian printing company, in the 1970s. At this time the company noticed the high rate of absenteeism amongst employees with young children and noted that the lack of childcare suitable for part-time and shift workers might be the problem. Following a survey of employees' needs a crèche was opened by the company close to the printing works; it is open from 5.45 to 22.30 to cater for shift workers, who make up 83 per cent of the workforce (Hogg and Harker, 1992).

It is also useful to consider why family-friendly policies have *not* been adopted by some employers. Key factors which have already been mentioned are the impact of the recession, attitudes towards working mothers and the extent of government provision. Other factors include resistance from management and other staff and assumptions about the link between working time and productivity (see Lewis and Taylor, Chapter 9).

The diversity of factors likely to have contributed to the development of family-friendly policies across Europe deters any superficial explanations as to the necessary criteria for their increase. In the 1990s family-friendly employment practices in Europe cannot be considered to be widespread but are increasingly becoming part of the business agenda. It is certainly the case that most initiatives have been adopted by large, especially multinational companies, but there are also examples of good practice in the small and medium business sector (Erler et al., 1994).

Lessons from Europe: Employer Initiatives

Many lessons can be learnt from the actual experiences of employers; the realms of comparison are usefully extended, therefore, when a European rather than national perspective is taken. Limited research available suggests common elements in becoming family-friendly are: overcoming internal resistance, gaining support at all levels, encouraging the take-up of schemes, and monitoring and evaluating their progress (Erler et al., 1994; Hogg and Harker, 1992; Harker and Brinkhoff, 1993). Clear recognition of the business case is vital if policies are to be fully integrated into the strategic business planning activities of companies. Case study material from companies around Europe offers useful insight on each of these points. To date a remarkable uniformity of experience within companies has been evident when companies from throughout Europe relate their progress towards family-friendly policies. The examples quoted in the following sections[6] have been chosen for their innovation but nevertheless usefully illustrate broader experience of implementing family-friendly policies.

Overcoming Resistance

Convincing management about the need for family-friendly policies requires acknowledgement of the changes that such policies will cause. The implementation of new initiatives inevitably requires initial work for personnel staff and managers and an alteration in their traditional management procedures. Some managers resist change because they fear that their management autonomy will be undermined by new working arrangements, particularly if they involve staff taking long periods away from the office or working non-uniform.

When Levi Strauss (Europe) sought to introduce its equal opportunities programme in Belgium in 1988, resistance from management was voiced. A series of 'focus' conversations with managers and departmental meetings were set up where management met to discuss policies and challenge assumptions. Real-life case studies were used to show the benefit of new ideas.

Resistance can also come from other members of staff who feel that they will not be benefiting from new policies. Some may feel that it is not the company's role to provide support for families: when BMW in Germany first proposed setting up a resource and referral service in the early 1990s some felt that the company should be 'making cars not babies'. The company sought to overcome internal resistance by introducing an information campaign through the company monthly newspaper, circulating a brochure about family-friendly policies and setting up information stands about work–family policy and practice in the company canteen.

Support at all Levels

Gaining support for the implementation of work-family policies from all levels of the company is essential if policies are to be implemented successfully. One of the greatest difficulties is changing preconceived ideas. Policies need to be integrated into the work plans of all departments rather than treated as a separate agenda where they will be ignored, forgotten or seen as a 'perk'. As one equal opportunities manager of a large engineering firm noted:

> The danger is if you don't move to that [change at management level] what you are left with is fields of policies; you can point to these policies but rarely have you fundamentally altered the culture, the value system, of the company. (Harker and Brinkhoff, 1993)

It is helpful to stress the business case for family-friendly policies when trying to convince senior managers of the need to deal with work–family policies as part of the strategic planning of the business. Some companies have explicitly costed the savings that they make by adopting family-friendly policies. Research undertaken at Hypobank in Germany, for example, calculated the replacement costs per employee to be approximately DM90,000 (approximately £37,000), totalling a loss of DM18 million every year, based on a 35 per cent return-to-work rate after maternity leave (Harker and Brinkhoff, 1993).

Encouraging Take-Up

Employers need to be conscious of the eligibility criteria of all their 'family-friendly' policies, as well as informal constraints, to ensure that men and women are encouraged to take up schemes. At the UK sites of the Swedish furnishings and household goods retail company, IKEA, a research project was established in 1991 to look at ways in which new fathers could be supported in the workplace. Introductory half-day meetings were held with personnel managers at all sites and presentations were made by the research advisers to store managers, departmental heads and staff representatives. The resulting project eventually shifted from one directed especially at fathers, offering individual and group support advice sessions, information packs and workshops, to a wider service for all staff. The wider service was seen as essential in securing the future of the new parents' project, offering an independent and, when necessary, confidential support service.

Simply implementing a scheme may not be enough and strategies for improving take-up are important. When Levi Strauss (Europe) introduced its equal opportunities scheme in 1988, a central feature was the fact that managers were assessed on how they implemented the programme as part of their management appraisal.

Monitoring and Evaluation

An assessment of how far policies meet the key objectives of family-friendly policies outlined above, at both local and national levels, is necessary in order to monitor and evaluate their impact for employees and employers alike. Surveying employees' needs before introducing a scheme is important. Listening to employees' needs can initiate action on family-friendly policies. A chance remark of an employee to the Chief Executive at Swift SC Telecommunications in Belgium led to the setting up of a workplace childcare scheme. At Morgan Automation, a small engineering company in the UK with nine employees, staff needs are individually taken into account. One of the directors is a magistrate which necessitates a flexible hours working arrangement. Work–family commitments are viewed similarly and employees are able to work the hours which fit in with their childcare commitments. Small and medium companies are unique in their ability to be flexible in their response to staff needs (Erler et al., 1994). This can lead to supportive and happy working environments for employees. However, dealing with personnel policies in an *ad hoc* way (as many of them do) can lead to discriminatory practice and stifle change towards a less gender segregated labour market. Maintaining the informal flexibility of family-friendly practices and at the same time formalizing their approach to family-friendly policies would seem to be a key challenge for the development of such policies in this sector.

Looking to the Future

Study of family-friendly policies in Europe has been limited. This is a little known area of social policy, a fact recognized by the European Commission, which has begun to focus attention on work–family policies and practices in recent years. There are many areas which deserve further attention. Here, three pressing concerns are highlighted: the need for consistent definitions of terms, moving away from the emphasis on women rather than family, and ensuring that new ways of working develop in a way that is consistent with the objectives of family friendliness.

Defining Family-Friendly Policies and Practices

There is little consensus throughout Europe on the terminology applicable to organizationally based schemes which support social networks with their familial obligations. Whilst it is useful to determine key objectives which policies must meet if they are to be considered to be family-friendly, clarity in the definition of 'family-friendly' is needed, particularly for the purpose of transnational comparisons. Better consensus in understanding of the various components of family-friendly policies and practices would also usefully elucidate the processes towards becoming a family-friendly employer. The term 'family-friendly' is a subcultural, multi-meaning term which has more popular usage in some European countries than others. Other terms such as 'reconciliation' are also used but inadequately defined and subject to differing interpretations: 'reconciliation' is used in Slovenia to stress the need for traditional (normally maternal) family responsibilities, whilst it is more widely used in Germany with reference to balancing work and family commitments. The ambiguities surrounding the terms are in part the result of cultural differences but may also be indicative of the lack of uniformity in the development of policies and practices in this area.

Gender Differences in Family-Friendly Policies

Throughout Europe, the take-up of family-friendly policies is gender specific. Since gender equality is a key objective of family-friendly policies, the challenge of the next decades is to remove the gender differences in work–family practices, to ensure that they are truly family-friendly and not especially targeted to be 'woman-friendly'.

The experience of the Scandinavian countries suggests that offering non-transferable rights to leave encourage fathers to take up leave. Certain groups of fathers have also been found to be more likely to take leave: those who are well educated and have good incomes. But as the European Commission Childcare Network has noted, ideologies about parenthood and employment, workplace attitudes, women's job satisfaction and labour market attachment, and the bargaining position between parents in the family are also likely to be contributory factors (Commission of the European Communities, 1994). In the Network's view the most significant factors are the payment attached to leave, the length of the leave, the availability of concurrent and non-transferable leave, the possibility of taking leave 'flexibility' (part time, for example) and development of leave policies in a broad strategy with the support of all the social partners (Commission of the European Communities, 1994). Exchange of experience throughout all Europe will help all social partners recognize the key factors necessary for removing gender distinctions in family-friendly policies.

New Forms of Working

The traditional male model of working is becoming a historical rather than a realistic model in practice. Nevertheless many employment initiatives throughout Europe have been based on this model. Recognizing the fundamental changes in ways of working and identifying measures which ensure that such employment is family-friendly is a challenge which is faced throughout Europe. Achieving a balance between the needs of the employee and the employer is central to that ambition. Holt and Thaulow in Chapter 6 suggest that family-friendly policies could be seen to have three distinct components in relation to the needs of parenthood: economic support (for example, job security, opportunities for promotion, access to a living wage), practical care (such as flexible working hours and childcare support) and emotional care (for example, mechanisms to support coping, emotional space). To date most attention has been paid to practical care offered by employers; considering the other pieces of the work–family jigsaw might usefully inform the search for a balance between employer and employee needs in the context of new forms of working.

In conclusion, this chapter has drawn out key objectives of family-friendly policies and identified processes which influence their development. There remain many questions which research has yet to answer about the relationship between different processes and their effectiveness. Identifying how family-friendly policies work is essential if adequate assessment of their effect is to be made. What role should government, employee representatives and employers play? What are the vital elements of a family-friendly programme? Furthermore, do family-friendly policies really work and for whom, and how should outcomes be measured? Our understanding of family-friendly policies and practices is still emerging. And yet, the demand for such policies and practice has been widely recognized by representatives of all social partners. The challenge we face as we approach the next century is responding to this demand in the most practical and effective way possible.

Notes

1 This chapter will largely deal with employment practices in members of the European Union, unless otherwise stated.

2 Family-friendly policies and practices in the European Union known at the time of writing are reported. This is recognized to be a fast changing area.

3 'Annual hours working' is where an employee's working hours are defined over a whole year and the employee has a certain amount of flexibility in when she or he works the hours required.

4 The full title of the Network is: The European Commission Network on Childcare and Other Measures to Reconcile Employment and Family Responsibilities.

5 Atypical employment is that which diverges from the standard full-time employment relationship.

6 Case study material has been taken from Erler et al., (1994), Harker and Brinkhoff (1993) and Hogg and Harker (1992).

References

Commission of the European Communities (1993a) *New Ways of Working: The Challenge for Companies and Families.* Final Report: Seminar 30 September to 1 October 1993.

Commission of the European Communities (1993b) *Mothers, Fathers and Employment 1985–1991*. DGV.B4 Equal Opportunities Unit.

Commission of the European Communities (1993c) *Childcare in Partnership: Local Authority/Employer Partnership Initiatives in the European Community*. Report prepared by Bronwen Cohen for European Commission's Family Policy Unit.

Commission of the European Communities (1994) *Leave Arrangements for Workers with Children: A Review of Leave Arrangements in the Member States of the European Union and Austria, Finland, Norway and Sweden*. European Commission Network on Childcare and other Measures to Reconcile Employment and Family Responsibilities.

Erler, G., Erler, W., Jaeckel, M. and Subocz, B. (1994) *Von Europa lernen: Innovative und familienfreundliche Personalführung in kleinen und mittleren Unternehmen: Erfahrungen aus drei europäische Regionen*. Munich: Fan Consult.

FNV (1994) *Part-Time Work: The Dutch Perspective. Policy and Perceptions of the Netherlands Trade Union Confederation FNV*. Amsterdam: FNV.

FNV News (1993) No. 8, December.

Harker, L.M. and Brinkhoff, A. (1993) *Making Family-Friendly Policies Work: The Seminar Report*. London: Daycare Trust.

Hewitt, P. (1993) 'Flexible working: Asset or cost?', *Policy Studies*, 14(3): 18–28.

Hogg, C. and Harker, L.M. (1992) *The Family-Friendly Employer: Examples from Europe*. London: Daycare Trust.

Pedersen, S. (1993) *Family, Dependence, and the Origins of the Welfare State: Britain and France 1914–1945*. Cambridge University Press.

Rajan, A. and van Eupen, P. (1989) *Good Practice in the Employment of Women Employees*. IMS Report no. 183. Institute of Manpower Studies.

Simkin, C. and Hillage, J. (1992) *Family Friendly Working: New Hope or Old Hype?* IMS Report No. 224. Institute of Manpower Studies.

Working for Childcare (1994) *Survey of Employer Sponsored Nursery Provision, Britain*. Working for Childcare.

5

The Restructuring of Work and Family in the United States: A New Challenge for American Corporations

Judith G. Gonyea and Bradley K. Googins

Work–family programs within the United States continue to evolve because of dramatic turmoil both inside and outside of the corporation. What began primarily as a response to working mothers faced with inadequate childcare is now framed by a whole new set of social and economic realities for both corporations and families. Recent trends in corporate downsizing, which have forced employees to work harder and assume more responsibility in the workplace, have heightened the stress of living and working. The decline in real family income over the past two decades has led to increased anxiety over job and income security, forced more women with young children into the labor force, and contributed to a broader social anxiety that is manifested in both social and political arenas. Public sector and community supports for families have also continued to weaken through a parallel downsizing of the government. Thus, many families have had to confront the shrinking of the public safety net as well as the continuing dissolution of informal community supports, due in part to the new demands and roles of work and workplaces.

Despite media publicity about the growth of 'family-friendly' companies, most employees – men and women – still face inadequate support from the public and private sectors in creating a healthy balance between work and family. To a large extent this is a result of business leaders', policy makers' and scholars' decisions to define 'family-responsive' narrowly as either additions to the corporate welfare system through fringe benefits or modifications in work schedules. As Kingston stresses, 'this operational definition has two significant implications: it obscures the full breadth of the ways business practices shape family lives [and] it narrows the contours of the policy debate' (1990: 441). It is our belief that the next important step to advance the work–family field or practice is a move away from work–family being defined narrowly as a 'benefit' to a broader conceptualization of work–family as a 'strategic business concern' for promoting a healthy workplace in the twenty-first century. To achieve this objective, however, human resource personnel and other work–family advocates must expand their focus beyond the implications of the demographic shifts in families and workers for corporate

America. Critical to this next stage is an understanding of the changing nature of the work – not only the restructuring of the work environment and jobs, but the rethinking of the concept of 'career' (Bailyn, 1992). Also key is a grasp of the current political and economic climates in which American businesses operate, particularly shifting cultural values regarding the concepts of public and private responsibility.

It is our contention that by gaining a better understanding of this new set of socio-political realities which are driving today's markets and communities, human resource personnel can move work–family to a more strategic position within the corporation and become a partner in reestablishing a new employer–employee social contract. In this chapter, we therefore first explore the nature of the shifting socio-economic and political climate in the United States and then put forth a series of strategies as to how the professionals in the work–family field can respond to and integrate these social forces into their mission in order to become a core concern of corporations.

The Socio-Economic and Political Climate

Changes in family structure and norms served to ignite the original work–family field in the 1970s. The increasing numbers of women in paid employment, the emergence of working mothers and dual-earner couples, and changing conceptions of gender and parenthood reconfigured work–family patterns in the United States (Pleck, 1985; Beach, 1989). In the 1980s and 1990s, however, dramatic changes within corporations and society are reshaping work–family patterns. These socio-political forces can best be captured under three general headings: the reaffirmation of the ideologies of individualism and familism; the downsizing of government; and the downsizing and restructuring of corporations.

A Reemphasis on America's Ideologies of Individualism and Familism

Cultural ideologies provide the context for how countries define problems and how they seek solutions. The United States represents a liberal individualistic society. The state, the economy, religion and culture all stress the concept of individual choice and freedom. In contrast, many northern European communities are examples of communal corporatism in which 'modernization is built upon a perception of the state as a national community, rather than a nation of free individuals' (Meyers et al., 1988: 144). The preeminence of the individual is ingrained in our national identity. Comparing America's and Canada's founding legislation, Clark (1993) notes that America's Declaration of Independence emphasizes 'life, liberty, and the pursuit of happiness' while Canada's British North American Act stresses 'peace, order and government'. Closely related to the principle of individualism is the ideology of familism – or the family ethic – which emphasizes family self-determination, privacy, and freedom from intrusion. Also incorporated into the ideology of familism is the concept of family responsibility – that is, when an individual cannot attain independence, family members are the next level of responsibility (Abramovitz, 1988).

These values of individualism and familism form the historical basis for the United States' residual approach to public policy. A philosophy that emphasizes that the state should only become involved after the family has assumed as much responsibility as possible for care of its members and the market has failed as well. In the 1980s and 1990s, conservatives have reasserted this agenda in the United States. The new right has stressed that the family's private domain is natural and normal and that government non-intervention is justified and acceptable. Correspondingly, governmental assistance should not be regarded by citizens as a 'right', but rather it should be seen as an exception and privilege (Walker, 1985; 1991). The right simultaneously carries the dual messages of being 'pro-family' and 'anti-government' (Langley, 1991). Under President Reagan, the focus was on eliminating governmental programs viewed as 'undercutting the family' (Seaburg, 1990). Seeking a 'kinder, gentler society', the Bush administration's message of 'a thousand points of light' also emphasized the role of family, church, and charitable organizations (as opposed to government) in the well-being of citizens. Yet this message does not just come from the right. President Clinton has also stressed concepts of personal sacrifice, voluntarism, and individual responsibility as important to achieving a stronger nation. Nor is the reemergence of a philosophy of individualism and familism restricted to the public sector. For example, Nash (1994) in her article 'The nanny corporation' cautions against the business sector's increasing entry (through employee assistance programs, mental health and alcohol counseling, childcare, etc.) into the private lives of their employees.

The ideology of familism, promoted by the right, is based on the idealized traditional, nuclear, middle-class family of a breadwinner father, a homemaker mother and dependent children. The family is viewed as 'a private place where all caring occurs, and which assumes the total availability of families' free domestic labor and time . . . Specifically that women are home with free time and available to provide care' (Hooyman and Gonyea, 1995: 112). Ignored is the fact that for many families, especially working-class families, immigrant families, and families of color, this image was never reality, nor does it currently represent the majority of American families. Rather, members of the new right express concerns that the diversification of family forms is leading to the moral and economic decline of society. Despite the growing diversity in America's families and women's entry into the workforce, they believe that the traditional nuclear family should remain the guiding metaphor for American social policy. They argue that the responsibilities and costs of care should be shifted back to the family rather than incurred by the state and stress that the state's primary responsibility to the family is to ensure freedom from state intrusion (Linsk et al., 1992).

The Downsizing of Government

The 1980s represented a time period in which the appropriate role of government was being reevaluated, not just in the United States, but internationally (Hula, 1991). Eastern Europe and the former Soviet Union experienced the collapse of socialist and communist governments. Within the United States, increasing international economic competition and shrinking public dollars led to government retrenchment and interest in privatization (Kreiger, 1988). In 1980, Ronald Reagan was elected to national office on the themes of the reduced government involvement in domestic affairs, the adoption of supply-side economics, and the return to traditional American values. His administration quickly passed the Economic Recovery Tax Act and the Omnibus Budget Reconciliation Act of 1981 which led to a reduction in federal taxes, a shifting of more responsibilities to the states, and the cutback or elimination of many domestic programs. To compensate for the loss of federal funds for social welfare, Presidents Reagan and Bush called for the creation of public–private partnerships and stressed the role of corporate philanthropy in addressing social problems. Faced with their own economic concerns, however, business leaders did not welcome this transfer of responsibility and have not moved to assume these new roles.

Despite the theme of less government, this did not mean that the Reagan and Bush administrations effectively cut federal spending. In fact, the combination of tax cuts and spending increases – higher defense and entitlement spending – under these two Republican presidents led to soaring annual deficits and a mounting federal debt. Equally important is that fewer federal monies were now available to be devoted to domestic concerns such as unemployment, homelessness, and hunger.

The 1992 election of President Clinton was supposedly about 'change'. Central to his presidential campaign were the issues of the improving of the national economy through reduction of the federal deficit and the creation of jobs as well as the introduction of national health care. While in his first two years in office Clinton did reduce the deficit slightly, a federal deficit approaching $5 trillion continues to loom over every public debate regarding the role of government. Midway through his presidential term, health care reform was derailed both by fears of 'bigger government' or government intrusion into citizens' private lives and by concerns regarding the public costs of universal coverage.

In 1995, the Republican-dominated House of Representatives raised the issue of a balanced budget amendment to the US Constitution. Although polls reveal that a majority of Americans support such an idea, support declines when it is linked with the need for higher taxes or government cuts in popular programs (Rezendes, 1995). Whether or not a balanced budget amendment is passed, it is clear that faced with a massive federal budget deficit, attention has increasingly focused on ways to reduce public expenditures. Clark cautions that faced with an increasing federal deficit and growing interest in cost effectiveness, 'familism offers a convenient justification to cloak the real reasons for withholding support' (1993: 27). As priority is placed upon finding less expensive and more efficient ways to care for dependent members of society, debates regarding private obligation and family responsibility will continue to intensify.

The Downsizing and Restructuring of Corporations

The globalization of the economy and the technological revolution have led to dramatic changes in the workplace through the downsizing, restructuring and reengineering of companies. Throughout the 1980s the manufacturing sector slashed millions of jobs due to plant closing, relocation and layoffs. *The Fortune 500* industrial companies have downsized and eliminated approximately one out of every four jobs. The US labor force has undergone a radical transformation. Only 18 percent of American jobs are now in the manufacturing sector (US Bureau of Labor Statistics, 1991). Almost 80 percent of the new jobs created between 1982 and 1992 were in the service and retail sectors, jobs which pay only one half of the average manufacturing wage. More than three quarters (78 percent) of Americans now work in the service sector and it is projected that by the year 2000 that figure will reach 92 percent (Schuping, 1992). Although services is a heterogeneous sector, encompassing diverse fields such as financial services, transportation, information technology, and retail services, much of the growth is anticipated in the lower-wages service jobs – janitors, house cleaners, waiters, retail workers and hospital orderlies (O'Reilly, 1992).

Throughout the past decade, American companies have sought to maintain or increase profitability by gaining greater control over their labor costs by adjusting the size of their workforce to respond to shifting market conditions. Companies began to downsize their workforce by relying more heavily on part-time and temporary workers as well as contracting out for services previously performed in-house. These flexible work arrangements are generally referred to as 'contingent work'. During the 1980s in the US part-time and temporary employment grew at a much faster pace than did full-time employment. Between 1980 and 1992, part timers increased by 39 percent, contracted services by 61 percent and temporary workers by 250 percent. Today, contingent workers represent 30 percent of the total workforce.

For employers, one of the primary advantages of contingent work is cost containment. Employers only have to pay for the work performed; rarely do they pay any discretionary benefits such as health insurance, paid leave, job retraining or pensions (Christensen, 1987). Although there are advantages to companies (and some individuals) in having greater flexibility in work arrangements, for many Americans (especially women and people of color who disproportionately fill their ranks) contingent work has resulted in greater job insecurity, lower wages, and fewer benefits (Bryant Quinn, 1991).

It is often noted that, during the 1980s, the income gap between the rich and the poor grew wider and more families fell out of rather than rose into the middle class (Center for Budget and Policy Priorities, 1989). Less understood, however, is that for many American families this decline is a result of losing their jobs in the ever shrinking core or primary labor sector and entering the rapidly growing contingent or secondary workforce. Corporate social welfare policies are a major source of social protection for American families, especially in a country which (unlike European nations) lacks national health insurance. Receipt of employee benefits is tied to the individual worker, but the protection extends to the worker's family (Hooyman and Gonyea, 1995).

> Health care plans help soften the impact of medical expenses and perhaps, encourage workers and their dependants to seek care that might otherwise be forgone. Retirement income allows workers to stop work and maintain certain living standards. Similarly disability benefits provide income to those unable to work, and survivor benefits protect against loss of earnings resulting from the death of a spouse or other relative. (Wiatrowski, 1990: 28)

Yet, individuals employed in the contingent or secondary labor force rarely have access to these benefits.

Even those workers still tied to the primary labor force are facing an increasing number of stresses. Working hours, for example, continue to increase, in part due to downsizing and reengineering. Hammer and Champy (1993), who coined the term 'reengineering the corporation' which became the management buzzwords of the 1990s, perceived the concept as a competitive business strategy to redesign work by combining fragmented tasks into streamlined processes saving time and money. However, Champy notes that: 'Some companies are just downsizing and calling it reengineering. They haven't changed a damn thing. I was doing a talk show, and a guy called in from Houston and said: "My managers say they are doing reengineering; all I know is I'm working twice as hard and twice as long, they've laid off half the people"' (Lancaster, 1995: B1). Job stress and job insecurity are, thus, new realities for workers in both the primary and the secondary labor sectors. The era of corporate reengineering and work redesign, coupled with the decline in real family income, has placed new stresses on American families. Concerns about childcare or eldercare (the original focus of the work–family field) are being overshadowed by a new set of work–family issues such as job security, income security, scarcity of time, and heightened stress in attempting to balance work and family responsibilities. Indeed, for most Americans, the most basic work–family issue is the ability to obtain a secure job that offers an adequate 'family wage'.

Work–Family at the Crossroads

In light of the changing socio-political landscape, the primary challenge today is how to reposition work–family within the corporation so that it is not just perceived as a benefit for the employee, but is also seen as a benefit for the corporation – that is, adding to the 'bottom line' of business. By most accounts, work–family has settled into a relatively comfortable niche within corporate life, perhaps best exemplified by the term 'family-friendly corporations'.

Work–family has gained an enormous presence in American corporations and now represents a relatively visible and well-entrenched part of corporate human resources. In larger companies, work–family manager positions have been created to provide leadership in this arena (Gonyea and Googins, 1992). Almost two-thirds of companies offer some type of childcare assistance, although mostly limited to dependant care spending accounts allowing pretax salary deductions, lunchtime seminars, and information and referral (Hewitt Associates, 1990). Lists such as *Working Mothers* magazine's '100 best companies' have contributed to the drive for family-friendly corporations. One might suggest that within some circles the case for the family-friendly corporation has reached the status of 'politically correct'.

Factors Contributing to Work–Family Remaining on the Periphery

Despite these successes, work–family does not rank as a primary business issue or concern. In the minds of most CEOs or corporate officers, the centrality of work–family to the organization remains very much in question. Instances where corporate leadership has driven the work–family issue into the organization's core identity and/or business strategies are rare (Lehman, 1995). It is our argument that within the United States the evolution of organizations to family-friendly environments remains incomplete. Factors contributing to work–family issues remaining on the periphery of the organizations include the following:

First, companies perceive of being family-friendly as part of their 'corporate welfare system'. Based on this corporate welfarism orientation, much of what companies do to meet employees' work–family needs occurs within a framework of individual accommodation as opposed to structural change. For many organizations, work–family benefits are understood within a 'paternalistic framework' in which it is felt that companies bear some responsibility to 'take care of employees and their families'. Addressing employees' work–family concerns is, therefore, accomplished through either offering individuals' the option of certain fringe benefits or flexible work arrangements.

Secondly, work–family programs continue to focus predominantly on dependant care issues. Ignored by corporations, or outside their traditional definition of work–family issues, is a wider spectrum of work–life issues that affect most employees such as achieving a healthy work–leisure balance, the link between job security and family economic security, personal growth and development, and broader quality of life issues. Given this narrower definition of work–family, coupled with the fact that family care giving is still viewed as primarily a 'woman's role', it should not be surprising that work–family programs are seen as benefiting not all employees, but rather just working women or, at best, working parents.

Thirdly, the perception of work–family programs as primarily a benefit for working women has several negative consequences. Although women may achieve short-term gains through family-responsive policies (i.e., more flexible working conditions, less job–family strain), there is a fear (perhaps quite real) that their use in the long run may result in discrimination against women in the workplace (i.e. obstacles to career advancement). Similarly, although working men express interest in having more flexible work arrangements that would allow them more time with their families, they are reluctant to use these 'mommy track' benefits (Hall, 1990). The issue of stigma surrounding the use of work–family benefits is widely reported (Hall, 1990; Gibbs, 1993). For both men and women, there is a concern that use of these benefits will call into question their commitment to work leading to negative job performance appraisals, lower salary increases, and lack of career advancement.

The perception of work–family initiatives as 'corporate welfare' (predominantly for working women) versus a 'business strategy' shapes both employers' reluctance to expand these benefits and employees' hesitancy to use them. Hall (1990) suggests that at the heart of the work–family issue is the question of corporate values. He argues that framing work–family balance as a 'parent problem' as opposed to a 'corporate problem' allows companies 'to look progressive by working on family issues without confronting important issues of discrimination – based not just on gender, but also race, ethnicity, and other kinds of differences' (1990: 13). A company that defines work–family balance as a corporate problem, Hall asserts, fosters the adoption of an organizational or structural change approach rather than an individual accommodation strategy.

In attempting to have work–family balance redefined as a central business concern, professionals in the work–family field might heed the words of reengineering advocates, Hammer and Champy (1993), that getting people to accept that the workplace will undergo radical change 'is not a war won in a single battle'. The key to success is creating compelling arguments that change is essential. For corporate leaders in the 1990s, the critical issues are global competition, the economy, new technology, cost cutting, and productivity and quality. Corporate leaders must therefore be convinced that investing in human capital is essential for corporate success: that is, 'the success of companies that try to produce *faster, better, and cheaper* depends, to a large extent, on how they respond to changes in the availability and quality of the workforce' (Mirvis, 1993a: 16).

Bridging business strategies with human resources priorities in the minds of corporate leaders will not be an easy task. Although most persons in senior management view the caliber of the workforce as an important factor in maintaining or achieving a competitive edge, they do not necessarily link this to HR strategies. Lawler et al.'s (1993: 44) analysis of information from 406 HR executives revealed that: 'getting the attention of top management' was a 'major barrier' for 14 percent and a 'barrier' for 47 percent; and a 'corporate culture that doesn't emphasize human resource issues' was a 'major barrier' for 20 percent and a 'barrier' for 56 percent. Of equal importance, however, is the fact that a substantial proportion of HR executives also appear unable to understand how HR functions contribute to the organization's competitiveness.

Lawler et al.'s data revealed that 'over one out of every four HR departments say that *none* of their company's business strategies are a major responsibility of their department'. They conclude that 'what emerges is a picture of the HR department as disconnected from mainline business concerns in the majority of the companies studied' (1993: 35).

Defining Work–Family Initiatives as Strategic Tools for Competitive Advantage

The statistics cited above are alarming. In a climate of global competition and cost cutting, human resource personnel must demonstrate to corporate leadership that investing in human capital is, in fact, linked to corporate success. The critical next stage is the recasting of work–family initiatives within the corporate culture from being viewed as primarily 'corporate welfarism' or strategies of individual accommodation into being perceived as 'strategic tools for competitive advantage'. To do so, stronger links will need to be created between work–family and business concerns of productivity and competitiveness. Such efforts will include defining the contribution of work–family to core business issues in the following ways.

Linking Work–Family to Employee Recruitment, Retention, and Work Performance

Even in a downsizing environment, recruiting and retaining a high-caliber workforce is a major concern of management. There is growing evidence that issues of work–family balance strongly influence individuals' choices about particular employment opportunities (Galinsky et al., 1993; Ransom et al., 1989; Marquart, 1988; Lambert et al., 1992). Although much of the emphasis has been on the gains that employees experience from flexible work options, as Parker and Hall emphasize, 'data suggest that the major beneficiary is the employer' (1993: 148). For example, the study of Dominion Bank's on-site childcare revealed that among the 40 interviewed supervisors, 70 percent felt it had improved morale; 40 percent cited gains in worker energy; 32 percent noted gains in work quantity; and 30 percent cited improved work quality (Stewart and Burge, 1989). A survey of 178 employers with corporate-sponsored childcare also found that 53 percent cited positive effects on absenteeism and 39 percent noted declines in tardiness (Burud et al., 1984). A study at the Chicago-based company Fel-Pro also found a positive relationship between workers' use of work–family benefits and company affiliation, support for co-workers, and demonstrating initiative on the job (Lambert et al., 1992).

The absence of trained, experienced workers generates losses of an estimated $100 billion annually in the United States (Bureau of National Affairs, 1989). For example, eldercare responsibilities of employees at TransAmerica Life companies are estimated to cost an average of $2,500 annually per worker (Scharlach et al., 1991). Company programs can make a difference.

The Union Bank study revealed that for employees with children under the age of five, users of on-site childcare had 4.6 fewer days absent per year compared to parents with other childcare arrangements. This reduction in absenteeism was estimated to have a cost saving of $19,000 (Ransom et al., 1989). The pharmaceutical company Merck estimates it recovers $3 for every $1 spent on family care (Fernandez, 1990).

Reframing work–family from an employee benefit to a strategic business concern affecting such issues as recruitment and retention creates a new perspective for both work–family professionals and firms. Moreover, the timing for such a transformation could not be more propitious. The reengineering and work redesign movements leave in their wake enormous opportunities to create new policies and structures by which organizations can address the new realities of work life. Whereas 'traditional' work–family benefits have been targeted toward childcare resources, the new strategic approach could use the unfreezing of the organization through reengineering to change a more basic set of structural and cultural barriers which continue to impede healthy and productive individuals and families. For example, the issues of face time and long hours create as serious a set of work–family barriers as does the absence of childcare. As long as work–family is conceptualized or perceived as primarily a benefit, these more fundamental issues will not be addressed. The transformation from benefit to strategy redefines work–family as a process by which work life and working conditions can be redesigned to achieve flexibility, responsiveness, and supports for both the organization and the employee.

Linking Work–Family to Valuing Employee Diversity as a Competitive Advantage

It is beyond dispute that the workforce of the twenty-first century will look very different from that of the previous century – in terms of both greater racial diversity and the greater participation of women. Mirvis poses the question: 'will companies hire more women and minorities into higher-paying, higher-status jobs, or will they be content with the status quo?' (1993a: 19). He notes that there is considerable difference in the ways companies approach increased workforce diversity. Some firms regard it as an affirmative action issue, others see it as good management, and yet others view it as a competitive advantage (Mirvis, 1993a). Morgan and Milliken note that: 'one has to see these changes as competing for agenda space with an array of other issues from which the company must select the important, not the trivial, and then formulate responses to those deemed relevant' (1992: 239). They suggest that a key obstacle to change in an organization is the failure to see changing workforce demographics as a potential productivity issue. This view is echoed by Parker and Hall who note that current work–family and diversity programs are isolated efforts and rarely connected to companies' strategic goals and, thus, 'the potential benefits to organizations are largely unrealized, and the benefits to individuals unnecessarily constrained' (1993: 123).

If workforce diversity is to be seen as a competitive advantage (versus an organizational problem), the challenge to corporations is to support strategies that enable employees to bring their whole selves to the job, their skills, experiences, values and attitudes. Broadening the concept of 'flexibility' beyond the typical dimensions of time, space or style, Parker and Hall suggest that flexibility can also be a means of promoting 'psychological availability': 'A flexible workplace enables employees to bring their "full" selves to work and to be psychologically engaged in the tasks, activities, and relationships that make up their jobs' (1993: 124). They argue that individuals have personal identities (as women, as Latinos, as gays or lesbians, etc.) and non-work roles (as care givers for children and/or parents, as church or community volunteers, etc.) in addition to their work roles; individuals carry these identities and non-work roles into the workplace every day; and people are more engaged in their work organization when they can express, rather than suppress, these identities in the workplace.

Based on this philosophy, flexibility becomes an approach of valuing differences and is linked in the organizational culture to core business outcomes. Employees who can bring their whole person into the workplace will be more productive workers. Further, a corporate orientation of 'valuing diversity' offers a single coherent framework for a number of human resource programs that are generally perceived as isolated efforts – dependant care benefits, work restructuring, management training programs, mentoring and career opportunities.

Work–Family as a Component of a New Employer–Employee Social Contract

For many American families, there is a growing sense of economic insecurity arising from changing social contracts in both the public and the private sectors. Public opinion polls consistently show that a significant proportion of working-age Americans do *not* expect Social Security (the federal government's old-age insurance program) to be solvent by the time they retire, and therefore seriously doubt they will receive benefits. The Republican Party's social vision, as reflected in Newt Gingrich's maiden speech as Speaker of the House of Representatives, is that private charities are more effective, less expensive and better for the people they help. McNamee et al. suggest that 'many health and human service charities fear a double hit . . . they will not only be expected to provide services once performed by the government, but they also will lose existing government funding, which typically represents 30% of their budgets' (1995: 65).

As the public social welfare 'safety net' has shrunk, so too has workers' sense of a social contract with their employer that hard work in the past would guarantee one a job in the future. The notion of cradle-to-grave job security for Americans disappeared in the 1980s. As Mirvis notes:

> Few companies can today ask for employee loyalty and many no longer seem to want it. In turn, employees have entered an era of 'free agency', in which they are

> being advised to keep their skills and résumés current and be prepared to move on when and where they can. We can only wonder whether the cynicism washing over the workforce might reach the point where corporate proclamations about the 'value of people' are going to be perceived as 'corpocrisy' – hypocrisy in corporate life. (1993b: 239)

As businesses become 'lean and mean' in order to increase productivity, some negative consequences of this strategy are beginning to be recognized. In a study of 10 downsized companies, Marks (1993) found that the most frequently reported problem – in 61 percent of the cases – was lower morale among the remaining workforce. Hammer and Champy, the authors of *Re-engineering the Corporation* (1993), also indicated in a recent *Wall Street Journal* interview that they may have underestimated the social impacts or human costs of downsizing (Lancaster, 1995).

A new social contract between employer and employee might be constructed around the concept of 'mutual flexibility' – recognizing that both employers and employees have need for flexible arrangements (Hooyman and Gonyea, 1995). For the corporation, changing technology and intense global competition require a flexibility to respond quickly to shifting market conditions. For employees, faced with unpredictable events such as sick children, ill parents, school plays and sports events, flexibility becomes an essential ingredient for achieving balance between work and home demands. For the firm, flexible staffing enables adaptability to insure a competitive advantage. For the worker, flexible scheduling enables the delicate juggling act to maintain a sense of equilibrium between work and home life.

As Lambert asserts, 'the interests of employers and employees are not always compatible, but neither are they always at odds' (1993: 243). A number of management experts have noted that in order for American companies to produce high-quality and innovative products, they will increasingly need employees who are willing to 'think' about their jobs rather than just 'do' them. An expanding body of literature suggests that workers are more likely to think about their jobs in innovative ways and make contributions to their company when they perceive the organization is supportive of them personally (Eisenberger et al., 1990). Not only do productive workers benefit the company, but they also view their home lives more positively than non-productive workers.

While cradle-to-grave (or even one year to the next) job security is no longer a central component of the employer–employee contract, 'mutual flexibility' may be the vehicle to demonstrate organizational support to employers. In practice, this will require a new dialogue in which both parties recognize each other's need, the differences between their needs, and most importantly, the need to devise a new set of tradeoffs that will lead to a satisfying of each. For some organizations, this may lead to the staffing of operations being negotiated by team rules rather than corporate policy. In fact, some examples of this have already begun to crop up in the form of sick time and vacation pools to cover a group of employees rather than individual workers. Under this arrangement, a team may be held to a number of hours agreed for the year, but to be arranged by the team in accordance with organizational production schedules and team members' personal and family needs. In another organization, mutual flexibility may lead to a redesign of work by which face time truly becomes irrelevant. Mutual flexibility may encompass a corporate commitment to strategic initiatives such as valuing workforce diversity, creating healthy work–family balance for employees, and skill training and reeducation. Although corporations can no longer offer employees a long-term commitment, the promise of a corporate culture that values a workforce which has a healthy balance between their work and personal lives may represent a cornerstone of the future employee–employer social contract. Such flexibility may be a means of promoting the 'psychological availability' of employees which, in turn, may lead to individuals not just doing, but thinking about their jobs (Parker and Hall, 1993). 'Achieving corporate competitiveness through mutual flexibility' could ultimately become the centerpiece of the new social contract for the American workplace.

Of course, mutual flexibility is neither a panacea, nor easily obtainable in practice. It becomes a critical element of the new social contract only in as much as both parties have the desire and the will to negotiate the tradeoffs that will be necessary. As knowledge workers become essential and valuable to firms, their ability to negotiate for flexibility increases. Such is not the case for contingent workers, whose power and ability to negotiate will continue to diminish, posing a serious problem for an increasingly larger group of employees for whom flexible scheduling is even more critical in negotiating the fragile worlds of work and home. Their fate will be left to a trickle down theory, which has often been the case of human resource policies and benefits. However, if mutual flexibility becomes a more standard practice among the core employees, it has a better chance of finding its way into other employee populations whose ability to negotiate is severely limited by the power relationships that influence their bargaining position.

Finally, as helpful as this concept can be in empowering both employee and employer in realizing their own goals, operationalizing mutual flexibility faces a number of organizational obstacles. To begin with, the absence of mechanisms by which these issues can be discussed, negotiated and implemented remains a serious organizational dilemma. Given the virtual demise of labor unions which traditionally could bring these issues to the fore both informally and formally through collective bargaining, there remains no viable formalized workplace vehicle by which a concept such as mutual flexibility can be surfaced and acted upon. The absence of formal structures severely limits the dialogue between interested parties. This often results in a top down approach whereby innovations in areas that would contribute to improved work life wait for insight and inspiration from above, missing the input and insight of the rank and file. Reaching a commonality of interests will require a new set of workplace structures that will encourage and promote joint problem solving around a growing set of mutual concerns at work and at home.

Also limiting the operationalization of mutual flexibility is the issue of power and control. Flexibility rests ultimately on who decides what flexible work arrangements will be implemented, and under what conditions. The current power distribution within most workplaces remains concentrated at the top of the organizational hierarchy. New participatory management schemes, and the team concept at the core of much of what has been termed reengineering, promise a broader distribution of power sharing. Unless there is a broader power sharing arrangement present in work organizations, any meaningful implementation of mutual flexibility is doubtful.

Conclusion

We have argued that the work–family field is now at a crossroads. Although work–family has settled into a relatively comfortable niche within corporate life in the USA, it is perceived by companies to be outside the mainstream or core business strategies and as primarily corporate social welfare. The next critical stage is to redefine work–family as a 'strategic tool for corporate competitiveness'. An important first step in transforming work–family from an issue largely peripheral to the core of the organization to one aligned with central business goals is the reframing of its agenda beyond a focus on mothers and women and an overreliance on programs and benefits. The discussion must be broadened to focus on all employees and must address more profound and difficult work–family issues such as deep-seated organizational attitudes, cultural norms, and the unintended negative consequences of existing corporate policies.

Restructuring work–family along strategic lines comes at the same time that the corporation is undergoing its own restructuring and redesign. Consequently, in the next decade, the field of work–family will be facing a very different work environment. These changes give rise to a rich set of questions for future research. What are the impacts of work redesign on workers and their families? If 'family-friendly' is the measure or standard of a benefits-driven work–family model, what are the appropriate standards and measures of a strategy-driven work–family model? And under what circumstances are workplace practices (i.e. work redesign) considered human resource investment strategies rather than human resource cost cutting strategies?

References

Abramovitz, M. (1988) *Regulating the Lives of Women: Social Welfare Policy from Colonial Times to the Present*. Albany, NY: State University of New York Free Press.

Bailyn, L. (1992) 'Issues of work and family in different national contexts: How the United States, Britain, and Sweden respond', *Human Resource Management*, 31: 201–8.

Beach, B. (1989) *Integrating Work and Family Life: The Home-Working Family*. Albany, NY: State University of New York Free Press.

Bryant Quinn, J. (1991) 'Living from job to job', *Newsweek*, 23 September: 41.

Bureau of National Affairs (1989). *101 Key Statistics on Work and Family for the 1990s*. Special Issue no. 21. Washington, DC: Bureau of National Affairs.

Burud, S.L., Aschbacher, R. and McCroskey, J. (1984) *Employer-Supported Child Care: Investing in Human Resources.* Dover, MA: Auburn House.

Center for Budget and Policy Priorities (1989) *Poverty Rate and Income Stagnate as Rich-Poor Gap Hits Post War High.* 18 October. Washington, DC: Center for Budget and Policy Priorities.

Christensen, K.E. (1987) 'Women, families and home-based employment', in N. Gerstel and H.E. Gross (eds), *Families and Work*. Philadelphia: Temple University Press. pp. 478–90.

Clark, P.G. (1993) 'Public policy in the United States and Canada: Individualism, familial obligation, and collective responsibility in the care of the elderly', in J. Hendricks and C.J. Rosenthal (eds), *The Remainder of Their Days: Domestic Policy and Older Families in the United States.* New York: Garland. pp. 13–48.

Eisenberger, R., Fasolo, P. and Davis-LaMastro, V. (1990) 'Perceived organization support and employee diligence, commitment and innovation', *Journal of Applied Psychology*, 75: 51–9.

Fernandez, J.P. (1990) *The Politics and Reality of Family Care in Corporate America.* Lexington, MA: Lexington Books.

Galinsky, E., Bond, J. and Friedman, D. (1993) *The Changing Workforce: Highlights of the National Study.* New York: Families and Work Institute.

Gibbs, N.R. (1993) 'Bringing up father', *Time*, 28 June: 53–61.

Gonyea, J.G. and Googins, B.K. (1992) 'Linking the worlds of work and family: Beyond the productivity trap', *Human Resource Management,* 31: 209–26.

Hall, D.T. (1990) 'Promoting work–family balance: An organizational-change approach', *Organizational Dynamics,* 18: 5–8.

Hammer, M. and Champy, J. (1993) *Re-engineering the Corporation: A Manifesto for Business Revolution.* New York: Harper Business.

Hewitt Associates (1990) *Work and Family Benefits Provided by Major U.S. Employers in 1990.* Lancaster, IL: Hewitt Associates.

Hooyman, N.R. and Gonyea, J.G. (1995) *Feminist Perspectives on Family Care: Policies for Gender Justice.* Newbury Park, CA: Sage.

Hula, R.C. (1991) 'Introduction: Thinking about family policy', in E.A. Anderson and R.C. Hula (eds), *The Reconstruction of Family Policy.* New York: Greenwood Press. pp. 1–7.

Kingston, P.W. (1990) 'Illusions and ignorance about the family-responsive workplace', *Journal of Family Issues*, 11: 438–54.

Kreiger, J. (1988) 'The British welfare state and Thatcher's new coalition', in M.K. Brown (ed.), *Remaking the Welfare State: Retrenchment and Social Policy in America and Europe.* Philadelphia: Temple University Press. pp. 139–64.

Lambert, S. (1993) 'Workplace policies as social policy', *Social Service Review*, 67: 237–60.

Lambert, S., Hopkins, K., Easton, G. and Walker, J. (1992) *Added Benefits: The Link between Family Responsive Policies and Work Performance at Fel-Pro, Inc.* Chicago: University of Chicago.

Lancaster, H. (1995) '"Re-engineering" authors reconsider re-engineering', *Wall Street Journal,* 17 January: B1.

Langley, P.A. (1991) 'The coming of age of family policy', *Families in Society*, 72: 116–20.

Lawler III, E.E., Cohen, S.G., and Chang, L. (1993) 'Strategic human resource management', in P.H. Mirvis (Ed.), *Building the Competitive Workforce*. New York: Wiley. pp. 31–59.

Lehman, E. (1995) 'Business must do more for working parents', *Parade Magazine*, 26 February: 12-13.

Linsk, N., Keigher, S., Simon-Rusinowitz, L. and England, S. (1992) *Wages for Caring: Compensating Family Care of the Elderly.* New York: Praeger.

McNamee, M., Greising, D. and Shah, M. (1995) 'The GOP's blind faith in charity', *Business Week*, 6 March: 65–6.

Marks, M.L. (1993) 'Restructuring and downsizing', in P.H. Mirvis (ed.), *Building the Competitive Workforce.* New York: Wiley. pp. 60–94.

Marquart, J.M. (1988) *A Pattern Matching Approach to Link Program Theory and Employer-Sponsored Childcare.* Ann Arbor, MI: University of Michigan.

Meyers, J.W., Ramirez, F.O., Walker, H.A., Langton, N. and O'Connor, S.M. (1988) 'The state

and the institutionalization of the relations between women and children', in S.M. Dornbusch and M.H. Strober (eds), *Feminism, Children and the New Families.* New York: Guilford.
Mirvis, P.H. (1993a) 'A competitive workforce: The issues and the study', in P.H. Mirvis (ed.), *Building the Competitive Workforce.* New York: Wiley. pp. 1–30.
Mirvis, P.H. (1993b) 'The findings and their implications', in P.H. Mirvis (ed.), *Building the Competitive Workforce.* New York: Wiley. pp. 220–47.
Morgan, H. and Milliken, F.J. (1992) 'Keys to action: Understanding differences in organizations' responsiveness to work-and-family issues', *Human Resource Management*, 31: 227–48.
Nash, L. (1994) 'The nanny corporation', *Across the Board*, 31: 16–22.
O'Reilly, B. (1992) 'The job drought: Why the shortage of high-wage jobs threatens the U.S. economy', *Fortune*, 24 August: 62–74.
Parker, V.A. and Hall, D.T. (1993) 'Workplace flexibility: Faddish or fundamental?', in P.H. Mirvis (ed.) *Building the Competitive Workforce.* New York: Wiley. pp. 122–55.
Pleck, J.H. (1985) *Working Wives/Working Husbands*. Beverley Hills, CA: Sage.
Ransom, C., Aschbacher, P. and Burud, S. (1989) 'The return in the child-care investment', *Personnel Administrator*, 34: 54–8.
Rezendes, M. (1995) '$5,000,000,000,000: A battle over the bulge – unusual alliances are forming in the debate over a balanced budget amendment', *Boston Globe*, 5 February: A1.
Scharlach, A.E., Lowe, B.F. and Schneider, E.L. (1991), *Eldercare and the Work Force.* Lexington, MA: Lexington Books.
Schuping, J.A. (1992) 'Industry-at-large: Information integration – key to business success', *Electronic News*, 8 June: 11–12.
Seaburg, J.R. (1990) 'Family policy revisited: Are we there yet?', *Social Work*, 35: 548–54.
Stewart, D.L. and Burge, P.L. (1989). *Assessment of Employee Satisfaction, Stress, and Childcare at Dominion Bankshares Corporation.* Blacksburg, VA: Virginia Polytechnic Institute and State University.
US Bureau of Labor Statistics (1991) *Employment and Earnings.* Vol. 38, January. Washington, DC: US Government Printing Office.
Walker, A. (1985) 'From welfare state to caring society? The promise of informal support networks', in J. Jonker, R. Leaper and J. Yoder (eds), *Support Networks in a Caring Community.* Lancaster, England: Martinus Nijhoff. pp. 41–59.
Walker, A. (1991) 'The relationship between the family and the state in the care of older people', *Canadian Journal on Aging*, 10: 94–113.
Wiatrowski, W.J. (1990) 'Family-related benefits in the workplace', *Monthly Labor Review,* 113: 28–33.

6

Formal and Informal Flexibility in the Workplace

Helle Holt and Ivan Thaulow

Flexibility is a key element in securing a family-friendly workplace. However, it is important to recognize that flexibility embraces not only a number of formal arrangements (including, for example, flexitime, childcare days, or parental leave), but also informal flexibility. Two aspects of flexibility are considered in this chapter: the well-known and well-defined 'flexitime', and the broader concept of 'latitude for adjustment' in the workplace. Both aspects of flexibility are examined in their formal as well as their informal guise.

The discussion of flexible working hours to meet family needs has in recent years occupied a central place in the Danish debate on family-friendly workplaces (Det Tværministerielle Børneudvalg, 1990, 1992; Andersen and Holt, 1990; Gregersen, 1991; Holt, 1993; Thaulow, 1989). This has largely focused on family childcare needs. The Danish research upon which this chapter is based also relates to the needs of parents for a flexible workforce. The concept of 'family-friendly' adopted in this chapter is therefore based on the reconciliation of the needs of the workforce with parental needs. We begin by presenting a model of family friendliness in terms of parental needs. There is much evidence of the needs which parents have for flexibility in the workplace (e.g. Lewis and Cooper, 1987). Against this background, the next section considers the formal and informal aspects of flexitime. Finally a description is provided of the formal and informal aspects of the total 'latitude' granted by workplaces to enable employees to balance working life with family life, along with some of the workplace cultural elements which form this latitude.

The Needs Model

Parent Needs

In determining what parental needs involve we will refer to the findings of the Nordic project 'Improved Balancing of Working Life and Family Life'. In this project, the definition of 'family-friendly' is expressed in terms of the extent to which workplaces meet three fundamental needs: the need to be able to provide economic support, the need to be able to provide practical care, and the need to be able to provide emotional care (Holt, 1994; Mærkedahl, 1993; Skjortnes, 1994).

Economic Support The need for economic support refers simply to the need for an income on which the family can exist. Although this aspect is largely overlooked in the debate on family-friendly workplaces, economic support is an absolutely fundamental need which cannot be ignored. In this context the family friendliness of the workplace lies in whether the pay is good, whether there is security of employment, whether there is possibility of additional income, and so on.

Practical Care The need for practical care refers to all the everyday care tasks which have to be performed: delivering and collecting the children, shopping, cooking, minding of sick children, visits to doctors and dentists, and so on. In this case the degree of family friendliness is determined by whether the workplace enables these care functions to be performed by the parents themselves or makes provision for them to be performed by others.

Emotional Care Finally, the need for emotional care refers to the need to provide the attention, stimulation and love which are so important, particularly during the child's younger years. In this instance the family friendliness of the workplace is measured by the steps taken to ensure, among other things, that the mental and physical working environment is such that parents are not so tired, stressed and generally drained when they arrive home as to have insufficient resources to provide emotional care.

The importance of this 'needs model' is that it highlights the fact that parents have several different types of needs, and that these needs are very diverse and therefore difficult to meet at the same time. A job which largely meets the family's economic needs will often be less well suited to meet the need for practical care. It is essential, not least in cross-national comparisons, to establish precisely what aspects of family-friendly practice are being discussed.

Although there are at least three different family needs, existing literature dealing with the balancing of working life and family life focuses overwhelmingly on the need for practical care. This also applies to the studies on which this chapter is based. *Accordingly, the description which follows deals solely with that aspect of workplace practice which relates to the need of families for practical care.* In the following, use of the term 'family-friendly workplaces' therefore refers to workplaces which in practice provide their employees with good opportunities to adjust their working life in accordance with the practical care needs of their families.

Workplaces and the Need for Practical Care

Workplaces can contribute to the provision of practical family care in two essentially different ways. One way is for enterprises to actively support activities which ease the burden on parents with regard to their care tasks. The other is for enterprises to provide parents with improved scope for performing these tasks without forfeiting their association with the workplace in the process.

The first method takes its point of departure in questions such as: do enterprises help their employees with childminding? Do they set up enterprise nurseries? Do they assist with obtaining places in community childminding institutions or provide economic support for childminding? These are some of the questions which figure in more recent literature dealing with family-friendly workplaces (Galinsky et al., 1991; Hogg and Harker, 1992). A family-friendly workplace is in this sense one which actively participates in parental care tasks by providing services or economic support, the family-friendly aspect being that someone takes care of the children so that the parents can concentrate on their work! This approach to family friendliness is particularly prevalent in countries where welfare state services are less well developed, and where women are still seeking full integration into the labour market. Specifically, these are countries such as the UK, Germany and the USA.

Enterprises can also contribute to the provision of practical care by granting employees such influence over their work and working hours that they themselves can provide the necessary care at home. Good examples of this are the freedom to vary working hours (principally via flexitime) or to work at home. In this case the family-friendly aspect is determined by the opportunity for employees, in combination with their work, to provide the necessary family care themselves. These approaches are typically prevalent in societies where women have achieved a central position in both the labour market and the political system, and where the welfare state, partly because of this, is well developed. This is very much the case in Denmark, which is the reason why the present chapter specifically deals with flexibility for parents in the workplace.

The differences between these two family-friendly (in the sense of 'care-friendly') approaches are striking. The first method may be economically demanding for enterprises, will often require collaboration with external parties, but will rarely affect the work itself and work organization. In contrast, the second method will normally cost enterprises virtually nothing and will require no external involvement. On the other hand it will often affect the division and organization of work within the enterprise.

Neither method is exclusive of the other. However, there is a certain logic in the fact that the discussion of, say, flexible working hours only becomes pertinent when women have entered the labour market in large numbers. It is only in this situation – when both mothers and fathers are in employment – that a real need arises for flexibility for family reasons. As suitable childminding opportunities are a prerequisite for the entry of large numbers of women into the labour market, it is probably true to say that the establishment of a suitable range of (public or private) services will typically arrive on the political agenda before the establishment of family-friendly working hours.

Flexible Working Hours

In the present context flexible working hours are working hours which may be varied by individual employees in accordance with their own or their family's needs, thereby enabling parents (albeit to a varying extent) to fulfil certain fundamental care needs within the family.

Formal Arrangements

An important part of this flexibility is enshrined in formal arrangements. These involve precisely detailed arrangements agreed upon in advance between employers and employees which give employees latitude to change their daily working hours at little or no notice. Such arrangements may comprise agreements on variable job arrival times or more far-reaching flexitime agreements. They may comprise agreements on reduced working hours for specific periods or agreements on care days when children are sick. They may possibly also comprise agreements covering maternity/paternity leave or general parental leave.

A good flexitime arrangement contains only a short core period, and allows employees both to accumulate and owe time. It allows employees to spend the time saved as hours off, days off or even weeks off – in accordance with their individual needs (Bielenski and Hegner, 1985; Magnusson, 1986). This kind of flexibility is important to families because they are often vulnerable to even small changes. Flexitime offers parents a safety valve in situations where minor changes threaten to spoil the carefully constructed jigsaw. Research findings show that it is often in these circumstances that the flexibility is actually used (Baier and Barlog, 1986; Lee and Kanunga, 1984; Thaulow, 1993).

Several studies indicate that flexitime can reduce the stress experienced by parents when they are together with their children (Bohen and Viveros-Long, 1981; Lee, 1981) and ease the daily transition of parents from family life to working life (Bohen and Viveros-Long, 1981; Winett et al., 1982). However, these positive results are neither unambiguous nor undisputed. Other surveys suggest that flexitime arrangements have no significant influence on either the transition between working life and family life or parental satisfaction with their family life (Shinn et al., 1989; Thaulow, 1993). Furthermore, recent Danish findings reveal the disturbing fact that post-work stress is *no less marked* among flexitime parents than among other parents (Holt et al., 1992; Thaulow, 1993). On the contrary, parents working flexitime experience more stress than other parents. In all probability this is because flexitime is often a component of more demanding jobs, where work has to be completed even if the formal working day is over. Use of flexitime is presumably closely connected therefore with pressure of work, overtime and stress at work. There is no evidence to show that people in such jobs would be less stressed if they worked fixed hours rather than flexitime.

Another disturbing phenomenon is that flexibility is increasingly used not to meet family needs but to meet the needs of their workplaces. Despite the fact that formal flexibility is intended to relieve the pressure on family life, it is often used by employees to stay longer at work when this is required (Thaulow, 1993).

But although problems can easily be identified, experience with flexible work hours is still predominantly positive. Some of the major findings from recent Danish studies into flexitime are presented in the following:

1. The vast majority of employees working flexitime are very satisfied with it. A recent study shows that flexitime employees are far happier with their work time arrangements than other employees (Thaulow, 1993). Over 90 per cent of employees with flexitime expressed satisfaction.
2. Although it may sometimes cause people to stay at work when they would rather go home, flexitime is often used to adjust working time to the needs of families. Flexitime is regularly used by fathers and mothers alike to deliver or collect children, or simply to spend time together with the family (Andersen and Holt, 1990; Thaulow, 1993).
3. Employees already working flexitime often say they would very much like to see the framework of the arrangement widened. They would prefer less core time, wider scope for time accumulation, and wider scope for using the time saved, for instance in the form of whole days off. By contrast, hardly any employees wish to relinquish flexitime (Thaulow, 1993).

Flexible work hours are not a miracle panacea for time pressure, but overall experience shows that most employees and their families find such arrangements extremely useful.

Informal Arrangements

A number of recent studies have shown that formal arrangements contain only some of the possibilities open to parents seeking to balance their work with their family needs. In the daily interplay between people at a workplace, a number of informal rules are created as to what is and what is not permitted (e.g. Carlsen, 1993). In other words, employees and management interact to create a workplace culture with a set of rules regulating which freedoms individuals may allow themselves to take. The scope of this informal flexibility is examined below, along with the way in which workplace culture can widen – but also narrow – the formal flexibility among employees.

A useful illustration of the significance of informal arrangements in the workplace is evident in a Danish study of flexitime working carried out among parents employed in the Danish civil service (Thaulow, 1993). One of the purposes of the survey was to examine whether employees with no formal flexitime arrangements were nevertheless able to vary their working hours in accordance with personal needs. The study revealed that roughly a quarter of the employees interviewed had formal flexitime arrangements. In addition, however, no less than one third of the remainder had informal flexibility arrangements by which they were able to vary their daily working hours in accordance with their personal needs. Informal flexibility was therefore more prevalent than formal flexibility among the civil servants interviewed. More than half the employees who had only informal flexibility arrangements were able to vary their daily work time by one hour or more. Time-wise, the informal arrangements were therefore almost identical in scope to the formal flexitime arrangements.

These results are supported by other studies (Holt, 1994; Madsen and Nayberg, 1992), as well as by the findings of an action research project undertaken by the authors (Holt and Thaulow, 1995). These studies show that the informal flexibility arrangements typically manifest themselves as verbal agreements between colleagues, and sometimes also between colleagues and their immediate superiors. These agreements typically involve permission to meet for work later the next day, or permission to leave some time before the end of working hours. In some cases this is of no practical importance to either colleagues or superiors, whereas in other cases it can mean a variety of changes in the work of fellow employees. A second typical example of informal flexibility is the swapping of duty shifts, while a third is a total decentralization of working-hour decisions to smaller, autonomous groups in which employees working within the same group may have the option of highly individualized working hours. Finally, there are employees who despite fixed work time come and go more or less as they please without prior arrangement with others.

Experience shows that informal flexibility is very largely used in the same situations as formal flexitime (Thaulow, 1993). Typically, this means when children are to be taken to or collected from care institutions or school, or when employees wish to be together with their families.

In part, informal flexibility also appears to be based on a mutual obligation between employees and employers. Although the civil servants have a fixed work time, more than half regularly vary their working hours in the interest of their job (Thaulow, 1993). This suggests that informal flexibility also has its price. This price appears to be an expectation of additional effort on the part of the employee when work so requires. The social acceptability of informal flexibility thus appears to be dependent on a degree of reciprocity.

Latitude for Adjustment in the Workplace

Flexibility may also be construed in a broader sense than merely flexible working hours. It can extend to the scope which exists for minding children when they are sick, taking maternity, paternity or parental leave, determining the timing of days off and vacations, working at home, and being accessible to the children even though at work. Again this can have both a formal and an informal dimension.

Formal Arrangements

The formal dimension embraces the legislation and collective agreements which regulate and cushion the collision between working life and family life. In Denmark, examples of such legislation include the laws regulating the rights of women and men to take maternity and paternity leave, legislation (the Working Environment Act) governing the number of hours which may be worked without a break, legislation governing the right to take parental leave, and legislation governing the requirement of local authorities to provide public daycare facilities for children when parents are at work.

Legislation is supplemented by collective agreements. These regulate the extent to which full pay is payable during maternity leave, whether an employee may take a day off on a child's first sick day, whether there is access to part-time work, and whether individual agreements on working hours may be established. Collective agreements vary considerably according to the occupational categories they cover. Further, national agreements can in turn be supplemented by local agreements relating to the individual workplace. In general terms the male-dominated trade unions still give top priority to pay, and thus the economic support of their members, while the female-dominated unions also give priority to working conditions which meet the family's practical and emotional care needs. Nevertheless, legislation and collective agreements are central to flexibility – in its formal dimension – within the individual workplace.

Informal Arrangements

The informal dimension comprises the unwritten rules, or workplace culture, which govern what is practice and what is permissible in the workplace. These informal rules exist alongside the formal rules. The informal rules may in some cases increase workplace flexibility, while in other cases they may limit the formal flexibility which already exists.

The workplace culture is, essentially, the sum of the norms and values that govern the individual's behaviour in the organization. These norms and values are created and develop through interaction between the people in the organization. People are to some extent bound by what others consider correct because the individual is dependent on acceptance by the community (Martin, 1992). The behavioural 'norms' are the informal rules in a workplace which govern, for example, the number of days that can be taken off work to tend a sick child. The behavioural 'values' are the underlying reasons for the existence of, say, a limit on the number of days' absence from work on account of sick children. For example there may be an underlying value to the effect that sick children are not the problem of the workplace. Part of the workplace culture thus determines the possibilities open to employees for adapting their work to their family needs (Jaeckle, 1993).

The sum of the formal and informal flexibilities may be termed the 'latitude for adjustment' between working life and family life. The individual parent will act within this latitude in the workplace, but at the same time help characterize it. All employees in a workplace will seek to achieve fulfilment of precisely their parental needs, but they will do so in an interaction with the other employees, all of whom have their specific needs.

Determinants of Latitude for Adjustment

Latitude for adjustment is largely determined by workplace culture, which in turn is influenced by the interaction between factors such as content and organization of work, gender composition of workplaces, career structures and occupational variables.

The importance of workplace culture in determining latitude for adjustment should hardly be surprising. This is known to influence almost all areas within an organization including, for example, working environment, career opportunities and productivity (Acker, 1990; Alvesson and Billing, 1992; Martin, 1992; Schein, 1986). Latitude for adjustment will be influenced by the content and organization of work. Very little direct research has been performed into the significance of these aspects for the balance between working and family life. Within the context of traditional organizational theory, however, the factors influencing the individual's experience of work autonomy have been examined (e.g. Mintzberg, 1983). A number of studies (Billing and Alvesson, 1989; Holt, 1994; Kvande and Rasmussen, 1990; Thaulow, 1994) show that several factors are involved. The first is the individual's position in the work hierarchy, that is to say, whether or not the person concerned is a manager or holds a key position. The second factor is the work content, which can be divided into varied, stimulating work and routine, non-stimulating work. The third and last factor is the method of work control, work typically being either time-driven or task-driven.

If these findings are transferred to the debate on latitude for adjustment it is seen that persons in managerial and key positions with varied, stimulating work and task-driven rather than time-driven jobs will basically have most latitude for adjustment. This is confirmed in an inter-Nordic study (Holt, 1994; Lie and Skjortnes, 1993), which shows that precisely these characteristics provide substantial latitude for adjustment. The same study also shows that the characteristics referred to are more prevalent in male-dominated departments than in female-dominated departments. This means that employees in a male-dominated workplace inherently have greater latitude for balancing working life and family life than do employees in female-dominated workplaces.

Case Studies

With reference to an inter-Nordic research project (Holt, 1994; Lie and Skjortnes, 1993; Skjortnes, 1993; Tungland, 1993), a number of specific examples of the ways in which the latitude for adjustment is broadened and narrowed in different workplaces are presented below. In Denmark and other

European countries it is still women who – despite their increased participation in the labour market – are principally responsible for the provision of practical and emotional family care (Andersen, 1988; Hjort Andersen, 1991). It will be seen that the division of work within families is reflected in the latitude for adjustment at workplaces, so that workplaces dominated by women seek to widen the latitude in the direction of practical and emotional care, while in male-dominated workplaces the provision of economic support receives precedence. Finally, an example presented from the same study shows that aspects of an occupation or profession can also have a major impact on the latitude for adjustment, but that at the same time this impact must be viewed in a complex interplay between many factors.

Female-Dominated Environments

Evidence from the study suggests that when women interact they widen the latitude for practical care. One case concerned female assembly workers in a large iron and steel company. These workers inherently have very little latitude for adjustment because their work is very much place-bound and time-driven. However they juggle with their breaks so that they can shop during their lunch break and still have time to eat. They also cover for one another if they are late for work, they help one another with post office and bank errands, and they are reasonably indulgent and understanding if one of their number works slowly owing to problems on the home front.

By contrast, nurses in an intensive care unit inherently have more latitude for adjustment than the assembly workers. However they too substantially widen the formal scope which they possess. Some might even go as far as to say that work is organized around the family situation of the nurses. Same-day swapping of shifts is possible, the number of working hours can vary in the course of a month, the nurses' children can daily enter the workplace, they can phone the workplace, the nurses can leave early if they need to, they can nip down town, and they can take time off at short notice for overtime worked.

In both these cases it is clear that the willingness to help and cover for one another is rooted in a mutual understanding and awareness of personal family circumstances. The women are attentive and know when someone's husband is away on business, when a fellow worker is having problems with her husband's alcohol consumption and needs support, and so on. Above all, they are familiar with the problems of adjustment since they themselves are in the same situation and therefore also wish to be flexible. The women widen the latitude for the provision of practical care, and attempt in this way to solve the adjustment problems in the workplace itself.

Male-Dominated Workplaces

Male-dominated workplaces are characterized by an inherently greater latitude for adjustment than female-dominated workplaces owing to the differences in work type and organization. However, the interaction between men has a tendency to narrow the latitude for the provision of practical care while widening the latitude for the provision of economic support.

In a case study carried out in an iron and steel company the smiths (skilled metalworkers) were seen to enjoy by far the greatest latitude for adjustment of any employee group. However, this latitude was not translated into the provision of practical care. On the contrary, their attitude was that maternity leave (by definition), and the care of sick children, are strictly the domain of women and not something with which men should concern themselves. This is a clear narrowing of the formal latitude for the provision of practical care. However latitude was generated for so-called 'pigeonhole projects', such as repairing the family's electrical appliances or tinkering.

Similarly in a case study concerning policemen substantial (formal) latitude for adjustment was again observed, but here too it was clear that individual behaviour is very much dictated by the workplace norms and values governing the purposes for which this latitude might be used. It is possible in principle for a policeman to swap duty shifts with his colleagues for a month and avoid, say, day shifts entirely. There is an enormous willingness to be mutually supportive in this way, but the reasons for extraordinary swaps of this type are not unimportant. Second jobs are the legitimate reason, as in the case of the policeman who has a farm on the side and who in August must be free during the day to do the harvesting. However needs geared to the provision of practical and emotional care do not represent legitimate grounds for such drastic swapping of shifts.

Day-to-day flexibility at the police station is immense. The men largely determine their own working day, which means they have good opportunities for carrying out a wide range of practical tasks. Priority is given to car washing, bank errands, hobbies and similar pursuits but domestic tasks such as bulk food shopping are rarely undertaken.

Similarly use of paternity leave is also frowned upon. The lack of a 'temp agency' and indeed any tradition for using temporary staff poses an additional problem. Leave situations mean that police inspectors still on duty are forced to work harder and take more unpopular shifts. As a result, it becomes even more difficult for individuals to justify a possible desire to take the 10 weeks' paternity leave which Denmark provides.

An identical pattern was discernible among hospital porters. A temp agency does exist for hospital porters, and their failure to avail themselves of paternity leave is solely attributable to their personal attitudes and the attitudes of the workplace.

Mixed-Gender Professions

The medical profession is nowadays a mixed-gender profession in Denmark, but there are still distinct reminders of the days when it was a typical male enclave. It is very difficult to achieve a balanced working and family life without a marital partner who is able to provide the family with the necessary practical and emotional care. None of the female doctors interviewed had such a husband. They were married to professional men, for example male doctors, who accorded their work a high priority. This posed major problems for the women, which they resolved by taking on the role of primary family care providers, while their husbands used the flexibility inherent in their job to pursue the research so important for a doctor's future career. The women, however, are effectively debarred from research during their children's care-intensive years. They either choose specialist fields where the need for research is smaller, or accept that for a time their career will stagnate. Doctors – both men and women – limit, for example, the number of care days they take to look after their children when sick. In the medical world, taking a large number of care days would send the wrong signals to people such as the senior physicians who hold the key to participation in research projects. Excessive family orientation is quite simply a bad signal. Where doctors are concerned, therefore, the latitude for adjustment is curtailed not by the interaction between men but rather by the career system, which was created at a time when doctors' wives stayed at home.

To summarize, the case studies referred to above show that practical care rather than economic support is prioritized in a female-dominated workplace, but that it is difficult to be a family- and care-oriented man in a male-dominated workplace. And it goes without saying that it is difficult to be a woman with traditional care tasks in a male-dominated workplace.

Significance of Employee Occupation for Workplace Culture

The examples described show that the content and organization of the work, together with the gender dominance in the workplace, influence the amount of latitude which exists for balancing working life and family life, as well as the use of this latitude. However, other factors may also exert a major influence on the various cultures in the workplace. Relevant factors include whether the work is task-driven rather than time-driven in the sense that work time will be finished when a task is completed rather than at a fixed time. Related factors are whether the work is viewed as an extension of leisure, whether there is likely to be a need to take work home, or whether working life and family life are likely to be viewed as two wholly different spheres. For example, a case study of electricians, where work is task-related and considered an extension of leisure, suggests that opportunities for adjustment, rather than being used for family needs, are often used to take work home because they are not prepared to let a technical problem go until it has been solved.

Conclusions

We have argued that a key feature of the family-friendly workplace is that it supports employees/parents in their efforts to provide the practical care their families need. An important way in which this support can be given is for the workplace to grant employees sufficient flexibility to adjust their work to meet this need.

Some flexibility can be created through formal arrangements. Formal arrangements for flexibility, and its use, have long been at the centre of the debate on family policy. However, formal rules and arrangements conceal a wide variety of informal rules, embedded in the workplace culture, which although not formally agreed upon or placed in writing, nevertheless have a strong behaviour-regulating effect. Informal rules to a large extent determine what possibilities employees really have for adjusting their working life to meet the needs of their families. Several studies indicate that informal flexibility is just as prevalent, and may even be more widespread than formal flexibility, and can be just as significant. This is true irrespective of whether flexibility is considered in its narrow sense, as flexitime, or in its broader sense, as the total latitude for adjustment within the workplace. Furthermore, the scope of adjustment possibilities contained in formal and informal flexible arrangements would appear to be roughly similar, just as both forms of flexibility are used for roughly the same purposes.

The total 'latitude for adjustment' provided by the workplace is very largely determined by the workplace culture. The workplace culture may in some cases restrict the formal adjustment possibilities which exist. It is clearly evident in certain male-dominated workplaces that while the formal adjustment possibilities are substantial, the workplace culture may prevent them from being utilized for the provision of practical care. Conversely, the workplace culture may in other cases substantially widen the formal possibilities for adjustment. This is evident from female-dominated workplaces where, despite relatively few formal adjustment possibilities, considerable 'latitude' has been created by virtue of the widespread acceptance by the women of their mutual care obligations.

This chapter has focused on the work and family needs of parents. Future research could usefully extend this model by examining the issues in relation to other forms of family or non-work obligations. For example, what is the latitude available to men and women in different contexts for eldercare? In addition, cross-national research would be useful to explore similarities or differences in factors affecting latitudes for adjustment in cultures beyond the Nordic countries. Nevertheless, it is apparent from the material discussed in this chapter that studies which deal seriously with flexibility as seen from the viewpoint of employees, or with the development of family-friendly workplaces, cannot be limited to the examination of formal arrangements and their utilization. Such studies should also include the *informal* aspects of working life. In other words, workplace culture must be integrated into future analyses of the facilities and services provided by workplaces for employees in general and parents in particular. If not, there is danger that the picture of reality presented will be not only greatly simplified – but also distorted.

References

Acker, J. (1990) 'Hierarchies, jobs, bodies: A theory of gendered organizations', *Gender & Society*, 4,(2).

Alvesson, M. and Billing, Y.D. (1992) 'Gender and organization: Towards a differentiated understanding', *Organization Studies*, 13(12).

Andersen, D. (1988) *Danskernes dagligdag 1987*, vols 1 and 2. Report 88:4. Copenhagen: Danish National Institute of Social Research.

Andersen, D. and Holt, H. (1990) *Fleksibel arbejdstid i den statslige sektor*. Report 90:16. Copenhagen: Danish National Institute of Social Research.

Baier, A. and Barlog, A. (1986) 'Flexible Arbeitszeiten: Erfahrungen mit verschiedenen Formen Gleitzeit', in *Forschungsberichte aus Sozial- und Arbeitsmarktpolitik*, vol. 8. Vienna: Bundesministerium für soziale Verwaltung.

Bielenski, H. and Hegner, F. (1985) *Flexible Arbeitszeiten*. Frankfurt: Campus Verlag.

Billing, Y.D. and Alvesson, M. (1989) *Køn, ledelse og organisation*. Jurist og Økonomforbundets forlag.

Bohen, H. and Viveros-Long, A. (1981) *Balancing Jobs and Family Life*. Philadelphia: Temple University Press.

Carlsen, S. (1993) 'Men's utilization of paternity leave schemes', in *The Equality Dilemma*. Copenhagen: The Danish Equal Status Council.

Det Tværministerielle Børneudvalg (1990) *Børnefamilien 1990*. Beretning fra Det Tværministerielle Børneudvalg. SIKON.

Det Tværministerielle Børneudvalg (1992) *Det kan lade sig gøre!* Copenhagen: Ministry of Social Affairs.

Galinsky, E., Friedman D. E. and Hernandez, C. A. (1991) *The Corporate Reference Guide to Work–Family Programs*. New York: Family and Work Institute.

Gregersen, O. (1991) *Flekstid*. Report 91:2. Copenhagen: Danish National Institute of Social Research.

Hjort Andersen, B. (1991) *Børnefamiliernes dagligdag*. Report 91:6. Copenhagen: Danish National Institute of Social Research.

Hogg, Christine and Harker, Lisa (1992) *The Family-Friendly Employer: Examples from Europe*. London: Daycare Trust.

Holt, H. (1993) 'The influence of the workplace culture on family life', in *The Equality Dilemma*. Copenhagen: The Danish Equal Status Council.

Holt, H. (1994) *Forældre på arbejdspladsen – en analyse af tilpasningsmulighederne mellem arbejdsliv og familieliv i kvinde-og mandefag*. Report 94:8. Copenhagen: Danish National Institute of Social Research.

Holt, H. and Thaulow, I. (1995) *Family-Friendly Workplaces*. Copenhagen: Ministry of Social Affairs.

Holt, H., Mærkedahl, I. and Thaulow, I. (1992) 'Do working time arrangements affect stress and well-being in the family?'. Paper presented at National Council of Family Relations Conference, Florida.

Jaeckle, M. (1993) *Making the Workplace Organization and Culture More Responsive to the Needs of Parents in Parental Employment and Caring for Children: Policies and Services in EC and Nordic Countries*. Copenhagen: The European Commission.

Kvande, E. and Rasmussen, B. (1990) *Nye kvinneliv*. Oslo: Ad Notam.

Lee, M.D. and Kanunga, R.N. (1984) *Management of Work and Personal Life*. New York: Praeger.

Lee, R.A. (1981) 'The effect of flexitime on family life – some implications for managers', *Personnel Review*, 10(3).

Lewis, S. and Cooper, C. L. (1987) 'Stress in two earner couples and stage in the life cycle', *Journal of Occupational Psychology*, 60: 289–303.

Lie, T. and Skjortnes, M. (1993) *Dårlig sveiset?* Report RF 276/92. Stavanger: Rogalandsforskning.

Madsen, B. and Nayberg, M. (1992) *Hvornår vil vi arbejde*. Viborg: Spektrum.

Mærkedahl, I. (1993) 'Gender and workplace culture in the work–family interface'. Unpublished paper. Copenhagen: Danish National Institute of Social Research.
Magnusson, M. (1986) *Utvidgad flextid: Större flexram, lördagsarbete, ledig eftermiddag, ökat självbestämmande*. Lund: TEM, University of Lund.
Martin, J. (1992) *Cultures in Organizations*. Oxford University Press.
Mintzberg, H. (1983) *Structure in Fives: Designing Effective Organizations*. Prentice-Hall.
Schein, E.H. (1986) *Organisationskultur og ledelse*. Copenhagen: Forlaget Valmuen.
Shinn, M., Wong, N., Simko, P. and Ortiz-Torres, B. (1989) 'Promoting the well-being of working parents: Coping, social support and flexible job schedules', *American Journal of Community Psychology*, 17(1).
Skjortnes, M. (1993) *Familieliv i et avishus*. Report 275/92. Stavanger: Rogalandsforskning.
Skjortnes, M. (1994) *Fra kvinneansvar til foreldreansvar*. Report RF 121/94. Stavanger. Rogalandsforskning.
Thaulow, I. (1989) *Fleksible arbejdstider – et internationalt perspektiv*. Working Memorandum 7. Copenhagen: Danish National Institute of Social Research.
Thaulow, I. (1993) *Børnefamiliernes arbejdstider – en analyse af fleksible arbejdstider i staten*. Report 93:3. Copenhagen: Danish National Institute of Social Research.
Thaulow, I. (1994) *At måle det udviklende lønarbejde – en empirisk analyse af udbredelsen og betydningen af det udviklende lønarbejde*. Report 94:5. Copenhagen: Danish National Institute of Social Research.
Tungland, E. (1993) *Innen rimelighetens grenser*. Report RF 187/93. Stavanger: Rogalandsforskning.
Winett, R.A., Neale, M.S. and Willams, K.R. (1982) 'The effect of flexible work schedules on urban families with young children: Quasi-experimental, ecological studies', *American Journal of Community Psychology*, 10(1).

7

Corporate Relocation Policies

Cary L. Cooper

The issue of job relocation is extremely important in discussions of work and personal lives, since it is at the interface between the organization and the family. We have many organizations now considering 'family-friendly' policies such as alternative work schedules, childcare and the like, but still maintaining inherently unfriendly policies like 'pressurized' or involuntary job relocation.

It is certainly the case that there are many situations in which employers will require employees to be mobile, for example, in the relocation of whole workplaces, in the transferring of specialized skills across the country or cross-nationally or in providing broader experiences for ambitious or high-flying staff. On the other hand, relocation of employees has also been used to get the employee to demonstrate his/her 'organizational commitment', a necessary hurdle to overcome, in a sense a 'no gain without pain' ritual on the way up the corporate ladder. When relocation is seen as an essential requirement for achieving a specific organizational goal, and the employee can explore the extent of impact on him/her and the family, the costs and benefits can be assessed and some mutually acceptable decision can be reached. When the relocation decision is imposed, however, and is based not on organizational need but on a show of organizational commitment, then the individual and the family are likely to suffer in the short and medium term, and the organization in the longer term, in the sense that a stressed workforce is a costly one (in terms of sickness absence, labour turnover, lost productive value). This chapter explores the specific problems of job relocation, particularly in relation to dual-career families, and considers what organizations might do to improve the situation.

The Stress of Job Relocation

Several health problems have been shown to be associated with job relocation in general, as Luo and Cooper (1995) have found in their review of the stress and relocation literature. First, mobile employees are prone to coronary heart disease. Syme et al. (1965; 1969) reported in two separate studies that urban, mobile, white collar men had an incidence of coronary heart disease almost four times higher than blue collar and stable groups, regardless of factors of heredity, obesity, smoking and physical activity. This has been substantiated in more recent research (Brett et al., 1993). Second, teenagers have more problems with moving than younger children, and mobile teenagers have less well-developed peer relationships than their stable contemporaries (Barrett and Noble, 1973; Brett and Warbel, 1978; Douvan and Adelson, 1966). In general terms, job relocations, therefore, resemble other commonly regarded stressful life events: they disrupt routines of daily life, and are accompanied by changes in social context; they provoke feelings of anxiety, uncertainty, loss of control and challenge; they activate various coping strategies to reestablish daily routines, and to manage these aversive feelings; they may lead to either personal growth or illness (Cartwright and Cooper, 1994).

As far as the family is concerned, the early literature reported little effect of job relocations on the employee's family, and suggested an attitudinal consensus between employees and their spouses (see Brett, 1980 for a review). However, in Munton's (1990) study, the top five relocating stressors reported by 111 relocating families were all concerned with social and familial issues. Indeed, three important factors found to account for the relocating stress were 'loss of social contacts', 'problems associated with spouse employment', and 'worries about children's education'. However, employees reported little stress associated with 'changes in the work environment'.

An American survey in high-technology areas has also recognized geographical moves as a major stressor for both employees and their families (Anderson and Stark, 1985). However, the authors pointed out that there has been little attention devoted to relocation problems beyond financial support. In a more recent survey conducted with five big companies and five major universities in the US, Galinsky and Stein (1990) examined seven major issues including job relocation faced by employees in balancing work–family life. Their findings indicate that although some leading organizations are responsive to work–family problems, many are still unaware of or unresponsive to work–family strain and conflicts associated with relocation.

As a stressful life event, job relocation is, therefore, a 'family issue' rather than one that only concerns the employee. Job relocation, as Luo and Cooper (1995) suggest, can be hazardous to family life in many ways. Geographic relocation necessarily involves the family in 'property trading', and this appeared as a major stress in Munton's (1990) study. Financial concerns are usually high on the agenda (Wheeler and Miller, 1990).

In a more recent study, Rives and West (1993) surveyed 224 male workers involved in a recent job relocation and their wives regarding the effects of the wife's labour force attachment on family relocation choice. Migration was deterred by the wife's labour force attachment, and was also affected by a worker's eligibility for a company buyout, tenure with the company, community attachment and family size.

Sometimes job relocation causes temporary or long-term separation, which can be a crisis point in a marriage (Marshall and Cooper, 1976). Continuing children's schooling can also be problematic. Moreover, if the family is a dual-earner or dual-career one, conflict over the spouse's work can be acute, especially in today's tight labour market. It is not difficult to see how job relocation can compel the entire family into a struggle to reestablish its daily routine. The task is demanding for dual-career families, but there are also specific problems for step-families and single-parent families (Anderson and Stark, 1988). Therefore, not surprisingly, overcoming these family problems can contribute significantly to the final adaptation.

There are therefore strong quality of life and business rationales for companies to modify their relocation practices, as stress can have substantial costs for organizations. There are also gender issues to be considered and these are discussed below, with a particular focus on dual-career families.

Relocation and Dual-Career Families

Clearly relocation policies can be unfriendly to all families at certain stages, in so far as they produce difficulties for employees, their spouses and their children, unless properly handled. However, decisions about job mobility and relocation can be particularly difficult for dual-career families, who are now the most typical family form. The problem of relocating can be considerable, even for single earners who have to take account of factors such as children's education and social networks. Added to this, career needs of the spouse can cause particular problems in dual-career couples (Cooper and Lewis, 1993).

Relocating decisions, like decisions concerning initial locations, tend overwhelmingly to be in the traditional vein – in other words, to favour the husband's career. As Gilbert (1985) put it in her book on men in dual-career families, it is not surprising that location and relocation decisions tend to reflect traditional attitudes as dual-career partners live in a largely patriarchal society; they are subjected to and influenced by the norms and values of this society as well as its structures. However, this does not necessarily mitigate the stress of these decisions, or the constraints on those who decide not to move.

It is more socially acceptable for a wife to follow her husband than vice versa, and wives are more likely to feel that they should put their family's needs before their own. In addition, the practicalities of the situation often favour husbands, as men are more frequently offered higher-status posts or higher salaries than their wives. For women in dual-career families, relocations can cause considerable frustration. A study of women managers in the UK found that the majority of those who were able to accept relocation were unmarried (Davidson and Cooper, 1983). Just under a quarter of all women managers interviewed were not mobile because of their partners' careers or because of other commitments.

The decision for men to refuse to relocate is non-traditional. Although women frequently accept constraints on mobility for family reasons, men have begun to do so only relatively recently. Consequently, there is still an expectation that men will be mobile (and that women will not be mobile, which can affect promotional decisions). Men who do not conform to this expectation are often regarded as lacking in professional commitment and their promotional opportunities may also be restricted. The constraints are nevertheless acceptable to men who value their participation in family life and accept the importance of their spouse's career. An engineer who accepted limited mobility, because his wife was a doctor in general practice, felt that there were sufficient opportunities for him within his geographical area. However, his involvement in childcare imposed further restrictions on him which he felt prospective employers had difficulty in understanding:

> I went for an interview recently and in the first few minutes after we sat down, the interviewer went over the three most important points. One was that I should be completely mobile; be free to work in London or Paris for a few weeks. I said no, I thought I had made it clear in my application form that I have a wife who is in practice here and I have a young child. I suppose they just assumed that my wife would take over. (Lewis and Cooper, 1989 : 59)

Decisions by men or women to refuse jobs which require mobility or to resist relocation are by no means always easy. Even for couples who have considered the question in advance, making the actual decision can be very stressful, and for those who have to confront an unexpected situation, it can perpetuate a crisis:

> When the organization I used to work for closed its Northern branch, I was offered a position in London. The alternative was redundancy. It was difficult because Carolyn had a secure position with the local authority here and, in fact, she earned more than I did. We talked about it a lot and considered the pros and cons. She didn't want to move and didn't think she could find an equivalent position elsewhere so easily. The stress of the decision-making caused us to argue a great deal and say a lot of acrimonious things we both regretted. Eventually, we decided to stay put. I was unemployed for nearly a year. I felt resentful, and I know she felt guilty. Somehow we survived and I found another position. (computer programmer, male) (1989: 59)

The situation which this man described was stressful, not only because the refusal to relocate resulted in a period of unemployment, but also because the decision had favoured his wife's career. It is not uncommon for wives to follow their husbands in their job, and then to have periods of unemployment before finding a position themselves. However, couples who relocate on the basis of the wife's career often experience problems, because their behaviour contradicts assumptions of gender-appropriate behaviour.

A solution which many couples are seeking, and a few organizations are offering, is to relocate as a couple. This might involve both partners applying for new jobs together in a given area, or one partner agreeing to relocate on the condition that the organization finds a suitable post, with no deterioration in promotion prospects, for his or her partner. This type of policy requires an enlightened and understanding attitude on the part of the employer, and may also involve considerable negotiation, planning and problem solving on the part of the couple themselves. The tortuous processes involved in achieving such a solution are illustrated by the experiences of Kathy and Richard. The impetus for the move came from Kathy:

> The college approached me about a year ago to ask if I would be interested in setting up a new department. They offered me a very attractive package which

> included the opportunity to work part of the time in the community, a car, a higher salary and relocation expenses. They also found a position for Richard. That was part of the package. Richard did not want to go, though. He's not as ambitious as me and he said he was happy in his present job. We talked about it for months and at one stage I was going to turn the job down. After all, what's the use of an interesting job if it ruins my marriage? My personal life is important, too. Eventually the college wrote to Richard, stressing that they really valued his experience, and wanted him in his own right. After all, he is an expert in his field. After that he decided to go. There were some difficult times before we actually reached a decision that we would both move. (1989: 60)

It appeared that Richard feared that he was being appointed as an incentive for his wife to move, rather than being valued in his own right. This fear was echoed by other spouses who were considering relocating as part of a couple. A female academic, younger and less professionally advanced than her spouse, voiced this opinion:

> There were two posts available at the same university and we did think that we might both apply. I wasn't entirely happy about the idea because we would have presented ourselves as a package; we both come, or not at all. John already has his PhD and a lot more publications than I have, and I was afraid they might offer me a job in order to attract him and I wouldn't have been considered on my own merit. (1989 : 1)

As more men and women refuse to relocate, or agree to do so only as part of a package involving their spouse, organizations may eventually be forced to recognize the realities of the dual-career lifestyle and take steps to make relocating decisions easier. However, it is likely that individuals committed to both career and family may continue for some time to be faced with dilemmas and tough decisions. There are ways, however, in which the dual-career couple and organizations may be encouraged to plan for the problems confronting this 'new workforce', which will be explored in the next section.

What Can Organizations Do to Help?

Companies can modify their relocation policies and practice in a number of ways to take account of work and family issues and reduce relocation-related stress for all employees.

Is Relocation Really Necessary?

Organizations should, first, question whether their relocation policy is necessary. Is it essential for managers to gain experience in a wide range of locations, or could more promotions be made within one area? Some companies have a policy of enabling people to gain necessary experience by working at a number of sites within commuting distance of their family home.

Gear Relocation Plans to Employees' Home Life Phase

Employees who are single, or whose spouses are also ready for a move, may welcome a change of location; but dual-career spouses should not be compelled to compete with those in different family circumstances. A more liberal attitude could be taken towards those who refuse to relocate at certain stages in the life cycle so that this does not prejudice their opportunities of promotion later in their careers. It is, for example, part of the written equal opportunities policy at the Littlewoods organization in the UK that employees who refuse to relocate will not be disadvantaged. Organizations could consider gearing their relocation plans to an individual's 'home life' phases. It is obviously the case that at certain phases of the life cycle, change is less disruptive than at other phases (children beginning school, spouse re-entering career). On occasion, moving a person may be inevitable and necessary (e.g. when an engineer possesses skills vital to a particular project), but in most cases any planned change could be considered in light of the individual and family circumstances, with a view to integrating them into the changes and demands of work.

Involve Family Members in Decisions

The spouse's role in the individual's job and career development has been almost ignored by employing organizations. It would seem reasonable that the spouse should be given 'the option' to get involved in the decision-making and information-sharing process concerning any move that may impinge on the family. At the moment, organizations are contracting with one element of the family unit but making decisions which radically affect the unit as a whole. By operating in this way they often cause conflict between the individual and his/her family.

Provide Equal Opportunities for Women as well as Men to Relocate (or to Refuse to Relocate)

Organizations will have to reconsider attitudes toward women executives. A recent study of 827 managers in the USA (Brett et al., 1993) showed that a major factor determining employees' willingness to relocate was the willingness of their spouses to do likewise. Women were as willing as men to relocate, but were given fewer opportunities. The implication is that if companies are to ensure a large pool of flexible managers, willing to move when necessary, they need to provide career development opportunities for women, as well as support systems for spouses. They will have to offer promotional moves to them on the same basis as male managers and will also have to provide women (and men) with the opportunities to refuse a transfer without damaging their promotional prospects or with the same support facilities as given to their male counterparts if they accept (e.g. helping to find the husband a job, temporary 'home help', relocation expenses, paying the differential on mortgage rates, etc.).

Provide Information to Reduce Uncertainty

The major sources of stress involved in any potential move stem from the uncertainty which is nurtured in organizations by misleading or often imprecise information about their career plans given to employees. It is frequently the case that organizations provide their employees with inadequate notice regarding geographic moves. This usually involves them in a period of separation from their family, which may adversely affect them, their family, and in the long run the company, which may suffer from less efficient work performance as a direct consequence of the domestic conflicts. Up-to-date, honest communications can only help to minimize the level of uncertainty about prospective developments and provide for greater acceptance and a smoother transition when it occurs.

Provide Assistance to Spouses in Finding a New Job

The most widely adopted policy among companies which recognize the problem is to offer assistance in finding a job for the spouse of the relocated employee. This may take the form of financial assistance for job seeking, or more direct help such as arranging job interviews. Organizations can research and make inventories of the career opportunities for partners in a particular location, or form a consortium of companies to create a job bank. Eventually, computer-assisted job searches may ease the trauma of relocation decisions.

Provide Flexible Forms of Work

Flexible and alternative work schedules can all be used to assist relocated employees or their spouses. If a decision has been made to live apart and commute, a compressed working week and three-day weekend reduce the time apart, while telecommuting will allow one partner to be flexible in terms of relocating with his or her spouse.

Provide Support

For those individuals (and families) who need to be moved, organizations should provide the support required. Many companies help with buying and selling houses, helping spouses find equivalent jobs, and allowing the individual and the family enough opportunities to familiarize themselves with the new location (Munton et al., 1993).

Counselling and advisory services are also offered to some families. Counselling and workshops are often conducted to help executives and their families cope with the stress of relocation. However, these tend to focus on traditional single-earner families rather than dual-career couples (Kamerman and Kahn, 1988). Counselling services geared towards dual-career families may help employees to deal with difficult decisions, feelings of guilt and the emotional stress of relocation policies.

Make It Easier for Couples to Relocate Together

We have seen that many couples seek to resolve location and relocation issues by attempting to move as a couple, which often involves both spouses applying for new jobs together in a given region. This task will be easier if organizations develop a policy of recruiting couples, recognizing the realities of new family structures. Indeed, as the number of professionals in dual-career marriages continues to grow, organizations will increasingly need to attract dual-career couples in order to recruit the best candidates. Sekaran (1986) makes a number of recommendations to organizations working to adapt to the changes in the nature of the potential workforce.

Some companies operate anti-nepotism policies which prevent the hiring of dual-career couples if their relationship is known. Such policies are outmoded and should be discarded; they not only create the potential for location dilemmas for dual-career spouses, but may also deprive organizations of the talents of highly suitable recruits.

Often organizations are loath to hire the spouse of an employee in a rival company, because of a presumed conflict of interests. A case brought to an Industrial Tribunal concerned a woman who complained of unfair dismissal after marrying an employee of a rival firm (*Coleman* v. *Skyrail Oceanic Ltd*, Court of Appeal, 1981). The Tribunal's findings that she had been discriminated against on the basis of marital status was not upheld by the Court of Appeal. Nevertheless, such practices can discriminate against married professionals. Sekaran suggests that organizations do away with conflict of interest policies by incorporating an oath of loyalty into employee contracts. In practice, she argues, couples seem to have evolved their own codes of professional conduct to protect both their own careers and the interests of the employing company.

Advertising procedures can be altered to attract dual-career couples. Companies should advertise the broadest possible range of job opportunities to increase the scope for partners to find positions simultaneously. In addition, advertisements could specify that dual-career couples are acceptable to an organization and that policies which facilitate the combining of careers and family, such as childcare or flexible working arrangements, are available.

An interviewing strategy should be adopted to assess ability and potential of candidates and avoid biased assumptions, particularly relating to married women. Questions about the husband's job, although unlawful, are frequently asked. Decisions should not be made on the assumption that the husband will be the major breadwinner.

Mechanisms for training interviewers should be established. Interview panels should include members of dual-career families and high-ranking people in the organization to ensure objectivity and fairness.

Dual-career partners, once recruited to the organization, can be encouraged to incorporate family decisions in career planning by, for example, career counselling and appraisal systems which acknowledge the legitimacy of non-traditional career paths. Organizations operating a policy of hiring both members of dual-career couples could, by careful planning, arrange the relocation of the couple as a unit.

Relocation Policy at One Company

Many companies which find it necessary to relocate people, both nationally and internationally, are coming to terms with dual-career issues and finding innovative ways of easing relocation decisions and transitions for employees and their spouses. At ICI, for example, it is company policy that the careers of those who decline to relocate at a particular stage of their family cycle should not be damaged. If international experience is thought to be really essential and employees are willing to consider compromises, the company may seek to provide experience through short-term contracts or by paying for extra trips back to see family. When couples do relocate they are compensated for spouse's loss of earnings for up to six months while a new job is sought. Assistance is also provided through a career consultancy agency for spouses seeking jobs. Advice is given on academic and professional qualifications and training needs, particularly for those coming to Britain from abroad, and any extra training which is required is funded. Help is provided with writing CV, training in interview techniques, and making contact with agencies to find employment. Trailing spouses have also been helped to set up a business in the new country. For employees relocated to other countries there may be constraints on spouse employment for legal reasons (e.g. in the USA) or cultural reasons (e.g. in Saudi Arabia). Help is provided for spouses within the constraints of the host country. This may include assistance in finding other activities such as further study or voluntary activities. ICI's experience is that assistance for trailing spouses, who are increasingly as likely to be men as women, can work well in easing the transition for dual-career couples.

Conclusion

This is a time of great social changes, and corporate planners will need to be insightful, creative and innovative in designing effective strategies to deal with them. It will be important for relocation policies to be clear and explicit as well as flexible. Their effectiveness should be carefully monitored to ensure that they continue to adapt and respond to the changing needs of the workforce.

References

Anderson, C. and Stark, C. (1985) 'Emerging issues from job relocations in high tech field: Implication for employee assistance programs', *Employee Assistance Quarterly*, 1: 37–54.

Anderson, C. and Stark, C. (1988) 'Psychological problems of job relocation: Preventive roles in industry', *Social Work*, 33: 38–41.

Barrett, C.L. and Noble, H. (1973) 'Mothers' anxiety versus the effects of long distance move in children', *Journal of Marriage and the Family*, 35: 181–8.

Brett, J.M. (1980) 'The effect of job transfer on employees and their families', in C.L. Cooper and R. Payne (eds), *Current Concerns in Occupational Stress.* New York: Wiley.

Brett, J.M. and Warbel, J.D. (1978) *The Effect of Job Transfer on Employees and Their Families: Baseline Survey Report.* Washington, DC: Employee Relocation Council.

Brett, J.M., Stroh, L.K. and Reilly, A.H. (1993) 'Pulling up roots in the 1990s: Who's willing to relocate?', *Journal of Organizational Behavior*, 14: 49–60.
Cartwright, S. and Cooper, C.L. (1994) *No Hassle! Taking the Stress Out of Work*. London: Century Books.
Cooper, C.L. and Lewis, S. (1993) *The Workplace Revolution: Managing Today's Dual-Career Families*. London: Kogan Page.
Davidson, M.J. and Cooper, C.L. (1983) *Stress and the Woman Manager*. Oxford: Blackwell.
Douvan, E. and Adelson, J. (1966) *The Adolescent Experience*. New York: Wiley.
Galinsky, E. and Stein, P.J. (1990) 'The impact of human resource policies on employees: Balancing work/family life', *Journal of Family Issues*, 11: 368–83.
Gilbert, L.A. (1985) *Men in Dual Career Families*. Hillsdale, NJ: Lawrence Erlbaum.
Kamerman, S.B. and Kahn, A.J. (1988) *The Responsive Workplace: Employers and a Changing Labor Force*. New York: Columbia University Press.
Lewis, S. and Cooper, C.L. (1989) *Career Couples*. London: Unwin Hyman.
Luo, L. and Cooper, C.L. (1995) 'The impact of job relocation: Future research', in C.L. Cooper and D. Rousseau (eds), *Trends in Organizational Behavior*, vol. 2. New York and Chichester: Wiley.
Marshall, J. and Cooper, C.L. (1976) 'The mobile manager and his wife', *Management Decision*, 14: 179–225.
Munton, A.G. (1990) 'Job relocation: Stress and the family', *Journal of Organizational Behavior*, 11: 401–6.
Munton, A.G., Forster, N., Altman, A. and Greenberg, L. (1993) *Job Relocation: Managing People on the Move*. Chichester: Wiley.
Rives, J.M. and West, J.M. (1993) 'Wife's employment and worker relocation behaviour', *Journal of Socio-Economics*, 22: 13–22.
Sekaran, U. (1986) *Dual Career Families: Contemporary Organizational and Counselling Issues*. San Francisco: Jossey-Bass.
Syme, S.L., Borham, N.O. and Buechley, R.W. (1969) 'Cultural mobility and coronary heart disease in an urban area', *American Journal of Epidemiology*, 82: 234–46.
Syme, S.L., Hyman, M.M. and Enterline, P.E. (1965) 'Cultural mobility and the occurrence of coronary heart disease', *Journal of Health and Human Behavior*, 6: 178–89.
Wheeler, K.G. and Miller, J.G. (1990) 'The relation of career and family factors to the expressed minimum percentage pay increase required by relocation', *Journal of Management*, 16: 855–64.

8

Developing and Implementing Policies: Midland Bank's Experience

Suzan Lewis, with Anne Watts and Christine Camp

This chapter presents a case study of one organization which has implemented work and family policies to address equal opportunities and business objectives, and more recently, the quality of life goal of stress reduction. Midland, like other banks, employs large numbers of women, although most senior positions continue to be held by men. Given the reliance on female labour, equal opportunities, especially in relation to gender, has been an issue for many years. The first Equal Opportunities Manager was appointed in 1979, following the sex and race legislation of the mid 1970s. Policies introduced during the early 1980s focused mainly on gender, but more recently this has broadened to include race, disability, age and sexuality, with equal opportunities increasingly being perceived as a business issue. In 1988, an Equal Opportunities Director was recruited, the executive level of the appointment giving prominence to the issue. This chapter describes the policies, the rationale for their development and the strategies for their implementation, and presents a brief evaluation of their impact and limitations to date and future agendas for change.

The Policies

Midland began a nursery programme in 1988 and now has over 100 nurseries in locations around the country, providing places for approximately 850 children of employees. The nurseries are open to children of 'primary carers' (male or female) who are full- or part-time employees. Quality of childcare is constantly monitored to ensure that standards are upheld. In addition, up to 60 holiday playschemes are available for school-age children. A career break scheme, introduced in 1985, was revised in 1989 and 1995. Initially developed to meet the needs to retain women, who otherwise would have left the organization for childcare reasons, the scheme was extended in 1989 to cover all caring situations.

Career Break Scheme

If an individual does not wish to return to Midland immediately at the end of her maternity leave, one option may be for her to take a career break. The

Priority Returner Scheme provides for a break of up to five years to cover all caring situations. During this time the bank encourages the individual to keep in touch and offers any key time opportunities that may be available. Every endeavour is made by Midland to offer a suitable job on three months' written notice of return, but no guarantee can be given, as opportunities are dependent on the business need. The bank will, however, give priority for an interview over external candidates, for any advertised positions. On return to employment, individuals can link up with their previous service, for service-related benefits.

Due to the changed business and economic climate, from 1996, the bank is no longer able to offer a separate scheme for management. But the Priority Returner Scheme is open to all employees who have satisfactorily completed their probationary service.

Family/Paternity Leave

All members of staff, both male and female, are entitled to time off, in an emergency, to care for sick, elderly or disabled dependants. Fathers may also use up to three days of the entitlement for paternity leave when their baby is born. Family leave consists of five days' paid leave per year on the following basis:

- The sick child must be 14 or under. If the child is older, managers must consider the individual circumstances.
- There must not be another adult carer available.

Maternity Leave

Under the revised statutory maternity leave regulations (1994) all women in the UK are now eligible for 14 weeks' maternity leave irrespective of length of service and hours worked. However, at Midland since 1990 the contractual maternity leave period has been for 46 weeks: 11 weeks before the birth and 35 after. Paid family leave has been available to all employees since 1989 and this is taken up more or less equally by men and women across the bank. Paternity leave was introduced in January 1996.

Flexible Working

There are also a range of flexible or atypical working arrangements. For example, over 1,000 people now job share, mostly at clerical levels but also up to and including middle managers. Part-time work has long been available and part-time employees now make up nearly 20 per cent of the total work-force. In 1992 Midland extended the range of its comprehensive pension scheme benefits to all part-time workers, irrespective of hours worked, on a full pro rata basis. This anticipated and predated legal developments, in this case the decision of the European Court of Justice (1994) on the rights of part-time workers (see Jeremy Lewis, Chapter 3).

Other Policies

Other recent developments include a working parents' network and an employee counselling service. The working parents' network, which was launched officially by the Chief Executive in 1994, has been meeting monthly at lunchtime in London since late 1992. The membership is approximately 70 per cent women, 30 per cent men. It provides a forum to share experiences and solutions to everyday problems faced by working parents and offers various support programmes, including parenting workshops, advice lines and literature. The aim is to extend this by establishing regional networks. The employee counselling service is available for all employees. Although it does not focus specifically on work and family, problems that arise at the work–family interface inevitably feature along with other problems which may affect working lives and for which employees can benefit from a confidential and free counselling service.

These policies have been developed within the equal opportunities framework, which also includes a wide range of policies on women's career development, harassment, race and disability, aiming to promote a diverse, healthy and productive workforce.

Rationale

The rationale for introducing work–family policies has changed over time as the business context shifts and different issues emerge. However, it has always been based on a business case and on the impact on the bottom line profits. Planning in the 1980s was dominated by the demographic argument (NEDO, 1988). The downturn in the market for school leavers, the historic basis of recruitment to the bank, was a prime concern in terms of future shortages in skilled labour. Retention of current staff became a key issue. This provided a window of opportunity and was used strategically.

Internal research in the 1980s indicated that Midland was losing the vast majority of its women employees after maternity leave. Of women taking maternity leave, 70 per cent were not returning to the bank, and they had on average 11 years' service with all the skills and experience that goes with that. The focus was on women at this stage, because women and not men were leaving the bank in large numbers. Childcare problems were identified as a major factor preventing women from returning to work. Based on research conducted by the Institute of Management Studies which showed that the replacement costs of an experienced employee were roughly equal to his/her annual employment costs (Forbes and McGill, 1988) it was calculated that it was costing the bank around £15 million a year to lose such a high percentage of women. This was the business argument used in persuading Midland's Board to commit to its nursery programme.

The demographic argument became less salient as recruitment fell during the economic downturn. The major issues of the late 1980s and the 1990s have been downsizing and development, rather than retention, and the rationale has shifted accordingly. For instance, the argument for introducing family leave was that when staff are reduced to a core, who are working at a high level of productivity, it is essential to be able to support them and give them the means to be able to cope with their non-work obligations, which would otherwise reduce their effectiveness at work. It was recognized that in addition to childcare, other emergency domestic arrangements could emerge which are often sudden and very severe, and that it is important that these difficulties are not exacerbated by financial hardships. Consequently paid leave was introduced and a range of flexible work options is being developed to enable people to continue to work while attending to these obligations. The stress experienced by members of staff with young children or other family concerns has also been recognized and was an important factor in the development of the working parents' network.

An emerging force adding to the business case is the ethical investment movement. Stakeholders, including customers, shareholders and corporate investors, are becoming increasingly critical in asking questions about company ethics and equal opportunities policies. For example, letters from pension fund managers ask about the commitment to equal opportunities, to satisfy investors. This all helps to build the business case.

Strategies for Development and Implementation

The process of implementation has involved researching needs, consultation and involving, advising, piloting and reviewing new schemes, before launching them at a national level. The business rationale is always stressed, emphasizing the rights and responsibilities of all employees. Regular monitoring and reviewing of the policies is an important and ongoing process.

Although most schemes are initiated by the equal opportunities department, a central strategy for development of policies is to consult and involve the business at all stages. The business argument is always supported by facts and figures to help position people's thinking. Policies are put forward, with the business argument, and sent out to the line and human resource functions for consultation. They in turn address their business issues which feed into the process. There is rarely 100 per cent agreement for all the policies but there is usually a critical mass which is sufficient to progress. The support of top management has always been crucial. In addition, the union (Banking, Insurance and Finance Union, BIFU) has been very supportive of the policies.

The initiatives are supported by a communications strategy covering policy and procedures. Equal opportunities training and booklets are also available. Equal opportunities is defined in these publications as good management practice – getting the best from all people, which makes sound business sense. In terms of maternity leave and returners, booklets remind managers of the retention and cost effectiveness argument. It is emphasized that nothing should happen which places the maternity leaver in a less favourable position than had she been in continuous employment.

This process ensures that the policies and the rationale for their introduction are well known. Inevitably, in any organization there will be some who are cynical about the value of family-friendly initiatives. Where resistance occurs it is treated in the context of employee relations, occupational health or other management processes. If, for example, there is an area which is not putting the policies into practice, efforts are made to find out what the business problem is perceived to be and to help sort out any difficulties. For instance, there were some initial fears among some sections of management that family leave might be abused. To counter this it was pointed out that if staff are abusing their rights then they may also abuse their own sickness absence rights, and this would be a management issue to be dealt with in accordance with normal practice. It is considered to be less likely that people will invent family emergencies than their own sickness. However, it is pointed out that even if this is not the case, to deny the majority the right to this leave because a few people may abuse it would not be rational. If there are problems, managers have recourse to disciplinary procedures if necessary, and employees who feel that they are wrongly accused or discriminated against have access to grievance procedures. Moreover, where there are high levels of sickness in a particular department, this is regarded as an occupational health issue and it may be necessary to examine what fundamental problems underpin this.

The development of the policies has been helped by support at the top. The appointment of an Equal Opportunities Director, with external credibility, adds credence to the initiatives. This has ensured that issues are not marginalized and enabled the rationale for the policies to be communicated at the highest levels.

It has been important to monitor the policies in practice, to be able to demonstrate their success in terms of take-up, retention and other criteria. For example statistics relating to actual take-up of family leave have demonstrated that fears of widespread abuse of the benefit are unfounded. Roughly 20 per cent of the workforce use the entitlement at any one time and average take-up is the equivalent of two days per member of staff. Some people take five days and others none at all. It is possible, of course, that the lack of take-up by some employees may be due to cultural barriers. This may be a problem to be addressed at some stage. However, the leave is taken almost equally by men and women, in all parts of the business, which suggests that it is increasingly acceptable in dealing with domestic emergencies.

Evaluation

It is recognized that policies and practices within the organization must be constantly monitored and developed, both to ensure that policies are fulfilling their original goals, and to address new issues as they emerge. Methods of evaluation have included periodic reviews and surveys, monitoring of statistics on take-up of particular policies, and qualitative research. The criteria for evaluating the effectiveness of family-friendly policies are a source of debate (Gonyea and Googins, 1992). At one level, effectiveness can be assessed in terms of cost effectiveness, take-up of leave and flexible forms of working, quality (of nurseries), impact on women's long-term career development, and the ability to sustain approaches in the light of changing internal and external conditions. At a more fundamental level, the impact on organizational culture in terms of shared beliefs and values must be examined.

Meeting Business Objectives and Sustaining the Initiatives in the Light of Internal and External Changes

In terms of meeting the business objectives the policies have been very successful. Retention rates after maternity leave have increased from 29 per cent in the early 1980s to approximately 80 per cent in 1995, making the initiatives very cost effective. The take-up of alternative forms of work is growing, albeit mainly among women. Flexible ways of working are also highly effective, as demonstrated by the business success of First Direct, a 24-hour, seven days a week banking service which is made possible by the use of shift work and other flexible forms of working. The impact of equal opportunities policies on the public image of the bank has also been considerable, and regarded as relevant to its commercial success. For example, in a period when all the banks were having very negative press Midland was receiving very favourable publicity on childcare and other initiatives. It was noted as a leading-edge employer, which is good for staff morale. These successes have helped to ensure that the vision which first fuelled the various equal opportunities initiatives has continued with changes in management. The initiatives were first developed when the bank was at a low point in its cycle. Equal opportunities became an important part of a broader change, which included recognizing the importance of women and was driven from the depths of recession. The changes thus became associated with the recovery and it has since been possible to sustain the initiatives in the face of internal and external changes.

Impact on Women's Career Development

The impact of career breaks and other forms of flexible work on women's careers has yet to be fully evaluated as the policies have not been in place long enough for long-term follow-ups to be carried out. Many women have returned from career breaks, but they have not yet moved up in the hierarchy in sufficient numbers for proper evaluation. A danger of an initiative such as the career break, if it continues to be taken up only by women while traditional working patterns remain the norm, is that it can create a 'mommy track' (Schwartz, 1989) – a slower career track for mothers. This may be acceptable to those women who reject the 'male model' of work (Pleck, 1977; Cook, 1992) and wish to find a more comfortable balance between work and family. However, by marginalizing mothers in this way it may also help to perpetuate work structures which may be incompatible with family life, and of questionable long-term value to the organization. Moreover, it is not clear that traditional hierarchical career structures will continue to be the norm in the future. With the trends towards delayering, downsizing and redundancy of senior people in their 50s, who have often sacrificed involvement in family to demonstrate total organizational commitment, the future seems less certain. Longitudinal research is needed into the impact of career breaks on women's careers, but the full picture should include a follow-up of men and women who work continuously without career breaks so that traditional careers can also be evaluated.

Impact on Organizational Culture

The impact of policies on organizational culture is always difficult to assess. Most organizations continue to be male-dominated, with men, many of whom have non-career wives, making the rules and perpetuating the culture (Cooper and Lewis, 1993), and Midland is no exception. There is widespread understanding and appreciation of the policies throughout the bank. Nevertheless some practical problems inevitably remain. In particular, the 'family-friendly' focus remains largely on women and the vast majority of take-up has been by women. The fact that 50 per cent of family leave time is now taken by men, and that approximately 30 per cent of members of the working parents' network are men, suggests a slight shift in Midland's culture, towards recognizing that men as well as women have family commitments, but there is clearly some way to go.

The reluctance of men to take up family-related benefits reflects both the organizational culture and the wider society. The take-up of flexible benefits and leave tends to be restricted in many organizations by traditional social expectations and by line managers who disapprove of accommodating work for family. Midland's workforce inevitably reflects the range of attitudes of the wider society. There is a high level of training to counteract stereotypical beliefs, but the culture is changing only slowly. The problems brought up by men who belong to the working parents' network indicate that some would like to take advantage of work–family benefits but feel constrained by the culture. They struggle to find a balance between making time for family, and convincing managers that they are committed to their career. In many sections of the bank, there is an expectation that commitment will be demonstrated by working long hours, and travelling away from home, as in many other organizations (see Lewis and Taylor, Chapter 9). Paradoxically this culture of long hours at the top coexists with a commitment to equal opportunities within the bank. It is recognized that a major challenge for the future is to find ways of organizing work so that men as well as women can meet their needs for family involvement while also helping to sustain business growth. The hope is that the family-oriented policies will encourage a sympathetic climate for any further developments as men's and women's roles and needs continue to change.

Future Agenda

The bank continues to strive to be an equal opportunities and family-friendly employer, but recognizes that this must be a long-term and ongoing objective. The emerging issue of men's roles in the organization will be a major focus for the future. For further progress to be made an important goal is for the organization to be more supportive of men at all levels who wish to be actively involved in family care. This may require a fundamental reconsideration of organizational practices. It is envisaged that a business argument will again prevail. More and more men wish to strike a balance between work and family (New Ways to Work, 1995), which is difficult to achieve in current organizational cultures, even when flexible policies are available. Ultimately, the stress which this creates will impact on productivity. It is important to challenge the culture of long hours of work which are not only family-unfriendly, but may also indicate ineffective organization of work. The way forward here may lie in an emphasis on tasks, targets and competencies rather than time in the workplace.

Conclusions

Midland Bank's experience illustrates some of the key factors in achieving some organizational change towards the goal of equal opportunities and family friendliness. A change agent at a high level within the organization has been important to galvanize a critical mass of support. In addition the benefits of consultation, training and persuasion are apparent. It has been particularly important to stress the business case and the cost effectiveness of equal opportunities practices in order to convince businesses to implement change. Midland's experience is a good example of how this type of change can have a very positive effect on the business. However, issues keep emerging in new forms, so even if policies are in place it is necessary continually to revisit them. The current challenge is to address men's needs for time for family and the culture of long working hours versus productivity.

Can Midland's experiences be generalized to other contexts or is it a special case? It is a large organization and the nature of its work is characterized by a need to foster a loyal and well-trained workforce. In smaller organizations, or those whose employees require less training and are therefore more easily replaced, the exact business arguments may be different or less clear-cut. The basic principles of integrating the business and social case, anticipating and responding to new business and work–family issues as they arise, the importance of a change agent in a position of power, and the processes of consultation, persuasion, training and constant monitoring, however, may be widely applicable,. The remaining challenges of changing organizational practices to meet the needs of women, men and the business itself are also widely shared.

References

Cook, A. (1992) 'Can work requirements adapt to the needs of dual earner families?', in S. Lewis, D.N. Izraeli and H. Hootsmans (eds), *Dual Earner Families: International Perspectives.* London: Sage.

Cooper, C.L. and Lewis, S. (1993) *The Workplace Revolution: Managing Today's Dual Career Families.* London: Kogan Page.

Forbes, A, and McGill, D. (1988) *Understanding Wastage.* IMS Report no. 105. Brighton: Institute of Manpower Studies.

Gonyea, J. and Googins, B. (1992) 'Linking the worlds of work and family: Beyond the productivity trap', *Journal of Human Resources Management*, 31: 209–26.

NEDO (1988) *Defusing the Demographic Time Bomb.* London: National Economic Development Office.

New Ways to Work (1995) *Balanced Lives: Changing Work Patterns for Men.* London: New Ways To Work.

Pleck, J. (1977) 'The work family role system', *Social Problems*, 24: 417–27.

Schwartz, F. (1989) 'Management women and the new facts of life', *Harvard Business Review*, 67: 65–76.

PART 3

BARRIERS TO THE EFFECTIVENESS OF CURRENT POLICIES AND STRATEGIES: MOVING BEYOND POLICIES TOWARDS CULTURE CHANGE

9

Evaluating the Impact of Family-Friendly Employer Policies: A Case Study

Suzan Lewis and Karen Taylor

As in any organizational change programme, it is important to evaluate the extent to which work family initiatives meet their objectives within a specific organizational context. As outlined in Chapter 1, objectives of 'family-friendly' initiatives may be narrow and short term, including enhanced retention of women with children or the reduction of absenteeism, or may be broader and longer term aiming for wider corporate culture change. The latter is clearly more difficult to achieve. Organizational cultures are grounded in deep-seated beliefs about gender, the nature of work, and the ideal employee, which reflect societal norms and are often implicit or even unconscious, and therefore difficult to challenge. The process towards achieving fundamental organizational culture change, to acknowledge and value both men's and women's family identities and commitments, is therefore unlikely to be quick or simple. It is useful to examine the role that formal policy changes can play in this process, to identify facilitators of and barriers to fundamental change and to explore ways of overcoming barriers. We need to recognize, however, that organizational culture is multiple and complex (Meek, 1992; Woodall, 1995) and that different stakeholders may have different perspectives on the change process. It is important to gain an understanding of these different perspectives and the influence that different stakeholders have in bringing about change or sustaining the status quo.

This chapter presents a case study examining the impact of formal work family policies in one organization, drawing on the perspectives of employees with family commitments and their line managers. As the workplace comprises just one part of an integrated work–family system, and experiences in the two domains are inevitably interrelated, we also examine the perspectives of other family members, in this case, the employees' spouses.

The Company and its Policies

The company in which the case study was carried out is the UK division of a multinational firm of chartered accountants. It had recently implemented a number of family-oriented policies in a context which might be termed 'family-unfriendly', i.e. there were no formal 'family-responsive' policies and informally employees are expected to work long and often inflexible hours in the office. However, the company had recently signed up as a member of the Opportunity 2000 campaign. This business-led campaign aims to enhance the representation of women at all levels of organizations, and stresses the business case for equal opportunities. It is grounded in research in organizations in the USA, the UK, and elsewhere in Europe which identified four key aspects of good practice contributing to the successful implementation of equal opportunities and associated culture change (Hammond and Holton, 1991). These are: commitment from the top, changing behaviour, building ownership of the changes, and making the necessary investment of resources. Membership of Opportunity 2000 signals commitment at the highest level of the organization, although there are no prescriptions about how the objectives should be achieved. The policies at this company were developed as a consequence of this commitment, by a woman partner in the firm, working together with the personnel department. A clear business argument was used to support the policy development: the firm was losing highly trained and experienced women accountants who tended to leave after having a baby. This was costing the firm money. The main short-term objective, therefore, was to retain women staff after maternity leave, although the broader goals of reducing stress and promoting gender equality in the company were also expressed, as means of enhancing business success.

Following a survey of needs and widespread consultation, the initial policies, described as policies for employees with family commitments, were developed comprising four elements: enhanced maternity pay for selected women employees; reduced hours working, that is a reduction of standard working hours by a maximum of 10 hours per week, with pro rata salary but full entitlement to other benefits; part-time working in excess of 10 hours per week which can be negotiated with appropriate managers; and a career break and retainer scheme. All benefits are at the discretion of management. At the time that the case study was carried out the policies had been in place for just over one year and a small but growing number of women with family commitments (and one man) were taking up the initiatives. The most popular option was the reduced-hours scheme, although a number of women had returned to full-time work with the additional maternity pay. In these cases women were nevertheless restricting their hours to 9 to 5, which in the context of this organization is informally regarded as less than full time. Other women were working part time, or were currently taking career breaks.

This study examines the impact of these policies from multiple perspectives at one point in time. In particular, we sought to identify areas of culture change, and obstacles to be overcome in achieving fundamental change in the work–family system. Interviews were carried out with women who were working reduced hours or part time, or who had returned early from maternity leave with enhanced benefits and were working full time without overtime. No employees had yet returned from career breaks. Although the family policy benefits, with the exception of the enhanced maternity pay, are, in principle, available to all employees, only one man (whose wife was terminally ill) was identified as working reduced hours, and he declined to be involved in the study. Most of the women interviewed had young children. One had no children but was helping to care for her elderly mother and disabled siblings. The majority of the women were chartered accountants working at junior or middle management level but there were some non-managerial women, including support staff. The women were employed in one of five offices throughout England and Scotland in a range of departments and functions. They were asked to name their line manager and to invite him/her to be interviewed. All the line managers interviewed were male and four were partners in the firm. (Most of the women in the study are also line managers, but we use the term in this chapter to refer to the women's line managers.) We also asked the women to nominate a family member to be interviewed so that we could explore the impact of the new ways of working on family dynamics and relationships, which may in turn influence experiences at work. As none of the families had children old enough to be interviewed, spouses or partners were nominated. (Only one single parent participated in the study.)

In-depth semi-structured interviews were used to explore the perceived impact of and barriers to the effectiveness of the policies from the different perspectives. Interviews with the women employees explored childcare and other care issues and domestic division of labour, experience of returning to work and of managing multiple roles, experience of the family and work policies in action, formal and informal policies and practices, support available at work and at home, and career development issues. Interviews with managers explored attitudes to the policies and to work–family issues in general, anticipated and actual experience of managing employees taking up benefits, informal and formal policies and practices, impact of the policies on the day-to-day running of the department and career development issues. Spouses were asked about childcare and other care issues and the division of labour, and about their views on the policies and the support that their partners received, and the impact these had on the household. We also spoke to one woman who had been refused reduced-hours work and to key change agents, and presented findings to and invited discussion with members of personnel departments throughout the company. This chapter focuses on some strengths and limitations of the policies and barriers to change, identified from the interviews.

Strengths of the Policies

The main reported strengths of the policies were that the policies: (1) formalize informal practice; (2) allow women to achieve a balance between career and family and reduce stress from multiple roles; and (3) enable the company to retain valued staff and therefore enhance return on investment in training. In addition, a consequence not anticipated was that (4) many of the women interviewed felt their work was now more efficient and productive than when they had worked long hours.

Negotiating Flexible Working Arrangements

Many of the women and their managers reported that the policy has enabled them to build on and formalize existing informal practices, which also included flexibility about when hours were worked and periods of working from home. Others felt that the policy provided a necessary framework for jointly negotiating a solution to work and family problems. The women felt that the policies gave them a greater sense of entitlement to ask for what they mostly perceived as 'concessions', although clearly men in the organization did not perceive this entitlement. The women's managers also reported that the policies increased the pressure on them to consider requests for shorter or more flexible hours. Nevertheless, some managers were reluctant to negotiate such arrangements and some refused requests where they believed they were not feasible.

Most of the women were prepared to be flexible by, for example, putting in extra hours when it was necessary to meet urgent deadlines, or being available on a mobile telephone when not officially working. In general the line managers were able to see advantages to the department of having a flexible resource. However, flexibility is not always conceived in a mutually beneficial way. One partner in the firm spoke of the advantage of this flexible resource during the recession in terms of reduced labour costs and had actually refused one woman who asked to return from reduced hours to full-time work.

Achieving a Balance

All the women working less than full time felt that this enabled them to achieve a better balance between career and family than would otherwise have been possible. They appreciated having time to spend with their children, and, perhaps because of low expectations of support from employers, were satisfied to receive reduced pay despite often getting through as much work as they had on full-time contracts.

> On Thursday nights I go home and have three clear days with [the children] . . . and it doesn't stop me doing my job at all. I can do my job as well as ever really.

The women with the more supportive managers, who were able to build some flexibility into their schedules, felt in control of their work and family demands, a factor which has been associated with reduced work family conflict and stress (Thomas and Ganster, 1995).

Achieving a balance depends on being able to manage family as well as work commitments. Work–family stress is lower for women when they are able to negotiate an equal division of family work, and this is more likely to occur when women define themselves and are defined by their partners as co-providers (Potuchek, 1992). Most of the women in our study were relatively high earners and this was reflected in a relatively high level of spouse involvement in domestic work, or in the employment of paid domestic help. The family commitments programme helped women to continue in their family provider role. In some cases, however, the pro rata salary associated with reduced hours working was used by the women and their spouses to justify men's greater entitlement to free time, and women's greater responsibility for family work. Other women were clearly identified as the main provider and received substantial domestic support from their partners. However, the social construction of men as being entitled to exemption from the more burdensome aspects of domestic work often still prevailed, as illustrated by the couple quoted below. The husband, a milkman, is very much the secondary earner, but retains the entitlement to select those chores which he is willing to perform.

> I love cooking so I am more than happy to cook most nights. I refuse to do any ironing. Flatly refuse. I don't mind putting stuff in the washing machine. (husband)

> I have to do the ironing which I hate . . . He's done it once I think. It took him so long and it was awful. He said 'I'm never doing it again.' So I do it. (wife)

The short-term equal opportunities objective of enabling women with children to continue in paid work was therefore being met as was, to some extent at least, the quality of life objective of reducing stress in multiple roles. However, gender ideology continues to influence behaviour at home and at work, and to reduce the potential impact of family-oriented policies on the reduction of women's 'double burden'.

Retention of Staff

The short-term business objective of retaining highly trained and experienced women was also being achieved, as indicated by turnover figures (which may have been confounded by the recession and the difficulty of finding new jobs) and by the interview data. Some women were very clear that they would have wanted to leave the firm after maternity leave if they had not been able to return on reduced hours or part time.

> If the company would not have offered me reduced hours I would just have looked for a job elsewhere.

The policies can help to enhance loyalty to the firm.

> I thought about looking for another job, but then I thought well they were there for me when I needed them . . . [my manager] was very good.

This is not an inevitable consequence of the policies, however. Rather, it appears to depend largely on the women's working relationship with their managers, and the ease with which they negotiated their particular arrangements.

Most of the women's managers emphasized that retention and loyalty represented an important return on investment.

> It costs a lot of money to train an accountant up to senior manager . . . clearly it doesn't make economic sense to miss that return on investment. (manager, male)

> I feel that there are a lot of very highly talented women where employers do not give them the support they should and therefore they are not working. To me, I am not being altruistic, I would be quite happy to have more than just Mary working on this arrangement because I think we can get high-quality people who add a lot of value to the firm and to the clients we try to serve. So I see serious benefits in that if we are flexible the talented people will repay by the contribution they make. To me that is a very compelling advantage. (manager, male)

We did not interview employees without family commitments, other than those in personnel functions, so we were unable to test the theory that offering assistance to employees in need will symbolize concern for employees in general and positively influence attachment of others to the organization (Grover and Crooker, 1995). However, there was a feeling among many of the interviewees that the scheme acknowledged the difficulties experienced by those with family commitments and therefore treated them as valuable employees which can enhance broader satisfaction with the organization.

> It's actually a nice statement on behalf of the organization that we do value and recognize that people do have places to go and homes outside this office block. (manager, male)

Effects on Work

Most of the women who were working reduced hours felt that they became more productive and more efficient, although this is not always recognized by their seniors. They felt that they were more productive, and were fitting more actual work into the normal working day.

> I would certainly say that I try to do as much in four days as some people might do in five days. I rarely take lunches unless I have to go out for something but otherwise I'm quite happy to work through lunch.

Many reported that the balance between their work and family enabled them to focus on doing a better job.

> In a way it's helped me, it's made me more conscious of what I've to do when, to help me sort out my work more than I did before because there was always the thought of, well, if there's an emergency you can do it Friday afternoon. Now I've got to have everything covered in advance so I think it's made me more organized, more focused.

Similarly, women who had negotiated informal arrangements to work at home on certain days reported being more productive on those days, as well as saving on travelling time and therefore creating more time for family.

Problems and Limitations of the Policies

Problem areas identified included: (1) take-up is restricted by the targeting of a limited and exclusive group of employees; (2) management discretion further restricts take-up and can create financial insecurity in relation to maternity leave; (3) not all line managers are committed to the scheme and many are concerned about attitudes of co-workers and clients; (4) the women's greater efficiency was not always recognized and it was felt that when this happened it could have negative effects on career progression.

Limited Take-Up of Initiatives

The limited take-up of options was not regarded as a problem by management at this stage, but clearly restricts any general impact on the wider company culture. Informal culture limits take-up by men, in this company as elsewhere (Haas and Hwang, 1995). To some extent the designation of the policies as being for employees with family commitments implies that most employees do not have such commitments and marginalizes rather than normalizes different ways of working. None of the line managers whom we interviewed had received requests from men to reduce their hours of work for family reasons, nor did they think it was likely to happen at the present time. Most said that if they were asked they would treat the request in the same way as one from a woman, looking at the feasibility of specific proposals. A number of managers, however, were adamant that it would not be acceptable for men to change ways of working, recognizing that this had the potential to shift initiatives from the margins towards a mainstream challenge to current ways of working. They remained convinced that the firm could not survive unless the majority were able to put in the long hours of work which they believed were necessary to meet clients' needs. A number of these managers also displayed little awareness of the reality of men's and women's changing roles and needs. One father of four young boys, whose wife was employed part time, reflected on the possibility of reduced hours for a father and asked 'but what would he do with the time?'

The varying attitudes towards men's family roles were also evident in discussions relating to the implementation of paternity leave. A senior female manager felt that men's parental needs should be addressed.

> I think the biggest single area where they don't do enough is . . . for fathers. There should be paternity rights, time off . . . they had somebody in our department who got screamed at because he had not been to a meeting because he had gone to hospital where his wife was having a baby.

Some of the partners in the firm agreed but others were firmly against the introduction of paternity leave.

> I wouldn't be in favour . . . At the end of the day the father can't be a substitute for a mother. I took holidays [when my children were born] I chose to have children . . . it's my responsibility.

This opposition was firmly located in traditional constructions of gender roles, and particularly the social construction of fatherhood in terms of the provider role, with involvement in family care as optional.

The policies informally excluded not only men but also women with family commitments other than the care of young children and women working in support roles or at junior levels. The fact that one man, one woman with eldercare and other care responsibilities, and several women in support positions had already come forward and successfully negotiated shorter hours suggests that pressure to broaden the applications of the 'family-friendly' policies may come from the grass roots level. On the other hand, employees may be deterred from making such demands because of a limited sense of entitlement to consideration of family needs in the workplace. Many of the women interviewed as well as the line managers felt that employers should not really be expected to take account of employees' family commitments. This may reflect the wider socio-political attitude in the UK that family is a private concern (see Moss, Chapter 2), which also restricts expectations about how the state could support families.

> I know there are other countries in the EC . . . have far better childcare facilities . . . but I suppose there's an argument *if you decide to have a child it should be your responsibility.* (manager, female; author's emphasis)

This ambiguity surrounding entitlement to consideration of family responsibilities may create low expectations of employers, an overvaluing of 'benefits' provided and a reluctance among employees to press to have the value of alternative ways of working recognized. It also illustrates the impact of the broader social context in which the organization operates.

Management Discretion

For those who did ask for reductions in working time, management discretion could pose a further barrier. Management discretion concerning take-up of the initiatives is not something that will be readily relinquished, as it is seen as a necessary safeguard against the threat of loss of power and autonomy for managers to run their departments. In particular it was felt that certain jobs and departments would not lend themselves to reduced hours working, for example, auditing which requires long hours of work at certain times of the year. This was regarded as a given by all associated with this department who were reluctant to discuss notions of flexibility.

From the women's perspectives, management discretion was particularly problematic in relation to maternity leave. The procedure with regard to the enhanced maternity leave was that managers could ask women to return early, with extra pay, if they believed this was appropriate, that is, if there was sufficient work for them to do. This could create financial uncertainty, particularly when the woman was the main breadwinner. One woman, who was the major earner in her family, needed to arrange mortgage payments while she was on maternity leave and was dependent on an early return to work. Her early return was not requested until quite late in the leave which caused her some distress.

> a worry to me at the time was . . . if they don't request your early return you don't get the bonus and because we basically needed that to pay the mortgage . . . I'd said to Personnel, 'how do I go about getting this confirmed?', and they said, 'well you can't, we'll write to you seven weeks after you've had the baby and if we say to you . . . we want you to come back early then you can say, "yes I will come back early", then you'll know you'll get the two months' salary', which I felt was a bit hit and miss.

Many of the line managers themselves were uneasy about their discretionary roles and commented that they needed more training and support in making decisions about staff with family commitments, managing the return from maternity leave and managing staff working reduced hours. They also felt the need for support relating to how to set objectives and appraise employees working reduced hours. The long-hours culture made it difficult to know what to expect from employees within a given time framework.

Line Managers' Concerns

Management support for and understanding of the women's situation and a good working relationship between the woman and her manager were crucial factors in the success or otherwise of the family-friendly schemes. Many of the women felt that managers had been understanding and sympathetic to the issues and practicalities of being a working parent while their managers themselves were appreciative of the women's continued commitment.

> From where I sit Julia seems to manage her home life very well and she certainly performs her professional duties to a very high standard of quality.

Other managers, however, had a range of concerns about the scheme, which made them appear less than supportive to the women. Some felt that the scheme might be open to abuse and feared that employees could take advantage, although in their personal experience, none of the women had done so. Often this was tied up with beliefs that mothers of young children should not be working, and that even with reduced hours their work and/or family would suffer. There was often a conflict between deeply held beliefs and what was actually being observed in practice. This, in turn, can create a biased view of the success of the scheme, and may become self-fulfilling.

> I think the manager I've got [on reduced hours] is doing a damned good job . . . but I don't see the other half . . . I don't see their lives falling apart . . . I feel, from being a parent, it isn't feasible to do it all. That's borne out by my experience here. (partner)

Managers who were not fully committed to the work–family policies quoted concerns about the attitudes of co-workers and clients. Most women said that their colleagues were supportive, but some did feel that co-workers see the scheme as a perk and do not understand that the time off work is not a holiday. Many line managers were concerned about co-workers' perceptions of fairness.

> My main goal is to work out an arrangement which meets Tina's needs and also is acceptable to other people in the office . . . If they were to see her going home early each day that would be disastrous for morale. One day a week when she is not here is more acceptable.

The construction of the policies as benefits rather than necessary supports together with a focus on input (time in the office) rather than output can fuel feelings of inequity, which can be exacerbated in times of economic uncertainty. Thus, while some managers perceived reduced hours as a useful way of creating more flexibility in the workforce, others reported being concerned that they might have to make some people redundant while apparently giving others 'benefits' such as part-time work.

Many of the line managers also anticipated problems due to the women managers' lack of availability to clients. The women themselves were aware of this as a potential problem. Some made efforts to ensure this did not happen, for example by being available at home on days when they were not officially working. None of the women felt that clients had been adversely affected, and they pointed out that full-time staff were not always available to speak to clients whenever they telephoned. Neither did their managers produce any concrete examples of how clients had been adversely affected or been dissatisfied with the service these women provided. A useful role for future research would be to examine the perspective of clients to establish whether their attitudes and expectations are indeed barriers to flexible working.

Women's Greater Productivity Is Not Always Recognized

Women's greater productivity and efficiency were often obscured because of a prevalent discourse of time as a commodity to be managed and 'given' to paid work and/or family and which symbolizes productivity, commitment and personal value. The difficulty in measuring productivity in most types of work is well documented, as are the problems of attempting to evaluate the effectiveness of family-oriented policies in productivity terms (Gonyea and Googins, 1992). However, productivity appears to be treated as largely unproblematic in this organization. The dominant culture is clearly one in which productivity is defined in terms of hours spent at the office, i.e. being seen to be working, regardless of whether this is reflected in chargeable hours.

> Within an accountancy firm, career-wise, there can be an element of, you know, doing long hours, to be seen to be doing long hours . . . I could quite easily see that your career in the office could be, well literally stopped if you're not prepared to put the hours in . . . get the work done. (manager, male)

The women's perspective that the reduced hours scheme not only enables them to work in a way that can be reconciled with family commitments, but actually enables them to work in a more productive and focused way, contrasts with the dominant culture. This culture, however, can obscure these positive outcomes: to the extent that commitment is defined in terms of time given to work, not just chargeable hours but also time spent in the office, women who work reduced hours or who do not work beyond 9 to 5 are, by definition, considered less productive and less committed than other staff.

> Someone on reduced hours is less committed . . . we have also got a problem with commitment with women coming back five days . . . they struggle in terms of giving outside 9 to 5 commitment . . . it's difficult for them to go side by side with a male manager . . . with a wife at home . . . they are able to give that extra hour or two. (partner)

Commitment is also often regarded as finite and non-expandable, implying that if someone has commitments outside work, this inevitably reduces their level of commitment at work.

> They have other commitments. You can't be a wife and a mother and a manager and do them all well. Something has to give. (manage, male)

Impact on Career Development

The construction of time as a commodity (Daly, 1992) defines those who do not give maximum time to the firm as less productive and committed, and hence less valued than those working long hours, who are constructed as giving their time more generously to the firm. This was reflected to varying degrees in attitudes to promotion of those working reduced hours in this study, and views were mixed about whether working reduced hours or restricting full-time hours to 9 till 5 will reduce women's opportunities for promotion. Some interviewees, both the women and their managers, were unhesitating in their belief that reduced hours would not affect promotion opportunities.

> When I was working reduced hours I had one of my best ever assessments. It clearly didn't affect my ability to do my job well, and that was recognized. (manager, female)

Other women and their managers, however, felt that while alternative working patterns help women to achieve a balance between career and family, their career progression will be affected.

> They made it very clear to me that while I'm on reduced hours I'll have no career progression here . . . [my boss] said to me if you don't come back full time you realise your career is on hold. (manager, female)

> She's a good manager, but she won't be promoted. She doesn't have the commitment . . . doesn't put in the time. (senior manager, male)

Starkey (1989) argues that an understanding of how time is constructed, manipulated and experienced is crucial to our understanding of organizations. Since family-friendly policies aim to challenge conventional notions of working time, the way in which time is construed within organizations is a crucial element of organizational context. The construction of time as a scarce resource and subsequent valuing of employees according to how much of this commodity is given to an organization leads to a valuing of time at work for its own sake and moves the focus away from the tasks performed or quality of performance. The economic associations of time as a commodity also mean that time is differentially valued, with time in market work being assigned greater value than time with family. Unless the discourses of time are challenged, therefore, family-friendly policies alone will have limited success in changing organizational culture, and the reduction of work–family stress and gender inequality at work and at home will be correspondingly restricted.

Is the Organizational Culture Changing? Pockets of Awareness

It is too early to judge the full impact of the scheme on the company culture. However, support from management is crucial for the success of any modifications to normal working practices. As is to be expected there are still some managers with entrenched views about whether women can, or even should, combine a career with parenthood. On the other hand some of the interviewees felt that the culture is changing to some extent. In particular, every manager interviewed appreciated that family crises were unavoidable and that providing these were rare (as they have proved to be) it was legitimate to miss work in these circumstances, which was presented as a shift from earlier norms. It could be argued that this would have occurred anyway, and may be unrelated to a policy on family commitments. Nevertheless, many of the women felt that there was a discernible positive impact in that those with family commitments were valued.

> I suppose [the culture] has [changed] in the sense that you feel valued by the firm, whereas if you had just gone off with the statutory amount [of leave] and been told that it's either full-time return or not at all, I think you would have felt that the difficulties are not being recognized. I feel that there is a place for you and they recognize the importance of the family to you. (manager, female)

It is of course not only mothers who have family commitments which can impinge on work at times, nor is it only women. At the present time, however, family commitments are largely viewed as a women's issue among those we interviewed, so any broader culture change is limited accordingly.

There are, however, pockets of awareness among the women and their managers in this study about the counterproductive nature of the dominant ways of thinking about time in the workplace, which suggests some questioning of informal values and might indicate a slight shift in the organizational culture.

> There is an element, I think, that if you are here from early in the morning to late at night and seen to be working hard, then this is seen as commitment, but I'm not sure that commitment equals effort in all cases. (manager, male)

> We encourage people to work too long. They say it didn't do Fred any harm . . . The reality is that by encouraging people to work long hours you reward inefficiency. (manager, male)

> If people can't do it in a normal day they are either under-resourced, they are inefficient or they can't delegate properly and manage their time. (manager, male)

> I very often feel that people stay in the office just for the matter of being seen. (manager, female)

Raising awareness of these issues may be an essential aspect of developing cultures which are family-responsive. However, the challenging of this discourse may be sensitive, as one male manager perceptively observed.

> You give the impression that you work a lot more . . . I give the impression that I do a lot more than I do. So, for a woman to stand up and say publicly . . . I work these hours and that's all I intend to do and I want some time at home with my family, that would be pooh-poohed, frowned upon. That's like the Emperor's New Clothes, it's like saying he's not wearing any clothes . . . it's like saying I don't need to work all those hours to be successful.

The Next Stages

The findings of this initial case study were fed back to the partner who was spearheading the changes and the personnel department, and were taken into account in developing further plans and strategies. Subsequently paternity leave has been implemented despite opposition by many partners. The extent to which such opposition will constrain take-up will need to be monitored. The objectives of the family commitments programme have also been extended. The initial objectives of supporting the equal opportunities and Opportunity 2000 goals, enhancing recruitment and retention and meeting business needs remain. In addition other specific objectives are articulated, including that of providing support for line managers in managing staff on reduced hours and enhancing consistency of implementation of the policies throughout the organization. In addition barriers have been made explicit and visible, with the objective of finding strategies for overcoming these, particularly the discourses of time and commitment which stress input rather than output, the perception of the issues as women's issues rather than concerns of all employees and in the business interest, the perception that flexible working will conflict with clients' needs, and the reluctance of some managers to take perceived risks. Clearly some barriers will be more difficult to address than others. Plans are being made for management training and support. The deep-seated attitudes to time and commitment may be more difficult to shift, but raising them as issues for discussion will allow the rationality of these beliefs to be questioned and success stories to be communicated. It may be possible to build on pockets of awareness of the inefficiency of long hours to challenge these ideas. It will also be useful to identify factors which promote this awareness. Further evaluation and reappraisal of objectives will be necessary as part of this ongoing process of organizational change. Although the policies described in this chapter were spearheaded by a partner in the firm, the policy development and communication emanated from the personnel department. There is some debate about whether personnel or human resource departments, which are often regarded as marginal to the real business of an organization, can bring about culture change (Liff, 1989). This may also have to be taken on board at some stage.

Conclusions and Implications

This case study illustrates the role of evaluation in the cycle of organizational change and the value of gathering in-depth qualitative data from multiple perspectives to highlight barriers to fundamental culture change. It demonstrates that change is a complex and uneven process and that although there may be one strong dominant culture, there is also considerable variation in attitudes and values.

One danger of qualitative studies of this nature is that of privileging some accounts over others (Hertz, 1995). Accounts from different actors were not always consistent. This can be illustrated in relation to the perception of managerial support in this study. Often there were conflicting assessments about how supportive managers were. In one case, for example, we received three conflicting accounts from a woman, her line manager and her husband. The woman claimed that her manager had been extremely supportive, which is why she had managed so well. Her manager felt, on reflection, that he could have been much more supportive. The husband maintained that his wife's manager was entirely unsupportive, commenting that he doubted if he even knew she had a family. There are many possible explanations of these conflicting accounts. Low expectations of support by the woman, cognitive dissonance, and socially desirable responses may all play a part. Nevertheless, it is difficult for us to draw conclusions about the 'objective' supportiveness of managers, and each of these different perceived realities will be real in their consequences. The difficulties in achieving an 'accurate' picture of organizational culture change should not be overlooked.

Despite these multiple realities it is nevertheless possible to identify barriers to further changes, consider possible strategies for overcoming them and propose new objectives, including realistically achievable short-term as well as long-term goals. Longitudinal research is necessary to chart the change process. The case study reported here is but one snapshot of the company's family commitments policy and practice at one point in time. It will be important to examine, for example, the extent to which the communication of success can convince the more sceptical line managers to change their behaviours or attitudes or both. It will also be important for future research to identify factors which are associated with 'pockets of awareness' among managers of the limitations of traditional organizational assumptions. Are these in fact different levels of awareness or just differences in willingness to articulate such beliefs? What is the impact of factors such as gender ideology, the managers' own family structures and the demands made on them to participate in family work on the ways in which work, family and time are conceptualized?

The study points to the importance of looking at the family as an essential piece in the work–family jigsaw. Family dynamics can modify the impact of family-friendly policies, and while it may not be within the remit of organizations to change families, neither should this factor be overlooked in attempting to gain a holistic assessment of work–family solutions. This study was limited in this respect by gaining only the accounts of spouses. As all forms of family interactions can impact on individual well-being and spill over to affect work and vice versa, future research should examine accounts of other family members including children, elders and others as appropriate. What does it mean, for example, for parent–child interactions if time is defined as a scarce commodity?

This case study also indicates a need for research to examine the perspectives of other stakeholders. More needs to be known about the perceptions of those employees who do not currently have demanding family commitments, in order to identify the circumstances in which family-oriented initiatives are likely to be perceived as inequitable or as signs of a caring employer, within specific organizational contexts. The attitudes and expectations of clients or customers also need to be better understood. The fear of losing clients is obviously a powerful disincentive to taking perceived risks. It is necessary to establish whether clients really are inconvenienced by flexible working or whether they may in fact be unaffected or even benefit. It is also possible that clients may value being consulted and involved in these changes, which may, in turn, help them to think about their own employees and business needs.

Finally, this study has highlighted the crucial impact of the ways in which time is constructed within one organization on the effectiveness of formal family-oriented policies. While this is likely to be common to other similar workplace contexts, the wider generalizability of the findings is limited by the study's focus on a professional setting and on women in relatively senior positions. An understanding of the ways in which time is experienced by industrial workers, who suffer the greatest time constraints and lack of autonomy (Starkey, 1989) and hence, for women in particular, extreme difficulties in managing work and family (Schein, 1994), as well as those working in other low-paid and often marginalized work, would enhance our understanding of the ways in which discourses of time may or may not block initiatives for work–family reconciliation. The reluctance of many managers in this study to permit different ways of working for employees below management level, however, suggests that a possible danger of an emphasis on the business argument for developing family-friendly policies, may be that fewer employees in these types of jobs, with arguably the greatest needs, will have access to such 'benefits'.

References

Daly, K. (1992) 'The discourse of time as a commodity: How fathers give time to families'. Paper presented at the National Council on Family Relations Conference on Families and Employment, Florida.

Gonyea, J. and Googins, B. (1992) 'Linking the worlds of work and family: Beyond the productivity trap', *Human Resource Management*, 31: 209–26.

Grover, S.L. and Crooker, K.J. (1995) 'Who appreciates family responsive human resource policies? The impact of family friendly policies on the organizational attachment of parents and non parents', *Personnel Psychology*, 48: 271–88.

Haas, L. and Hwang, P. (1995) 'Corporate culture and men's use of family leave benefits in Sweden', *Family Cooordinator*, 44: 28–36.

Hammond, V. and Holton, V. (1991) *A Balanced Workforce, Achieving Cultural Change for Women: A Comparative Study.* Ashridge: Ashridge Management Research Group.

Hertz, R. (1995) 'Separate but simultaneous interviewing of husbands and wives: Making sense of their stories', *Qualitative Enquiry*, 1–4: 429–51.

Liff, S. (1989) 'Assessing equal opportunities policies', *Personnel Review*, 18: 27–34.

Meek, V.L. (1992) 'Organizational culture: Origins and weaknesses', in G. Salaman (ed.), *Human Resource Strategies*. London: Sage.

Potuchek, J. (1992) 'Employed wives orientation to breadwinning: A gender theory analysis', *Journal of Marriage and the Family*, 55: 133–45.

Schein, V. (1994) 'Working in the margins: Voices of mothers in poverty'. Paper presented at the 23rd International Congress of Applied Psychology, Madrid.

Starkey, K. (1989) 'Time and work: A psychological perspective', in P. Blyton, J. Hassard, S. Hill and K. Starkey (eds), *Time, Work and Organization*. London: Routledge.

Thomas, L.T. and Ganster, D.C. (1995) 'Impact of family supportive work variables on work family conflict and stress: A control perspective', *Journal of Applied Psychology*, 4: 806–15.

Woodall, J. (1995) 'Organisational restructuring and the achievement of an equal opportunities culture'. Paper presented at Opportunity 2000 and University of Cambridge Conference on Culture Change in Organisations, June.

10

Constructing Pluralistic Work and Career Arrangements

Phyllis Hutton Raabe

To what extent are reduced work time and other alternative, flexible work arrangements compatible with high productivity? Can people reduce their work time and be as – or more – productive? Can a workforce – including professionals and managers – have diverse and flexible work schedules, be productive, and achieve career progression? Many people answer no to these questions and assume, for example, that reduced work time necessarily means proportionately less productivity and career plateauing. In a context of varying assertions on these issues, does *evidence* exist supporting the efficacy claims of reduced work time and alternative work and career arrangements? A main purpose of this chapter is to present some evidence from Europe and the United States that positive forms of reduced work time and alternative career paths can be constructed that benefit employees, families and work organizations. I begin by briefly considering the limitations of current work and family programmes and then outlining the constraints of traditional 'standard work' assumptions and components of an alternative 'pluralistic' model.

The Stalled Revolution in Family-Friendly Employment: The Structure of Standard Employment and Careers as a Work–Family Problem

The contemporary workforce in advanced industrial societies is changed and more diverse not only in gender, ethnicity and race but also in work–family situations (Galinsky et al., 1991, 1993; Lambert, 1993). In the past the paradigm was of a male-dominated workforce with elastic time and schedule availability to work organizations (itself largely enabled by women's caring for families and homes) (Hochschild, 1989; Seron and Ferris, 1995). By contrast, both women and men now are likely to have commitments to active involvements with family – children, elderly parents, and other relatives – as well as to work and careers. As such, the availability to the work organization has to be balanced with these other commitments arising both simultaneously and sequentially over the life course (Conference Board, 1994; Voydanoff, 1987). To some extent this diversification in the workforce has given rise to changes in the way work is organized, including the development of work–family policies which support the integration of family and work activities (as discussed in earlier chapters in this volume).

There has been substantial growth in work–family policies, and some societies (for example, Sweden) and some employers in particular (for example, 'star' companies in the USA) are renowned for their policies and constitute highly supportive work–family environments (Galinsky et al., 1991; Haas and Hwang, 1995; Kamerman, 1991; NRWF, 1994). While some workers are advantaged in policy supports, many others are greatly disadvantaged in lacking or having inadequate leaves, childcare or eldercare services, or flexible and alternative work and career options (Brannen et al., 1994; Ferber et al., 1991; Lambert, 1993). Furthermore, job insecurity and associated stress have increased with the trend of organizational downsizing, and organizational 'survivors' often experience added stress, work overload and long work hours (Galinsky, et al., 1993; Lewis and Cooper, 1996). Particularly in relation to providing flexible, diverse and equitable work arrangements, even many of the organizations regarded as most 'family-friendly' have stalled in organizational development (Bailyn, 1993; Friedman and Galinsky, 1992; Haas and Hwang, 1995; Olmsted and Smith, 1994). In fact, valid assessments of 'family-friendly' organizations may need to *deduct* points for 'family-harmful' workplace practices such as work overloads, lack of equitable, flexible work arrangements, and not considering redeployment and training of workers before downsizing.

Regardless of whether the impetus for the implementation of 'family-friendly' policies comes from the workplace organization or from national or international policy, the success of such initiatives may rest largely upon the attitudes to and valuing of those policies within the workplace organization (as discussed in other chapters in this book). In developing work–family policies in organizations, managers more readily implement policies that are seen as having organizational benefits such as improving work productivity, job performances, and retention (Galinsky et al., 1991; Lambert, 1993; Raabe, 1990). For organizations, the ultimate focus is on work outcomes: 'family-friendly' policies which support the integration of family and work activities are instrumental in relation to attaining organizational goals. Childcare and eldercare programmes and work–family counselling and educational seminars are supported on the basis that they contribute to workers being at work and working productively (Lambert, 1993). However, greater problems often have arisen in relation to allowing time from work for 'family caring' or other non-work activities through the use of leaves, reduced work time and other alternative work arrangements (Galinsky et al., 1993; Schor, 1991). While family leaves, part-time work, job sharing, compressed work weeks, flexible schedules and work-at-home programmes exist at many work organizations, these are 'non-standard' work arrangements, and their existence and use have generally been associated with work penalties, including lower pay and poorer conditions, and with career limitations. Moreover, reduced work-time options are frequently unavailable in upper-level professional and managerial work, and consequently many forgo professional and managerial career interests and development in order to obtain family time (F. Schwartz, 1989; D. Schwartz, 1994).

When leaves and reduced work time options are available to professionals and managers, their *use* often has meant career subordination: plateauing, derailment, 'career suicide' (F. Schwartz, 1992). Given the prevalent stratification of jobs in work organizations, this policy construction has been highly damaging to women users who have been relegated to subordinated status in what have been labelled 'mommy/family' career tracks, and it has constrained men's use of leaves and part-time work (Pleck, 1993; Hall, 1990). As one man put it:

> I am committed to my profession, and I want to be taken seriously, but I don't want to be working all hours. I want some time with my children. I wish it were possible to work part-time without losing my foot on the ladder. (Cooper and Lewis, 1994: 16)

Even in a highly supportive work–family environment such as Sweden, workplace cultures remain highly gendered (Haas and Hwang, 1995). Women's use of leave and part-time work have been associated with career penalties. These career penalties create problems for women and also are a major disincentive to men's greater use of family leave and part-time work, and thus, a barrier to greater family involvement by men and to improved gender symmetry (Haas and Hwang, 1995).

At the root of these difficulties there is often a fundamental organizational reluctance to alter conventional work and career structures as the norm, particularly for professionals and managers. This reluctance frequently persists even where firms are 'family-friendly' in terms of implementing many formal policies to support the integration of family and work activities. The implicit if not explicit message has been that it is permissible to combine family and employment – but only in certain kinds of work and in conventional work and career configurations. In this climate an insistence on altering standard working ways and careers often is only possible at the expense of career achievement. As such, a major component of further progress in reconciling conflicts between family, work and career requires a shift away from the institutionalization and privileging of 'standard' work and career arrangements towards a pluralism of work options and career paths (Morgan, 1986; Sirianni, 1991; Sussman, 1990). In this 'pluralism' there is *equivalence* of a variety of arrangements, and as such, it can encompass both those who want to work in standard work and career formulations and those who prefer alternative constructions at a point in time or over time (such as leave components and work in reduced time arrangements in viable careers).

The pluralism model has clear advantages for those employees struggling to integrate family, work and careers. The remainder of this chapter considers some assumptions underpinning the standard and pluralism models of working time, and presents some evidence that pluralistic practices can benefit *both* workers and employers.

Conflicting Standard and Pluralistic Paradigms of Work and Careers

Tenets of Current Standard Work and Careers

Given increased endorsements of reduced work time and other alternative work and career arrangements, a question arises as to why there have been extensive organizational lags in cultural and structural changes. Organizations have tended to have negative evaluations of reduced work time and other alternative arrangements and their practitioners – particularly in terms of professional and managerial work. These negative evaluations seem to rest on beliefs that current 'standard' formulations of work and careers are not only 'normal' but necessary for achieving the most effective and productive work outcomes. These fundamental conclusions about traditional, 'standard' work contain a variety of components (Bailyn, 1993; Friedman and Galinsky, 1992; Lewis and Cooper, 1996; Raabe, 1991, 1993). In particular the following assumptions are prevalent:

1. Work, particularly professional and managerial work, needs to be in standard formulations that involve long hours of work. This is because long hours of work are necessary for maximum effectiveness and productivity: quantity of work time is directly correlated with quantity and quality of work output. The longer one works, the better the work accomplishment.
2. Long hours of work in continuous standard careers are necessary indicators of high work and career commitments (see Lewis and Taylor, Chapter 9).
3. People need to be available at workplaces and working in standard, predictable ways to achieve productive work.
4. Managers need to work long hours in order to manage effectively. This is because effective managers are always available for consultation, problem solving, resource facilitation, coordination and control.
5. Current standard work and career structures are necessary for optimal work productivity and profitability.

Tenets of Pluralistic Work and Careers

Standard work and career assumptions have been criticized as mistaken and inadequate – particularly in relation to the development of less routinized post-industrial work and to changes in the contemporary workforce (Appelbaum and Batt, 1994; Bailyn, 1993; Hage and Powers, 1992; Parker and Hall, 1993; Parks, 1995; Rodgers, 1992; Sirianni, 1991).

By contrast, a pluralistic view of work and careers counters standard assumptions with revised conclusions about work and career arrangements:

1. Today's standard work and career arrangements are social, historical constructions, and as such can be reconstructed in alternative forms.
2. Work and career structures that may have been appropriate and most effective in the past may not be necessary or optimal under present conditions – particularly in less routinized post-industrial work.

3 Presence at work and time involved in work are inadequate and unnecessary indicators of work interest, motivation and accomplishment.
4 Reduced work time is compatible with high productivity. In many work situations, the *quality* and management of time and work are more important to task accomplishment than quantity of time.
5 Rather than being detractions, non-work activities (e.g. family, recreation, leisure) can contribute to work productivity.
6 In comparison with current standard definitions, work can be redesigned in reduced forms and integrated into functional equivalents – or improvements – of standard configurations.
7 Variety and flexibility in work arrangements are manageable and compatible with work productivity.
8 The above conclusions are applicable to professional and managerial as well as other forms of work.

Evaluation: Evidence about the Viability of Reduced Work Time and Pluralistic Work and Careers

Today's standard work hours, and definitions of work commitment, jobs and careers, are social creations and historical products (Hinrichs et al., 1991). Many workers are restive with the continuation of rigid, uniform, work and career practices that may have fitted routinized, industrial work in the past but which seem outmoded and counterproductive today – especially in relation to the increased complexity, creativity and flexibility involved in post-industrial work (Bailyn, 1993; Rodgers, 1992). However, while standard forms of work and careers *can* be reconstructed into new arrangements, many managers continue to question the comparable efficacy of such work and career innovations (Loveman, 1990; Haas and Hwang, 1995; McColl, 1988; Parker and Hall, 1993). As such, it is important to examine situations where workforces – including professionals and managers – work in reduced work-time schedules and other diverse arrangements and the extent to which they can be productive and achieve career progression. Below I discuss two examples of such situations, the first from the former West Germany, and the second from experiences of part-time managers and professionals in the US and Europe. This section draws on interviews carried out with German and US managers.[1]

Evidence from Germany

The experience of post-war West Germany provides some important evidence in support of the pluralism model. For example, in the course of the Federal Republic of Germany's 'economic miracle', significant productivity improvements were associated with reductions in working time (Hinrichs, 1991; Peters, 1990; Wever and Allen, 1992). By the late 1980s, reductions in the standard work week and the development of vacation, holiday and leave times meant that the average full-time German worked eight weeks less a year than the comparable American (Schor, 1991). While annual work time decreased, productivity was maintained or increased (Hinrichs, 1991; Schor, 1991; Wever and Allen, 1992). It also is important to note that this reduced work time occurred within the definition of full-time work, and, unlike the typical construction of part-time work, compensation was not reduced but maintained or increased. While technology and a highly trained workforce were important contributors to productivity gains, certain management and workforce orientations and practices also were significant. These German experiences provide some supportive evidence for propositions of the pluralistic paradigm about the efficacy of reduced work time and pluralistic work and career arrangements. Specifically, evidence from German experiences supports the following conclusions:

1 Reduced work time is compatible with maintained or increased productivity; the *quality* of the management of time and tasks is more important to task accomplishment than the quantity of time.

Originally pushed by German labour unions for work sharing purposes, decreased average worker work time and resulting diverse work schedules have led to increased organizational productivity. According to one corporate executive:

> Work is now done more quickly and intensely – in a more concentrated way. In the past, there was more unproductive work time. If workplaces avoid unproductive work time, there are advantages for both sides. (cited in Raabe, 1993)

2 Non-work activities can contribute to work productivity.

Managers interviewed in German companies reported that family involvements and vacations are paradigmatically considered 'good'; they are seen not as distractions from work accomplishment but as important to a balanced life and as a resource for improved work productivity. German executives generally take at least three weeks of annual vacation, which contrasts with the US experience where managers frequently are reluctant to take a week of vacation (German and United States interviews, 1991–2).

3 Diversity and variability in work arrangements are compatible with work productivity, and workforce 'flux' (diverse and variable work arrangements) can be viably managed.

Because of decreased weekly and annual work times, German work organizations have extensive experience with a variety of shifts and other work-time schedules (for example, Siemens offered 18 formal options in 1990). Workforce flux is also increased because people are on vacations at different times and are departing to or returning from leaves. Managers reported that as experience with workforce flux has grown, it has come to be seen as a 'fact of life' that can be managed through co-worker cooperation and the reallocation of tasks. As one manager put it,

> the focus should be on the coverage of work; then, how it is 'peopled' can be flexible. Organizations are learning to deal with uncertainties [leave takers, vacations] and integrating part-time pieces. (German interviews, 1991)

German managers also tend to have an annual view of productivity which recognizes that while there are different rhythms of short-term productivity, high productivity can be achieved over time.

Evidence about Reduced Work Time in Managerial and Professional Work: Existence, Productivity and Career Progression

In Europe and the United States, increased numbers of professionals are taking leaves, working part-time, and job sharing. This is the case for accountants, attorneys, physicians and others (Association of Part-time Professionals, 1995; NRWF, 1991b, 1992a, 1992b; New Ways to Work, 1990, 1993a); Loveman, 1990; Hogg and Harker, 1992).

Management work has seemed especially resistant to reduced work-time configurations owing to traditional expectations about the necessity of long hours and the pervasive supervision involved in management work (Bailyn, 1993; Rodgers, 1992; Schwartz, 1989). Nevertheless, part-time managers exist at companies and in government. For example, in the United States, 120 managers had been on SelectTime schedules at NationsBank in 1992, there were several part-time managers at Hewlett-Packard, and part-time managers at Wells Fargo included the Chairman of the Board and a division Senior Vice-President (NRWF 1991a; Galinsky et al., 1991; United States interviews, 1992). A 1991 survey of large companies found that 53 per cent had part-time managers (Parker and Hall, 1993). In New York State's 'Voluntary Reduction in Work Schedule' programme, thousands of professionals and managers have reduced their work schedules by five to 30 per cent since 1984 (Ackley, 1993; Dudak, 1993). In the United States federal government, there were 342 part-time managers in 1993 and 293 in 1994 (US Office of Personnel Management). In Germany, several part-time managers were reported at Bayer, Hoechst, and Deutsche Bank in 1991 (German interviews, 1991).

While part-time managers clearly exist, subsequent issues concern their productivity and career promotions. In assessing the productivity and job performance among part-time professionals and managers, it is first helpful to expose some of the flawed assumptions about the continuous availability of full-time managers and professionals to work associates and clients. As one German manager put it:

> Currently when managers are gone – travelling and at meetings – we already have 'part-time' managers – but it's not called this! (German interviews, 1991)

Another German manager observed that:

> Part-time management works. It's a question of organizing and of colleagues. Every manager has to leave the office – for vacation, sickness, travel – and relies on and shares responsibilities with others. 'Part-time management' is simply an extension and systemization of this idea. (German interviews, 1991)

Similarly, attorneys in the United States arguing for part-time positions pointed to the frequent scheduling conflicts between clients and inaccessibility to associates and clients that occur and are managed in full-time practice (Deutsch, 1991).

Much more research is needed on conditions associated with productive white collar work generally and, specifically, in relation to the integration and management of leaves, reduced time schedules, and other alternative work arrangements (Galinsky et al., 1991; Gonyea and Googins, 1992; Schwartz, 1994). However, there is existing evidence which indicates high work efficiency and effectiveness by people returning from leaves and working in equitable reduced-work time and other alternative work arrangements (Olmsted and Smith, 1994; Schwartz, 1994; Catalyst, 1993; Galinsky et al., 1991; Friedman et al., 1992; Lambert et al., 1993; NRWF, 1991c). Workers in such arrangements typically report greater focus, concentration, and motivation – and high degrees of productivity. Professionals, managers and other workers often assert that they accomplish as much work on a reduced work time or other alternative work arrangement as they did in standard work (see also Lewis and Taylor, Chapter 9). In one recent example from a 1994 survey, 85 per cent of part-time managers in the US federal government said they accomplish as much work as a full-time manager (Raabe, 1995).

Assuming that part-time professionals and managers are able to work efficiently and effectively, a further issue arises as to whether they also can have viable career development and the extent to which there are easy transitions back to full-time work and/or equitable alternative part-time career paths. Organizations predominantly have treated part-time workers as contingent and secondary workers in a two-tier labour force, and this has meant disproportionately lower wages and benefits and constrained work and career opportunities (Olmsted and Smith, 1994; Barker, 1993; Tilly, 1992). However, there are some indicators of alternative practices in which the part-time work of professionals and managers is compatible with career development. In the United States, some law and accounting firms provide more flexible career paths including options to be a part-time *partner* (New Ways to Work, 1990; Loveman, 1990; NRWF, 1991b). A longitudinal study of part-time professionals found that 53 per cent received a promotion between 1989 and 1992 (Catalyst, 1993). A survey of female certified public accountants found that, in contrast with the negative perceptions of non-users, 71 per cent of the users of flexible work arrangements (including part-time work) reported minimal damage to promotions (Hooks, 1989). A 1994 survey of part-time managers in the United States federal government found that 29 per cent had received a promotion as a part-time manager (Raabe, 1995).

Part-time college and university faculty typically have been contingent and marginalized workers (American Association of University Professors, 1981; Lomperis, 1990). However, a 1991 survey of United States academic institutions found some evidence of pluralistic career paths: 29 per cent of the colleges and universities permitted the expansion of time for achieving tenure to accommodate maternity or parental responsibilities, 36 per cent provided accommodative scheduling (reduced workloads) to meet family needs, and 11 per cent had a policy of tenure for part-time faculty (Raabe, in press).

In voluntary reduced work time programmes, such as that of New York State, professional and managerial employees temporarily reduce their work time while remaining in the same career path (Olmsted and Smith, 1994). In Sweden, leaves and part-time work are components of women's career continuity and progression, and they do not constrain later movement into full-time jobs (Sundstrom, 1991), although it should be noted that there is a high level of gender segregation in the Swedish labour force, in comparison with the UK and the US (Sandqvist, 1992). In Britain, career breaks and associated part-time work have the potential to be components of career continuity and development (see Lewis, Watts and Camp, Chapter 8; New Ways to Work, 1992, 1993a, 1993b), although the schemes have not yet been in place long enough for long-term evaluations to be carried out and the extent to which the take-up of this option is limited by career concerns is not known. In both Scandinavia and the UK, annual hours programmes can constitute pluralistic work time and career arrangements (Olmsted and Smith, 1994).

Thus there is considerable evidence that reduced hours of work do exist at management and professional levels and that in some cases this is associated with career development. Nevertheless, further research is now needed to learn more about the experiences of part-time managers and professionals and the conditions of success as well as the barriers to viable career progression.

Conclusion: Reduced Work Time and Pluralistic Work and Careers Can Benefit Workers, Families and Work

Today's changed workforce includes women and men interested – in varying degrees and ways – in combining family involvements with work and career commitments. A variety of societal and workplace policies can support the integration of these family and work activities and in combination can constitute varying levels of family-friendly employment. However, the structure of what has been constructed as standard work involves practices such as long hours and rigid, uniform work schedules that can obstruct time for family caring, disempower family members and create the potential for stress. Further, when organizations *are* willing to moderate hours and rigid schedules, these facilities often can only be used at the risk of accepting career constraints. In this context, the organizational development challenge is to become family- and career-friendly by constructing equitable pluralistic work and career arrangements that provide time for family caring and which are institutionalized equivalents to standard work and career forms.

Current standard work and career patterns can be seen as a form of institutional discrimination that privileges some workers (those without active family involvement) and disadvantages others who want and need to work in alternative ways. Standard policies and practices 'discriminate against a growing number of people . . . [and] enforce a particular view of how work should be done, at the exclusion of other equally legitimate views' (Sussman, 1990: 25). Further, these policies and practices are 'not neutral . . . not fair . . . not harmless . . . and not functional any more' (1990: 26).

However, change in the nature of work need not be seen as benefiting the employee only at the expense of the employing organization. Long work hours and rigid work and career requirements can undermine motivation, creativity and work quality, and therefore can be dysfunctional and counterproductive (Bailyn, 1993; Dobrzynski, 1995). Conversely, equitable pluralistic work and career arrangements can be seen as more congruent with achieving quality work outcomes (Bridges, 1994). A major point here is that although mechanistic, standard modes 'can work', pluralistic forms are likely to be more appropriate and yield better outcomes, particularly with the juncture of changes in work (the increased importance of motivation, innovation and quality productivity) and the changed workforce (with broadened active family involvements) in advanced industrial societies.

However, many organizational leaders remain reluctant and uncertain about changing to pluralistic work patterns and careers (NRWF, 1993). Others feel that they lack knowledge about how to change, being 'at a loss regarding how to put these strategies into place' (Haas and Hwang, 1995: 35). In this context, greater knowledge about positive experiences and the conditions of integrating leaves, reduced work-time practices and other work variations in pluralistic modes that are beneficial to workers and work organizations is important for the advancement of such arrangements. Much 'social learning' in this respect already has occurred in Europe and the United States as organizations have implemented family leaves, reduced work time and other work alternatives (e.g. New Ways to Work, 1992; 1993a; 1993b; Olmsted and Smith, 1994). In so far as mutual benefit, pluralistic 'successes' exist and are known, they are important in demonstrating that such nonstandard work and career arrangements are both achievable and efficacious. Some evidence about the explicit conditions and characteristics of practices conducive to successful results has been presented elsewhere (e.g. Bailyn et al., 1994; New Ways to Work, 1992, 1993a, 1993b; Olmsted and Smith, 1994) and in this chapter's research findings on the reduced work-time experiences of West Germany and of many part-time professionals and managers. Specifically, in relation to conducive conditions, reduced work time seems to be associated with maintained or increased productivity when: (1) reduced work time is accompanied by maintained (or understood as equitable) compensation and benefits; (2) reduced work-time practices are defined as legitimate and 'normal' (not defined as atypical but incorporated as a form of standard work and careers); (3) reduced work-time practices are seen in the organization as an element of 'mutual benefits' for all workers and for the work organization; and (4) time and activities outside of employment (e.g. family involvement, vacations) are seen not as detractions but as likely resources for improved work.

More research and findings about specific conducive organizational conditions and favourable environmental factors such as public policies (labour laws, taxes, social programmes) are likely to be important for the advance of pluralistic practices. For example, the success of the pluralistic model may be affected by the level of state support, such as through legislation on equal employment protection for non-standard work to discourage employers from treating non-standard workers as peripheral to the organization. It will also be important for future research to elucidate the *process* of achieving change in organizational norms and behaviours, and to identify the efficacy and/or limitations of the pluralistic model for a wider range of occupations and sectors. Most research has been with relatively large corporations and more needs to be known about small and medium enterprises. While more research about pluralistic practices and conditions is important, some existing examples of such evidence discussed in this chapter support these conclusions: (1) reduced work time can be compatible with maintained or increased productivity of individuals or organizations; (2) professional and managerial work exists in part-time, efficacious forms and can be associated with career advancement; and (3) diversity and variability in work arrangements can be viably integrated and managed.

Work organizations are currently experiencing a contest between hierarchical organizational practices that privilege some and disadvantage others, and alternative, more pluralistic, equitable modes (Appelbaum and Batt, 1994; Hinrichs, 1991; Olmsted and Smith, 1994; Parks, 1995; Shostak, 1994). Increased evidence is being marshalled that the latter are more congruent with post-industrial work and attain superior results – that 'worker friendly organizations outperform others' (Olmsted and Smith, 1994). Such evidence is likely to be significant for further organizational changes to a win–win process in which equitable, pluralistic practices are 'worker-, family- and career-friendly' – and also benefit organizations.

Notes

1 In addition to other research, a major source of research findings discussed in this section is my study of 'Work Innovations and Outcomes' in Germany and the United States in 1991 and 1992. Interviews about reduced hours, other alternative work arrangements and leaves, and the effects of such options on work productivity and career achievement – particularly in relation to professionals and managers – were conducted with representatives of the following companies: Bayer, Hoechst, BASF, Siemens, Deutsche Bank, and Commerzbank (Germany), and Hewlett-Packard, Hoechst-Celanese, Levi Strauss, Miles, Inc., NationsBank, Siemens US, and Wells Fargo (United States). Additional interviews in Germany were held with professional staff of the DGB (German Trade Union Federation), the Federal Ministry of Labour and Social Affairs, and the Confederation of German Employers' Associations. Partial findings from this study have been presented in papers at professional meetings.

References

Ackley, M.L. (1993) Phone interview. State of New York, Governor's Office of Employee Relations.

American Association of University Professors (1981) 'The status of part-time faculty', *Academe*, February–March: 29–39.

Appelbaum, E. and Batt, R. (1994) *The New American Workplace: Transforming Work Systems in the United States*. Ithaca, NY: ILR Press, Cornell University.
Association of Part-time Professionals (1995) '4.7 Million Professionals Work Part-Time, BLS Reports', *Working Options*, 15(5): 1.
Bailyn, L. (1993) *Breaking the Mold*. New York: Free Press.
Bailyn, L., Kolb, D., Eaton, S., Fletcher, J., Harvey, M., Johnson, R. and Perlow, L. (1994) *Executive Summary: Work–Family Partnership – A Catalyst For Change*. Ford Foundation/ Xerox Project.
Barker, K. (1993) 'Changing assumptions and contingent solutions: The costs and benefits of women working full- and part-time', *Sex Roles*, 28(January): 47–1.
Brannen, J., Meszaros, G., Moss, P. and Poland, G. (1994) *Employment and Family Life: A Review of Research in the UK (1980–1994)*. London: Employment Department.
Bridges, W. (1994) 'The end of the job', *Fortune*, 19 September: 19, 62–74.
Catalyst (1993) *Flexible Work Arrangements II: Succeeding with Part-Time Options*. New York: Catalyst.
Conference Board (1994) *Work–Family Roundtable: Lifecycle Support*. New York: Conference Board.
Cooper, C.L. and Lewis, S. (1994) *Managing the New Work Force*. San Diego: Pfeiffer.
Deutsch, C.H. (1991) 'The fast track's diminished lure', *New York Times*, 6 October: F25.
Dobrzynski, J.H. (1995) 'Should I have left an hour earlier? On mixing work and life: These workaholics tell all', *New York Times*, 18 June: 3,1.
Dudak, J.J. (1993) *Voluntary Reduction in Work Schedule Program*. State of New York, Governor's Office of Employee Relations.
Ferber, M.A. and O'Farrell, B. (with Allen, L.R.) (1991) *Work and Family: Policies for a Changing Work Force*. Washington, DC: National Academy Press.
Friedman, D. E. and Galinsky, E. (1992) 'Work and family issues: A legitimate business concern', in S. Zedeck (ed.), *Work, Families and Organizations*. San Francisco: Jossey-Bass.
Friedman, D.E., Galinsky, E. and Plowden, V. (eds) (1992) *Parental Leave and Productivity*. New York: Families and Work Institute.
Galinsky, E., Bond, J.T. and Friedman, D.E. (1993) *The Changing Workforce*. New York: Families and Work Institute.
Galinsky, E., Friedman, D.E. and Hernandez, C.A. (1991) *The Corporate Reference Guide to Work–Family Programs*. New York: Families and Work Institute.
Gonyea, J. and Googins, B. (1992) 'Linking the worlds of work and family: Beyond the productivity trap', *Human Resource Management*, 31: 209–26.
Haas, L. and Hwang, P. (1995) 'Company culture and men's usage of family leave benefits in Sweden', *Family Relations*, 44(1): 28–36.
Hage, J. and Powers, C.H. (1992) *Post-Industrial Lives*. Newbury Park, CA: Sage.
Hall, D.T. (1990) 'Promoting work family balance: An organization-change approach', *Organizational Dynamics*, 18: 5–18.
Hinrichs, K. (1991) 'Working-time development in West Germany: Departure to a new stage', in K. Hinrichs, W. Roche and C. Sirianni (eds), *Working Time in Transition*. Philadelphia: Temple University Press.
Hinrichs, K., Roche, W. and Sirianni, C. (eds) (1991) *Working Time in Transition*. Philadelphia: Temple University Press.
Hochschild, A. (1989) *The Second Shift*. New York: Avon.
Hogg, C. and Harker, L. (1992) *The Family-Friendly Employer: Examples from Europe*. London: Daycare Trust.
Hooks, K.L. (1989) *Alternative Work Schedules and the Woman CPA: A Report on Use, Perception, and Career Impact*. Chicago: American Woman's Society of Certified Public Accountants.
Kamerman, S. (1991) 'Child care policies and programs: An international overview', *Journal of Social Issues*, 47(2): 179–96.
Lambert, S.J. (1993) 'Workplace policies as social policy', *Social Service Review*, June: 237–60.
Lambert, S.J., Hopkins, K., Easton, G., Walker, J., McWilliams H. and Chung, M.S. (1993)

Added Benefits: The Link between Family Responsive Policies and Job Performance. University of Chicago Study of Fel-Pro, Inc.
Lewis, S. and Cooper, C.L. (1996) 'Balancing the work home interface: A European perspective', in *Human Resource Management Review*, 5(4): 289–305.
Lomperis, A.M.T. (1990) 'Are women changing the nature of the academic profession?', *Journal of Higher Education*, 61(6): 643–77.
Loveman, G.W. (1990) 'The case of the part-time partner', *Harvard Business Review*, September–October: 12–29.
McColl, H. (1988) 'What a caring company can do', *Across the Board*, 25(7,8): 38–42.
Morgan, G. (1986) *Images of Organization.* Newbury Park, CA: Sage.
New Ways to Work (1990) 'Update: Alternative work schedules in law firms', *Work Times,* 9(1): 1, 4–5.
New Ways to Work (1992) *Taking a Break: Introducing Employment Breaks*. London: New Ways to Work.
New Ways to Work (1993a) *Change at the Top: Working Flexibly at Senior and Managerial Levels in Organizations*. London: New Ways to Work.
New Ways to Work (1993b) *Changing Times: A Guide to Flexible Work Patterns for Human Resource Managers*. London: New Ways to Work.
NRWF (1991a) 'Bank adds manager training to "SelectTime" program', *National Report on Work and Family*, 4(4): 2–3.
NRWF (1991b) 'Boston firms expand benefits intended for professional employees', *National Report on Work and Family*, 4(18): 3–4.
NRWF (1991c) 'Flexible work arrangements found successful for managers', *National Report on Work and Family*, 4(3): 4–5.
NRWF (1992a) 'Firms battle corporate culture to achieve work/family balance', *National Report on Work and Family*, 5(6): 3–4.
NRWF (1992b) 'Influx of women into medicine may bring flexibility to field', *National Report on Work and Family*, 5(9): 1, 7.
NRWF (1993) 'CEOs said to stand in way of work/family programs', *National Report on Work and Family*, 6(10): 2.
NRWF (1994) '*Working Mother* magazine names top 100 companies for 1994', *National Report on Work and Family*, 7(18): 3–4.
Olmsted, B. and Smith, S. (1994) *Creating a Flexible Workplace*, 2nd edn. New York: ANACOM.
Parker, V. and Hall, D. (1993) 'Workplace flexibility: Faddish or fundamental?', in P. Mirvis (ed.), *Building the Competitive Workforce.* New York: Wiley.
Parks, S. (1995) 'Improving workplace performance: Historical and theoretical contexts', *Monthly Labor Review*, May: 18–28.
Peters, T. (1990) 'The German economic miracle nobody knows', *Across the Board,* April: 17–23.
Pleck, J. (1993) 'Are "family-supportive" employer policies relevant to men?', in J. Hood (ed.), *Men, Work, and Family.* Newbury Park, CA: Sage.
Raabe, P.H. (1990) 'The organizational effects of workplace family policies: Past weaknesses and recent progress toward improved research', *Journal of Family Issues*, II(4): 477–91.
Raabe, P.H (1991) 'A legacy of the mommy track debate: Illuminating possible "standard work" myths'. Paper presented to the American Sociological Association Meeting, Cincinnati.
Raabe, P.H. (1993) 'The work/family revolution, challenges to "standard work" – and German insights about work-time innovations and productivity'. Paper presented to the American Sociological Association Meeting, Miami.
Raabe, P.H. (1995) 'Part-time managers: A way to be "career and family friendly"?' Paper presented to the Eastern Sociological Association Meeting, Philadelphia.
Raabe, P.H. (in press) 'Work/family policies for faculty: How "career- and family-friendly" is academe?', in J. Loeb and M.A. Ferber (eds), *Academic Couples.* University of Illinois Press.
Rodgers, C.S. (1992) 'The flexible workplace: What have we learned?', *Human Resource Management*, 31(3): 183–299.
Sandqvist, K. (1992) 'Sweden's sex-role scheme and commitment to gender equality', in S. Lewis, D. Izraeli and H. Hootsmans (eds), *Dual-Earner Families.* London: Sage.

Schor, J. (1991) *The Overworked American*. New York: Basic Books.

Schwartz, D. B. (1994) *An Examination of the Impact of Family-Friendly Policies on the Glass Ceiling*. New York: Families and Work Institute.

Schwartz, F. (1989) 'Management women and the new facts of life', *Harvard Business Review*, 67: 65–76.

Schwartz, F. (1992) *Breaking with Tradition: Women and Work, the New Facts of Life.* New York: Warner.

Seron, C. and Ferris, K. (1995) 'Negotiating professionalism: The gendered social capital of flexible time', *Work and Occupations*, 22(1): 22–47.

Shostak, A. B. (1994) 'Management as usual . . . not!', *Journal of Management Inquiry*, 3(1): 54–7.

Sirianni, C. (1991) 'The self-management of time in postindustrial society', in K. Hinrichs, W. Roche and C. Sirianni (eds), *Working Time in Transition*. Philadelphia: Temple University Press.

Sundstrom, M. (1991) 'Part-time work in Sweden: Trends and equality effects', *Journal of Economic Issues*, XXV(1): 167–78.

Sussman, H. (1990) 'Are we talking revolution?', *Across the Board*, July–August, 24–6.

Tilly, C. (1992) 'Dualism in part-time employment', *Industrial Relations*, 31: 330–47.

Voydanoff, P. (1987) *Work and Family Life*. Newbury Park, CA: Sage.

Wever, K.S. and Allen, C.S. (1992) 'Is Germany a model for managers?', *Harvard Business Review*, September–October: 36–43.

11

Work–Family Issues as a Catalyst for Organizational Change

Joyce K. Fletcher and Rhona Rapoport

This chapter presents findings and perspectives from an action research project in three US corporations, each with a record of being 'family-friendly'. We describe the project with particular reference to one of the corporations – the Xerox Corporation, a large international high-technology firm headquartered in the US. In this chapter we will present the context and background of the overall project, describe the organizational change effort at this one corporation, present an argument based on our findings (namely, that work-family issues can provide a catalyst for fundamental organizational change) and suggest general principles for achieving this type of change.

Project Background

The Xerox study is one of three collaborative action research projects funded by the Ford Foundation to examine the impact of work and family policies as they are being implemented in leading-edge US corporations today.[1] The project was born of a concern that the current approach to creating 'family-friendly' organizations, which focuses on providing an array of work–family benefits, not only is inadequate to deal with today's complex work–family issues but might actually be undermining rather than advancing the goal of gender equity.[2] The purpose of the project was to move beyond the current concept of family-friendly organizations by exploring the connections between work structure, gender equity and work–family integration. The intent was both to increase our understanding of how these issues are related and to engage with corporations in action projects to address cultural and structural barriers to work–family integration and gender equity. The plan was to leave in place an ongoing change process that would help organizations link more effectively to their changing social environments.

Limitations of Family-Friendly Work–Family Policies and Programs

There is no doubt that the recent development of work–family benefits is an improvement over the long-standing tradition, rooted in the work of organizational theorists such as Talcott Parsons and Max Weber, of excluding families from organizational concern because they were assumed to be antithetical to the trend towards rationalization – the heart of capitalist market-oriented systems. The recent evolution of family-friendly policies such as maternity leave, parental leave, flexitime, on-site childcare facilities, and childcare or eldercare referral services, is a step forward in that it combines humanistic considerations with rational self-interest by providing workers with what they need to keep working productively and gives the organization value for the investment in their training by retaining them. Although these benefits are helpful and even crucially important to many employees, we argue that their limited scope does little to address the complexity of work–family issues facing society today. These issues include the crisis in childcare, the undermining and devaluation of family life, the overemphasis on work in the public arena as the most important measure of self-worth, and the persistence of stereotyped gender roles that constrain both women and men in integrating their work and personal lives.

There are a number of reasons why these complex issues cannot be addressed through the sole use of a 'policies and benefits' approach to work-family integration. First, a benefits approach tends to focus on *symptoms* rather than root causes. So, for example, benefits like providing sick or weekend childcare allow parents to meet the obligations of work as currently defined but do nothing to question these obligations or the cultural assumptions on which they rest. Indeed, providing this service as a benefit reinforces the image of an ideal worker as someone who is 'work primary' and can make outside responsibilities disappear at a moment's notice. Furthermore, it keeps the issues at the individual level and does nothing to question fundamental, systemic work practices that require such inflexible, all-encompassing demands. In the same vein, it can be argued that setting up 'mommy track' benefits, such as career breaks aimed at mothers, reinforces the notion that those who want to integrate work and family life are an aberrant subset of workers who are less promotable than those who choose to focus primarily on work.

Another limitation of a benefits approach to creating family-friendly organizations is that it inadvertently undermines organizational efforts to achieve gender equity in the workplace. Since providing work–family benefits was done largely in response to women's increased participation in the labor force, these issues have come to be seen as 'women's issues' (Friedman and Galinsky, 1992). As a result, those men who would like to participate more fully in family and community responsibilities often feel constrained from using these workplace benefits. This leads to a situation in which men are disadvantaged in their desire to contribute and achieve in the family and the community. And women, because they still assume a disproportionate share of family and community responsibilities and so must use some of these benefits, suffer negative career consequences; they are disadvantaged in their ability to contribute and achieve in the workplace.

The third limitation of a benefits approach to work–family integration is that it does nothing to link the structure of work to larger societal issues such as the crisis in care (Hamburg, 1992; Hochschild, forthcoming; Minow, 1995); the decrease in social capital and civic engagement (Putnam, 1995); the gender inequitable division of labor in the home (Hartmann, 1995; Hochschild, 1990); and the rising number of hours and focus on time spent at work (Bailyn, 1993; Kanter, 1995; Schor, 1991). On the contrary, a benefits approach to the integration of work and family implictly reinforces the image of organizations as closed systems, affected by the larger social context when it comes to issues such as global competitiveness or government trade policies but closed to an examination of how organizational structures and practices impact the social fabric, including the well-being of community, educational institutions and family life itself (Friedlander, 1994). Thus, to the degree that work–family integration is conceptualized as an issue of individual accommodation, organizations remain unaware of their influence on factors that seriously impact the ability of society to produce, maintain and adequately prepare the next generation of organizational citizens. This closed system approach leads to a situation in which organizations can benefit from the fruits of the unpaid labor force without sharing proportionally in the costs (Schor, 1995), or as Shirley Burggraf (1995) so aptly described it, a situation in which organizations and economists are free to act as if they 'still don't know where babies come from'.

Yet another limitation of this approach is that benefits, no matter what their supposed connection to productivity and employee satisfaction, remain marginal to core business issues and strategic decisions. As the word 'benefits' implies, these policies typically are seen as 'extras' given to employees to increase satisfaction or retention but only indirectly related to broader business goals. Keeping these issues 'below the line' (Bailyn, 1995) not only casts them as marginal to business goals, but also implies that they are separate and adversarial and that solutions to problems that arise from this separation reside in individual accommodations related to family situation rather than systemic issues related to work (Fletcher, 1995). Thus, strategic decision making, reengineering initiatives and work process innovations proceed independent from the life situation of the organization's workforce; the connection – and possibly synergy – between the two is typically ignored (Fletcher and Bailyn, 1996).

The action research project overviewed in this chapter sought to go beyond these limitations inherent in the traditional, individually focused benefits and policies approach of many family-friendly organizations. More specifically it sought to explore these issues in their broader context by reframing issues of work–family integration not as individual issues related to a particular *family situation* but as systemic issues related to *organizational norms, work practices and structure.* One of the central goals of the project was to articulate a new vision of the ideal worker, one which reflects the reality that each worker lives in an interdependent world of paid employment and private interests and responsibilities, and to *use* this vision of the ideal worker not as a problem to be solved, but as an opportunity to challenge and innovate work practices in ways that would enhance both productivity and gender equity in organizations. The business imperative to engage with this project was envisioned not as an issue of employee benefits and satisfaction, but as a way of discovering new ways of doing business that would capture the synergy between the two spheres of life and be beneficial to both work and family concerns.

The Xerox Corporation, which already had in place a number of traditional family-friendly benefits, agreed to look at work–family integration in relation to these broader societal issues. The 'Work–Family Partnership: A Catalyst for Change' project started with a collaborative definition of the issues, framed by the researchers and a Collaborative Action Research Team (CART) at Xerox. Instead of seeing what policies might be needed to deal with work–family issues, the joint decision was to treat those issues as an opportunity to innovate work practices. Our goal was to use a work–family lens to identify general work and cultural assumptions that made it difficult for *all* employees – not just those with dependent children and eldercare responsibilities – to integrate their work and personal lives. Once these cultural barriers to integration were identified we intended to work collaboratively with people on-site to design experiments and changes in work practices that would address these barriers. Our belief was that this could be accomplished with no loss – and perhaps some gain – to business productivity. As we will describe, we actually underestimated the benefits of this approach to productivity and effectiveness. At each of our sites we found that using a work–family lens as a catalyst for change resulted in work practice innovations that not only enhanced work and family integration but yielded significant bottom line business results. Our findings indicate that this approach – in which business concerns are central and are tied inextricably to the work–family issues that provide the impetus for change – is a strategic opportunity to achieve a more productive, equitable, flexible workplace. Moreover, we have learned a great deal more about the approach that is necessary to achieve this positive, win–win result. The rest of the chapter summarizes our method, the findings and what we have learned.

Work–Family Partnership: A Catalyst for Change

Work with the Xerox Corporation on this project has taken place at three sites that span the functions of the company: a product development team (PDT) in Webster, NY; a customer administration center (CAC) in Dallas, TX; and a district partnership of sales, service and business operations (SSO) in Dallas/Fort Worth, TX. At each site we interviewed managers, supervisors and line workers, conducted surveys, spent days shadowing individual employees and attended a full range of technical and staff meetings. Unlike many work–family studies, we interviewed all types of workers in the target work groups, not just those with young children or other dependant responsibilities. The focus of our data collection was on understanding the structure and culture of work, particularly those elements that make it difficult for workers to integrate work and personal life. The distinctiveness of our approach was evident in the reactions we got from people when we started asking them about their work and the particular work culture and structure of their part of the business. Invariably, they would say something to us like, 'I thought you people were supposed to be studying work and family issues, why are you asking me about work?' We found that meeting this resistance with an invitation to join us in a process of mutual inquiry helped us all to reframe these issues. Once we explained that we were taking a new approach and wanted their help in identifying systemic, practice, structural and cultural barriers to work and family integration rather than individual barriers related to particular family situations, we found people could readily identify work factors that made integration difficult regardless of family situation.

As we began to identify and understand the cultural assumptions, beliefs and norms that were clearly problematic for employees' work–family concerns it became clear that these same assumptions were also problematic for other business concerns. *A key feature of our method was that at each of the sites when we fed our initial findings back to management we emphasized this new, work-focused link between business goals and work–family integration.* The general focus of each of these feedback sessions was to highlight the connection of these issues by showing how cultural and structural barriers to work–family integration were barriers to other business goals as well, such as time to market, quality and empowerment. After these initial feedback sessions, we worked collaboratively both with management and with groups at other levels within the organization to design specific interventions to innovate work practices, to address some of these barriers to work–family integration.

The results of each of these interventions indicate that work–family *is* an effective lever to innovate work practice in ways that create a more productive, equitable, flexible workplace. Indeed, when we challenged the assumptions about work that were identified as key cultural barriers to the integration of work and family we found people able to innovate in ways that increased not only morale and flexibility, but productivity as well. For example, at the PDT site our initial cultural diagnosis revealed a work culture characterized by crisis and an individual orientation to the work. We found that although projects are organized by subsystem teams, autonomy, independence and individualism are highly valued. It is commonly accepted that the way to get ahead is through individual heroic action or solving 'high-visibility' problems. Unrealistic deadlines, or what people call 'stretch schedules', create a high-energy, crisis mentality typified by emergency meetings, often called early morning or into the evening, and a work day filled with constant interruptions as priorities change to accommodate new crisis situations. This crisis mentality is clearly problematic for work–family integration since the 'best' workers in this environment are those who can immediately put work concerns ahead of all others and respond immediately to crises at any time of the day or night.

Management was well aware of many of these aspects of the work situation. They recognized the implications for quality and efficiency and often voiced the need to move from what they called 'crisis mode' management. However, in the past their approach had been to focus on planning and process documentation, an approach that resulted in more tightly scripted behaviors and procedures but did not challenge the behaviors themselves or their underlying assumptions. Using work–family issues as a lens, however, focused attention on the *cultural* norms around crisis mode – issues such as the individualistic approach to the work, the skills that were valued and rewarded, the behaviors that were seen as evidence of competence, the norms around how one demonstrated 'caring' about the project. Moreover, using this lens we were able to show how these norms actually reinforced the crisis mentality through the reward system and tacit definition of the 'ideal worker'. Working with a group to identify work practices that were characteristic of *problem prevention* challenged the norms of prizing *problem solving* skills and strategies over the often less visible work that prevented the problems from arising in the first place. It gave people the language to talk about these 'invisible', more collaborative, less individualistic behaviors and skills as evidence of competence and led to a questioning of the organizational reward and promotion structures that 'disappear' this desirable behavior.[3]

We also challenged the 'long-hours, high-reward' aspect of the culture by working collectively with a group of software engineers in what we called the 'time experiment'. We suggested that they engage with us in a short-term experiment in which their hours at work would be constrained. Our assumption was that if hours were constrained, people would have to devise new ways of working. Interviewing and brainstorming with them about how to design this intervention led to a deeper understanding of how time is used at work. It became clear that the crisis mode of working, which implictly rewards emergency, high-energy problem solving, leads to some unproductive uses of time. Engineers continually interrupt each other to have their immediate concerns met, with no thought given to the impact their behavior is having on the whole project. Since the day is filled with interruptions, most engineers have to find time off-hours to do the 'real' work of writing codes. As a result they often come in early, stay late, come in on weekends or even in the middle of the night to get the quiet time they need to get their individual work done. While this situation is problematic both for work and family integration and for time-to-market concerns, it became clear in talking to the engineers that simply constraining time at work would not address the issue. We worked jointly with them to devise a way of separating the day into 'quiet time' and 'interactive time'. Three times a week for several hours, engineers agreed not to interrupt each other spontaneously, but to evaluate, prioritize and if possible delay their requests for help or information. This restructuring led to a clearer differentiation between unnecessary interruptions and the kind of interactions that benefit the well-being of the overall project. It gave the engineers time to work on their individual deliverables during the work day, while at the same time helping them to appreciate the significance of interactions that are essential for learning, coordination and problem prevention. This intervention led to several positive outcomes: the team experienced its first ever on-time launch of a new product; managers found they interrupted engineers less with no negative results; the team received several excellence awards for the quality of the product; and the engineers reported feeling more in control of their time and how that influenced their personal life. As one noted: 'It's not that I spend fewer hours at work – but now I can finish what I need to and don't have to take the worries home.'[4]

Using the work–family lens at the customer administration center (CAC) revealed a very different work culture and led to a different type of intervention. Unlike the PDT which has more male than female engineers, this site employs a largely female workforce doing administrative paperwork and processing. The culture is one of control, measurement and inspection. Tightly scripted procedures exist for dealing with customers and running meetings as well as billing and leasing processes. The ideal worker at this site is someone who always shows up, never has problems and does not ask for flexibility. Although an array of work–family benefits such as a compressed work week, more flexible hours and part-time work are theoretically available, managers tightly control the number of requests granted. They tend to approve only a very limited version of flexitime and, even then, only for those employees who 'deserve' it because of their past performance. Employees deal with the situation by 'jiggling the system' on an individual, *ad hoc* basis to achieve the flexibility they need, often using sick time or vacation time. The costs to the CAC are considerable in terms of unplanned absences, lack of coverage, turnover, backlash against people who take the time they need, and mistrust of an organization that claims to have benefits but makes their use so arbitrary and difficult.

We found that this pattern of behavior, which we called the 'disempowerment loop', is problematic not only for work–family integration but for other business issues as well, such as innovation and the move to empowered work teams. The culture of control leads to a very narrow definition of business need and the close monitoring of productivity fosters management caution and an emphasis on short-term results. This situation disempowers workers and teams, reinforcing existing practices and stifling innovation: managers are reluctant to relax control for fear that short-term productivity will suffer and front line workers are reluctant to take risks because they fear management will not support them.

Reflecting on these findings helped management understand why they had been having difficulty moving to empowered teams. In an effort to break this disempowerment loop, they opened up the use of work–family benefits to *all* employees, regardless of family status or manager discretion. The research team worked with a group to help set up a process whereby work teams can manage, collectively, the work–family boundaries of their members. The results have been dramatic. Nearly everyone has worked out a different schedule. The site has experienced a reported 30 per cent decrease in absenteeism, customer responsiveness has increased as times of coverage have been extended, measures of employee satisfaction have improved and divisions between employees decreased as apparent favoritism is reduced. In addition, the more general move to empowered teams has been advanced: self-managed teams that previously had little responsibility are now active participants not only in decisions about work schedules but in other business issues such as team selection and evaluation.[5]

At our third site (SSO), using a work–family lens helped identify cultural barriers to effective partnering among sales, service and business operations. Ever more ambitious sales targets, an increasingly competitive environment and the need for immediate and constant availability to customers creates a work environment at the SSO of enormous stress and pressure, which makes work and family integration difficult. We found that despite the label 'partnership', individualism is the norm and collaboration within and across the sales, service, and business operations functions is quite limited. Finger pointing and blame are common as employees in each of the functions are on their own in dealing with work problems and meeting family demands. This specialization and functional separation mean that information about customers is rarely shared and help with family issues or emergencies is not common. After interviewing, shadowing and observing members of all three functional areas, the research team suggested establishing a cross-functional team that would sell, service and support a particular product line. The expectation was that restructuring the ways the functions worked together would help work–family integration *and* would service customers more effectively. When this recommendation was made to the groups, there was quite a bit of resistance to the idea. Specialization is such a strong norm that, at first, people could not see any benefits or opportunities in operating across functions. As we brainstormed with them, however, and allowed people to surface their fears and challenge each other on the 'impossibility' of collaboration, enthusiasm for the idea started to grow. With the impetus of helping themselves as well as the business, the team began to meet, share information and work together in new and unexpected ways. Service started helping sales identify new marketing opportunities and problem sites. Through better communication with sales, service employees can now better plan for installations, removals, upgrades, and software fixes. Business operations people, by being informed about what is occurring, can better support the other functions. As the different functions began to collaborate, they found many ways that they could cover for each other and be more responsive to customers. Both men and women note that this type of teamwork is having a positive impact on their family lives. They now can count on each other for coverage and by having more complete and honest information they can plan and predict family time with greater confidence that those plans will hold. As a result of these efforts, sales in the group have increased over budget, and service to customers has improved. Significantly, these results were achieved despite downsizing and growing external competition.[6]

One of the interesting features of the intervention at the SSO is that the idea of cross-functional teams had been tried, unsuccessfully, some time before. We believe it succeeded this time because of the way in which using a work–family lens marries individual and business needs. Framing the intervention as an experiment to enhance personal as well as business goals not only unleashes enthusiasm for the project, but also determination and persistence in making it work. As one participant notes, 'there is tremendous energy now to make this thing work. I mean, I really care about this because if it succeeds, then maybe I'll be able to live a normal life and see my kids once in a while. We are going to *make* this work!'

Project Learnings

We believe this project challenges traditional organizational approaches and definitions of family-friendly organizations in a significant way. Each of the interventions described above shows how using a work–family lens is a strategic opportunity to join business concerns with the new realities of employees' lives, resulting not only in decreased employee stress around issues of work–family integration but increased productivity and effectiveness. The implication for future research and action projects related to work–family and employee stress is to move from an employee 'benefits' focus (changes to allow employees to better meet the needs of work as currently defined) to one that examines the nature of the work (changes that center on work practice innovation). This focus on the nature of work has the additional benefit of potentially addressing many of the unintended consequences of the employee benefits approach discussed here and in other chapters in this book. These include such things as the gender inequitable definition of work, commitment and time, the backlash effect of policies and programs that are only available to a subset of employees, and the career impact on these employees of using the policies. Indeed, the findings from this project suggest that work–family policies and practices that focus only on individual accommodations related to dependant care, parental leaves, sick child care, etc., while important, not only do not address these broader concerns but are quite limited in their ability to affect strategic business concerns. On the other hand, interventions that surface assumptions about such things as ideal workers, time, commitment, crisis management and empowerment have a potentially significant effect on a full range of strategic concerns, including employee stress, work–family and gender equity.

Surfacing and working with these assumptions to challenge work practices, however, is no simple task. We believe that engaging this process requires an action research approach that is truly a collaborative partnership, where organizational members are willing to walk with us through each step, to own the process, to learn together and make decisions jointly. This collaborative process has the following key features.

Surfaces Basic Assumptions about Work Practice

Using a work–family lens to surface assumptions about work practice requires engaging people in a process of reflection on aspects of the work culture and structure that make it difficult, either directly or indirectly, to integrate work and personal life. The first step in this process is to frame work and family issues as systemic issues about work rather than individual issues about family situation. This means helping people explore the work culture in ways that will surface such issues as how work is structured, what skills and behaviors are rewarded, how one demonstrates competence and commitment, how time is valued and used, and where one experiences pressures and stress. We believe this *process of reflection* is facilitated when led by someone outside the immediate work group, who can question and probe assumptions about work that are usually taken for granted. An outsider, whose presence is sanctioned by management, not only has the ability to break the usual silence around these issues and give people permission to talk about their feelings and their personal dilemmas but also is in a unique position to make the connection between individual experience and these systemic, cultural conditions. Such a person must be out of the immediate power system and be unafraid to say things that in another position might jeopardize her/his job.

Applies the Findings to a Salient Business Need

How work and family issues play out at a given site or in a given work group is a local issue, dependent on the nature of the task, the size and composition of the group and the specific pressures and resource constraints the group may be experiencing. In order to begin to design an intervention, it is important to make the connection between team members' experiences in integrating work and family and the concrete, salient business needs the group is facing. Again, we believe an outsider who can reflect the cultural implications of individuals' personal experiences can facilitate this process. The role of the outsider is to help the work group come to a *collective understanding* of the systemic implications of their individual experience and how it can be brought to bear on whatever business need the group is facing. Arriving at this shared understanding of the situation is critical to the process of designing interventions that question current work practice. We found that in talking to individuals, they could only go so far in questioning the systemic factors that determine routine work practices before they began to feel hopeless that anything could really change. But discussing these factors as a collective created a different dynamic. Individuals challenged each other's assumptions and previously unquestioned limitations on what is fixed and what can be changed and made specific suggestions on ways assumed constraints could be addressed. This not only encouraged *out-of-the-box thinking,* it also helped people believe that fundamental change might be possible.

Creates Safety and Minimizes Individual Risk

It is important in the process of designing local interventions to give voice to different perspectives and air conflicts about the findings and their implications. This means sharing and discussing the findings in a spirit of openness and collaboration where fears and concerns can be raised and new possibilities entertained. By giving people permission to talk about their feelings and their personal dilemmas in the context of redesigning work, we found that a surprising level of energy, creativity and innovative thinking gets released. However, it can be risky to suggest work practice innovations are based on difficulty with work–family integration because these issues are so rarely discussed openly. Difficulty with work and family integration is usually assumed to be an individual problem, related to a problematic family situation. Raising these issues may be difficult for people who fear they will be branded as less committed or dependable if they acknowledge these difficulties. By the same token, managers, who are used to seeing these issues as zero-sum, where gains for the family mean productivity loss for the business (see Lewis and Taylor, Chapter 9), may fear they will bear all the risks of innovation.

Although our findings indicate that these fears of productivity loss are unfounded, we believe that collaboration and *sharing the risks* across levels of hierarchy are important aspects of the process. In concrete terms, this means getting some sign from upper levels of management that they are willing to suspend, at least temporarily, some of the standard operating procedures that have been identified in the work groups as barriers both to work–family integration and to productivity. This sign from upper management is another critical component of the process as it helps people believe that change at the cultural level is possible and protects individual managers from bearing all the risks of innovation. At our sites, these signs took different forms. At one site it was the suspension of a complex operations review process; at another it was the suspension of work rules that narrowly defined how customer needs could be met and the granting of a grace period to accommodate possible short-term productivity losses; at the third site it was the suspension of rules about how functions relate to one another. The point is, for this type of intervention to work, people need concrete evidence that they are *truly empowered* to control some of the conditions that affect their own productivity and managers need some assurance that they will not be penalized for relinquishing this control.

Uses Collaboration at All Levels to Design Solutions

Using a work–family lens to promote organizational change requires a process of reflection that raises some difficult and emotional issues for people. We found that assumptions about work that drive organizational practices and norms touch core beliefs about society, success, the place of work and family in our lives and even gender roles. At each phase of the project we encountered *resistance* to engaging in this deeper process of reflection. We met resistance to connecting work and business issues with family concerns, to the cultural diagnoses offered, and to the pilot projects we proposed. We found that resistance – whether from organization or research team members – almost always meant we were on to something and it was important to acknowledge and engage with this resistance collaboratively rather than trying to work around it. Working *with* this type of resistance means listening and learning from people's objections, incorporating these concerns or new ideas and working together to establish a mutual agenda. This process of learning together and exploring possibilities led to creative options none of us had foreseen.

Although this collaborative approach of learning together was the greatest source of energy for the project, ironically it was itself also the greatest source of resistance. At each phase of the project we were pushed to act more like consultants – to come up with solutions, action items or a 'six-step' plan. Offering collaboration in place of 'expert' advice was often met with anger and frustration and a sense that this process was taking too long. We, too, often felt ambivalent about our role and at times nearly succumbed to the temptation to shorten the process by simply telling them what to do. Once engaged, however, we found that the process of collaboration yielded work practice innovations that were implemented quickly and efficiently. We believe that this type of collaboration is key to the outcomes achieved. It is not a process that can be short-changed but instead is a methodology that depends on something we have come to call 'fluid expertise': trust, openness and a true willingness to learn from and be influenced by each other.

Ensures Mutual Benefits Are Sustained

Because family issues are so rarely connected to broader business goals there is a danger that once new work practices become routinized, benefits to the family might recede in importance or lapse altogether. Since the success of the interventions depends on capturing the synergy between individual and business goals, this lapse would seriously undermine the potential for continuous learning and improvement. Therefore, as work practice innovations become routinized, it is important to continue to keep the double agenda on the table and ensure that benefits continue to accrue to employees and their families as well as the organization. This means that at all levels, the organization and its employees must learn how to translate the beneficial effects of changes at work into benefits for personal and family life, or else individual energy that is unleashed will dissipate and lead to cynicism.

Passes On Process Not Product

One way to keep this mutual agenda on the table is to focus on the process, rather than on specific work innovations that are developed by work groups. We found that as people reflect on how business needs were met in the different sites, there is a tendency to want to pass on to other teams the *outcomes* of the process, such as quiet time or cross-functional teams, *rather than the process itself.* The danger in consolidating the learning in this way is that it may undermine the synergy that comes from marrying individual and business goals. Indeed, we found that it is the *process* of looking at work through a work–family lens and reflecting on the way that group members' personal experiences can be brought to bear on business problems that encourages innovative solutions to local business needs. The energy to implement these solutions, and to persist in working out the inevitable glitches and problems that arise, comes from understanding how collective success can translate into personal benefits. Exporting the innovation alone, short-changes this process and seriously undermines its chances for success.

Summary

Success in using this approach depends on encompassing each of the six features described above: using a work–family lens to surface basic assumptions about work practices, applying these findings to local business needs, sharing the risks of innovation across levels of hierarchy, using a collaborative approach, realizing mutual benefits and focusing on the process not the product. Achieving mutual benefits depends on *local* knowledge, participation and expertise and results in innovations unique to each team. This is not a process that can be short-changed. Rather, it is a process of arriving at shared understandings and collective action through listening, reflection and mutual learning. Our findings indicate that this approach is a strategic opportunity to achieve a more productive, equitable, flexible workplace, one that benefits men, women, business, community and society.

The project described here took place within a large international firm headquartered in the US. Further action research is needed to explore the applicability of this approach in other contexts. However, we believe these generic principles can be adapted and made applicable to many different kinds of organizations – large corporations and small businesses, philanthropic organizations, small public agencies and even large government bureaucracies. The important condition will be that the partners in the organization recognize that current practices are problematic for achieving the goals of gender equity and work–family integration and be willing to join in a process of mutual inquiry, exploration and action-oriented interventions to address these problems.

Conclusion and Discussion

The collaborative interactive action research study reported here was a pilot study with encouraging results. Our conclusion is that using work–family as a catalyst for change can result in work practice innovations that enhance both business and employee goals. *Indeed, the key finding from this project is that work and family goals need not be adversarial but are potentially synergistic.* At each of our sites the work practice innovations that groups designed not only facilitated members' work and family integration but had positive effects on bottom line issues such as effectiveness, productivity and customer satisfaction.

As a pilot, financial support for this project was shared between the Ford Foundation and the actual corporations involved. However, as corporations like Xerox begin to recognize the bottom line benefits of a synergistic approach to work and family, interest has developed in taking over the financial responsibility for extending the process to different parts of the company.

And already, the dissemination of findings from this project is creating interest in other organizations who are findings ways – with little or no foundation support – to be involved in a similar process.

On a less optimistic note, we must add that despite these initial successes, it is not easy to institutionalize this synergistic approach and spread the learnings throughout the corporation. Current organizational structures and norms as well as formal and informal practices tend to reinforce work and family spheres as adversarial and undermine efforts to reframe them as synergistic. The fears and apprehensions that were noted above as a key part of the process – fears about short-term productivity loss, fear of bearing the risks of innovation, apprehension about allowing a collective approach to integrating work and family through changes in work practice – do not disappear as the result of one intervention but surface over and over again. Cultural beliefs about gender roles, the definition of the 'ideal worker', assumptions about how one demonstrates commitment to work, and assumptions about the necessity of keeping work and personal life separate, are so entrenched they threaten to overwhelm efforts to change. As Maureen Harvey, a member of the research team who has worked for many years in organizational development, constantly reminds us, challenging the organizational manifestations of these cultural beliefs is no easy task. The possibility, indeed the likelihood that such challenges will dissipate, be coopted or be subverted is to be expected. As she and others (Harquail, 1995) suggest, challenging such deeply held cultural assumptions requires a strategy of 'small wins' (Weick, 1984) and a determination to share 'success stories' (see Phyllis Raabe, Chapter 10 in this book).

We believe that taking on this challenge is worthwhile because of the potentially significant benefits of using this approach. The significance lies in its ability to go beyond the limitations of traditional family-friendly approaches in order to address some of the complex societal issues involved in the current separation of work and family. Focusing on work practices provides a vehicle for addressing the ways in which cultural assumptions about the separation of work and family are reflected in organizational structures and norms. Challenging these assumptions with concrete changes in business practices that yield positive results suggests that organizations have much to gain by designing work with integrated people in mind. Changes of this type advance the goal of gender equity by making it possible for both men and women to integrate their work and personal lives, thus diminishing work–family integration as a 'women's issue' and freeing men to be more involved in family and community. This has the potential to address some of the broader social issues described earlier, such as the crisis in care and civic disengagement, by creating work environments that permit greater family and community involvement.

Despite this potential, using this synergistic approach does not guarantee that progress on these larger issues will be made. Even if changes in work practice free men and women to be more involved in family and community, what assurance is there that they will spend their time in these activities?

Even if work organizations change so as to make life more gender equitable within them, how can they affect the gendered division of labor in the family and the rest of society? These are important questions that require exploration and further study. We have hope that the 'small wins' reported from this study will spawn future work, exploring these issues more fully.

As authors of other chapters in this book note, the problems related to the artificial separation of work and family are extensive, destructive and often self-reinforcing. We believe using work–family issues as a catalyst to innovate work practice can be an important leverage for change with potentially positive – and far-reaching – effects. Furthermore, we believe that although work and family are inextricably linked, it makes sense to start this type of change process in organizations. People spend a lot of their lives at work, and work organizations are good leverage points for broader social change because they affect what goes on in families, in education and in the community. Large, international corporations are particularly important in this way. While they cannot be held responsible for all the ills of society, they do have a very strong influence, particularly in today's increasingly globalized economy. In fact, the way international corporations deal with work–family issues now may have important effects in other parts of the world where they are represented. If they do not want to export the problems arising from the current way of looking at work and work–family integration, they need to rethink some of the issues discussed in this chapter. For those of us who have been toiling in the field of work–family integration for years, we believe the time is ripe to begin working not only with these large international corporations, but with all types of work organizations to accumulate increasing numbers of 'small wins'. This will require tenacity, a belief in the potential benefits of this approach, a willingness to use a different, more collaborative way of organizing the work of action research teams, and – above all – perseverance to try, try and try again, despite the difficulties and inherent resistance to this synergistic approach to integrating work and family.

Notes

The authors wish to acknowledge the helpful comments and suggestions of Lotte Bailyn.

The project was funded by Ford Foundation grant 910–1036. The action research team at Xerox included Lotte Bailyn, Deborah Kolb, Susan Eaton, Joyce Fletcher, Maureen Harvey, Robin Johnson, Leslie Perlow, and the consultant to the project, Rhona Rapoport. Although this chapter is authored by only two members of the research team, the fieldwork, the interventions and the development of the ideas and analysis of the findings presented here are the result of a collaborative process in which each team member participated. For a complete report on the project see Bailyn et al., 1996.

1 The other projects included one conducted by the Families and Work Institute at the Corning Corporation and one conducted by Artemis Consulting at the Tandem Corporation.

2 Gender equity is a complex concept. In general we use it to refer to a fair allocation of opportunities and constraints between men and women. To achieve this, different areas of people's lives need to be revised both separately and in relation to each other (see Rapoport and Rapoport, 1975). Work, family and community relations are all involved. To many in the business world, gender equity means pay equity between women and men, or getting women to the

top, or numbers that need to be defended against the critics. These are all part of what we mean, but not the essence. Gender equity concerns men *and* women. This is *not* a woman's issue. Men's overidentification with work as a source of self-esteem feeds gender inequity just as does the presumption that women are responsible for family and community. In a gender equitable society neither sex would depend for its sense of worth on only one sphere. In such a society, social institutions would value and support *both* domestic and economic enterprise. A work–family benefits approach to integrating the two spheres does this.

3 See Fletcher (1994) for an analysis of the activities and work practices associated with a problem prevention orientation to work.

4 See Perlow (1995) for an in-depth description of this intervention and an analysis of ways time is used at work.

5 For a more detailed description of this intervention and an analysis of how issues of control and power affect empowerment see Johnson (1994).

6 This work at the SSO was done primarily by Susan Eaton and Maureen Harvey.

References

Bailyn, Lotte (1993) *Breaking the Mold: Women, Men and Time in the New Corporate World.* New York: Free Press.

Bailyn, Lotte (1995) 'The impact of corporate culture on work–family integration'. Paper presented at the Fifth International Stein Conference, Drexel University, Philadelphia, November.

Bailyn, L., Rapoport, R., Kolb, D. and Fletcher, J. (1996) *Re-linking Work and Family: A Catalyst for Change*. Working paper 3892–96. Cambridge, MA: MIT Sloan School of Management.

Burggraf, Shirley, (1995) 'The feminine economy and the economics of work and family in the 21st century'. Paper presented at the Bunting Institute Fellows Program, Radcliffe College, Cambridge, MA, January.

Fletcher, J.K. (1994) 'Toward a theory of relational practice in organizations: A feminist reconstruction of "real work". Doctoral dissertation, Boston University.

Fletcher, Joyce (1995) 'The work–family business imperative: Where's the beef?'. Presented at Symposium entitled 'Can we have it all? Examining the interdependence of work and family', Academy of Management Meeting, Vancouver, BC, August.

Fletcher, Joyce and Bailyn, Lotte (1996) 'Challenging the last boundary', in M.B. Arthur and D.M. Rousseau (eds), *Boundaryless Careers*. Oxford University Press.

Friedlander, Frank (1994) 'Toward whole systems and whole people', *Organization*. 1: 59–64.

Friedman, Dana and Galinsky, Ellen (1992) 'Work and family issues: A legitimate business concern', in S. Zedeck (ed.), *Work, Families and Organizations*. San Francisco: Jossey-Bass.

Hamburg, David (1992) *Today's Children: Creating a Future for a Generation in Crisis*. New York: Random House.

Harquail, Celia Virginia (1995) 'Group advocacy: Organizational voice on behalf of a constituency'. Paper presented at the Academy of Management, Vancouver, BC, August.

Hartmann, Heidi, (1995) 'Economic transformation in the U. S.: Key questions for the 21st century'. Talk given at the Radcliffe Public Policy Institute Conference entitled 'The new economic equation: Redefining the economy, the workplace and the family', Radcliffe College, Cambridge, MA, May.

Hochschild, Arlie (1990) *The Second Shift: Working Couples and the Revolution at Home.* New York: Avon Books.

Hochschild, Arlie (forthcoming) 'Traditional, post-modern, cold-modern and warm-modern: Contending ideals of care', in *Care and the Modern State*. Utrecht, Holland.

Johnson, R. (1994) 'Where's the power in empowerment? Definition, difference and dilemmas of empowerment in the context of work–family management'. Doctoral dissertation, Harvard University, Cambridge, MA.

Kanter, Rosabeth Moss (1995) *World Class: Thriving Locally in the Global Economy*. Simon and Schuster.

Minow, Martha (1995) 'How have economic changes affected family life?'. Talk given at the Radcliffe Public Policy Institute Conference entitled 'The new economic equation: Redefining the economy, the workplace and the family', Radcliffe College, Cambridge, MA, May.

Perlow, L. (1995) 'The time famine: An unintended consequence of how time is used at work'. Doctoral dissertation, MIT, Cambridge, MA.

Putnam, Robert (1995) 'Bowling alone: America's declining social capital', *Journal of Democracy*, 6(1): 65–78.

Rapoport, Robert and Rapoport, Rhona (1975) 'Men, women and equity', *The Family Coordinator*, October.

Schor, Juliet (1991) *The Overworked American.* New York: Basic Books.

Schor, Juliet (1995). 'Brave new world: Patterns of work, family, time and consumption for the 21st century'. Paper presented at the Work/Life Issues Conference, Northeastern University, World Trade Center, Boston, MA, March.

Weick, Karl (1984) 'Small wins: Redefining the scale of social problems', *American Psychologist*, 39: 29–31.

CONCLUSION

12

Rethinking Employment: A Partnership Approach

Suzan Lewis and Jeremy Lewis

This book has considered the need for changes in organizational practices and values to reflect: the profound structural and social changes which have taken place in families and organizations; shifting gender expectations; the changing composition of the workforce; market and workplace trends, and the revolution in the nature of work, in the context of which the beliefs about the separation of work and family spheres are no longer tenable. It has addressed the question of how to achieve cultural change in organizations: that is, how to encourage the development of values and beliefs about the relationship between work and family which are congruent with the experiences and needs of today's workforce. The authors have considered issues of work–family reconciliation on a number of different levels. These range from the formality of law and of workplace policies to the informal flexibilities and attitudes which contribute to the workplace culture. Issues of reconciliation have also been discussed from a number of differing perspectives – ranging from the needs of today's workforce to the interests of business and the need to preserve competitiveness. Combining these considerations and the experience of case studies where principles associated with work–family reconciliation and a collaborative partnership approach have been implemented at a local level, evidence is emerging that win–win solutions are attainable.

The Synergy Case

Employee Interests

The contributors have argued that from the perspective of both business and today's workforce there is a good case for fundamental organizational change in order to facilitate reconciliation between work and life beyond work. From the perspective of the employee much has been written in the work family literature about the need for support for caring responsibilities. This remains an issue, particularly in societies without an infrastructure of publicly provided care or with an ideology of public responsibility for families. But this is not the only family need of employees and it is important to widen the focus. While the needs of those who seek to combine career development with caring responsibilities may be very different from those whose primary concern is to combine family care with holding down a job in order to earn a living wage, certain needs are widely shared. Employees have basic needs for a secure and adequate income, for satisfying non-stressful work and for time to achieve a balanced life. In the current context uncertainty about job security is a major source of stress for individuals and families, and in some forms of work this exacerbates the need to demonstrate commitment by over involvement in work and reduced time for family or other commitments. Employees also need flexibility and autonomy to empower them to balance their commitments in work and beyond. A major concern throughout the book is the growing casualization of work in which flexibility is defined from the employers' perspective in terms of the ease with which they can hire and fire. This takes no account of employees' needs or indeed of wider social needs for healthy families and communities (Lewis and Cooper, 1996). We need to know more about the impact of new ways of working, including contract work and other forms of insecure employment, on families and on morale and productivity in the workplace, in order to be able to assess the real costs and consequences.

Business Interests

The narrow, one-sided construction of flexibility may meet some short-term business needs in social systems which encourage employers to treat part of the workforce as peripheral to the organization, with poor conditions and few rights. It is unlikely to meet long-term needs for a stable and coordinated workforce. In the context of global competitiveness, organizational restructuring, the drive for quality, automation and the demise of many routinized jobs, contemporary organizations rely increasingly on a workforce which is unstressed and optimally focused, productive and creative. This necessitates a recognition of employees' needs as whole people. While a growing number of organizations have recognized that it is in their interest to adopt policies which might be regarded as family-friendly and this has sometimes helped some people to manage work and family, these policies have not brought about fundamental changes in organizational behaviours or values. This is because the policies continue to be widely regarded as benefits, conferred upon women or at best parents, and are therefore perceived as being marginal to the organization, rather than a central business concern. Attention to business interests has often focused upon specific business goals such as the retention of women employees or reduction of absenteeism. Without detracting from the significance of these concerns, they can be viewed within the context of a broader approach which challenges the appropriateness of traditional work structures for contemporary workers and their organizations. This involves deconstructing taken for granted notions of the ideal employee, 'standard' jobs and careers, the questioning of tried and tested ways of doing things, and different ways of looking at and understanding organizations. The wider approach, in effect, involves rethinking employment to meet the work–family challenge.

We have seen that there is now a developing body of evidence to suggest that businesses and employees can both reap rich rewards from undertaking this process. Some evidence has been presented that systemic changes, based on an understanding of local needs developed after a process involving wide participation, have the potential to lead to business success for those who are willing to take perceived risks and try out innovative new practices. This is because jobs can be designed around rational systems rather than tradition or custom, and because jobs are performed in ways which fit in with employees' needs as whole people. Indeed while the benefits approach to family-friendly policies is perceived as incurring costs, albeit ones that can usually be offset by their benefits, this process of rethinking employment can be viewed more directly as part of a competitive strategy for improving the performance of the employing organization while also meeting the interests of the modern workforce.

Processes for Achieving Change

Understanding the process of achieving change is important for the success of any innovation. Essentials of the process for rethinking employment emphasized throughout the book include dialogue, collaboration and partnership. Partnerships provide not only a sharing of responsibility and resources, but also multiple perspectives and ideas in reframing issues and exploring solutions. There are a number of different partnerships both within and beyond organizations which can contribute to the process of change.

Partnerships in the Workplace

Within the workplace a partnership approach can help all sides to see the need for and importance of mutual flexibility, that is willingness to give and take on both sides, which several contributors argue is the key to the success of new approaches to work. Partners include unions and other employee groups, work teams and management. In addition the informal collaboration which often takes place between colleagues and is essential to informal flexibility and latitude is highlighted, and on a more formal level the role which an outside researcher or consultant can play as a partner and a catalyst for change is discussed. The sharing of issues in the collaborative process appears to be important not only for convincing management of necessary changes, but also to involve colleagues in designing ways of working together as teams, and to avoid backlash from those who may perceive others with family commitments as receiving more favourable treatment. The partnership approach makes it incumbent on employees to find ways of being flexible by, for example, working longer hours at genuine times of specific needs, or being available by telephone at certain times, and for employers to be flexible about where and when work is accomplished, although in both cases this may be within certain parameters. It implies rights and responsibilities on both sides. This approach suggests a need for a collaborative rather than a confrontational model of employee relations in order to reach agreement about the types of flexibility which will simultaneously meet the needs of employers and employees. The ease with which this can be achieved may vary across national contexts. Research is needed to compare the process in cultures where, for example, industrial democracy tends to take the form of collaboration such as through workers on the board or where there is a tradition of greater emphasis on collective bargaining, to consider how best to adapt the partnership model in different contexts.

It is also important to look at the nature of the partnerships involved in bringing about change, and to consider who is currently excluded. As we are working at the work–family interface, we should consider involving family members in discussions about change. One example suggested in the book is the need to consult spouses about relocation decisions. There are clearly many other organizational decisions which impact on families, and since family stress spills over to affect work, it is logical even within the business argument that family members should be given the opportunity to have a voice. It may also be useful to further extend the stakeholders involved in decision making. For example, organizational decision making inevitably takes account of the needs of clients, customers and investors and yet they are rarely consulted about changes affecting the workforce in matters of reconciliation of work and family. Assumptions are often made about how they would react, which may or may not be well founded. It may be important to consult these groups about the perceived impact of innovations, or even to involve them in consultations at an earlier stage. And everyone, in the roles of consumers or other stakeholders, can bring an influence to bear on organizations by communicating the valuing of ways of working which are likely to benefit the wider society. The ethical investment movement, for example, could be a force for change.

The Role of Public Policy

The importance of a partnership approach extends beyond the organizational context, to take in socio-political and legislative contexts. Public policy makers at local, national and, at least in the case of the European Union, international levels also have important roles to play as partners responsible for sustaining an environment conducive to work–family reconciliation. Their roles include providing incentives to employers to rethink employment, or disincentives to employer practices which do not permit reconciliation, as well as taking responsibility for measures which are essential for family welfare and therefore beyond the limits of corporate responsibility.

Public policy makers also have a role to play in influencing organizations towards rethinking employment practices. While we would argue that in many cases a win–win solution can be achieved in relation to work–family reconciliation, some employers may be reluctant to accept change in the absence of legislation. There are a number of rational and irrational reasons for employer reluctance. It may be because of fear of change, because of perceived or actual costs, or because of an existing legal framework which perpetuates a perception of atypical workers as peripheral or simply as a cheap and dispensable source of labour rather than as a valuable business asset. Further the business case may appear less persuasive in industries which do not rely to a great extent on human resources, or possibly in small businesses. We also need to recognize that many of the issues involved in bringing about change are issues about power – about an equitable distribution of power and about recognizing the deeply gendered nature of workplaces. The business case is a rational one. However, organizational decision making is often not rational, depending more on the views of dominant elites than on reason (Pettigrew, 1973). Resistance is often as much about threats to power as it is due to beliefs that traditional ways of working are most effective. The latter can be demonstrated to be false; the former may be more difficult to overcome. A double or many pronged approach may therefore be necessary to bring about changes in organizational behaviour and values.

Against this background, public policy makers have an important role to play on several levels. From a negative perspective, by conferring the same employment rights upon those engaged in atypical forms of work as are enjoyed by other workers, the law can counter a perception of such workers as peripheral to the business interest. The law can also play a role in laying down a background framework of rights such as a right to equal pay, minimum leave requirements and control over working time. Further change towards work–family reconciliation, for example in permitting paid leaves, can also be regarded as an important part of the fostering of an environment in which individuals are offered the opportunity to choose how to shape their lives and are given a range of healthy life options. Beyond this it may be that the law can play a role in requiring employers to focus upon the issue of the way work is organized and to grasp the nettle of change. In the United Kingdom, for example, indirect discrimination law and, to a lesser extent, health and safety regulation may provide this stimulus.

It is important to consider what are the limits of corporate responsibility and who should bear any costs of, for example, family care, along with families themselves. Family welfare is primarily the responsibility of government and not employers, albeit employers may have a partnership role to play. To the extent that reform is perceived as a benefit to society as a whole it may be unfair to expect employers to take responsibility. We would argue that the provision of basic rights to leaves for family reasons and an infrastructure of quality care are primarily a public responsibility in an ideal world. However government responsibility for meeting these costs will be difficult to achieve in contexts where an ideology of individual and family responsibility, and of limited public expenditure for support in families, is strong, (although in the case of the UK, European policy and legislation have a potentially strong role to play in bringing about changes). Here again it is helpful to focus upon the role of partnerships. A number of interesting partnerships between companies and local government have been described in the book. Given different cultural norms and ideologies, the appropriate role of local and national government is likely to continue to vary in different contexts.

Gender Equity in the Family

In order to successfully pursue work–family reconciliation it is also necessary to pay attention to the nature of partnerships at the family level, irrespective of how families are structured, and particularly to issues of gender equity in the family. While the bulk of the responsibility for unpaid work is assumed by women there is a danger that policies geared towards work–family reconciliation will be marginalized. Indeed some of the benefits to be gained from reconciliation, notably a less stressed and more highly motivated and focused workforce, may be undermined where there continues to be overload due to an uneven distribution of non-work responsibilities.

Gender equity in the family does not necessarily imply equal inputs, but inputs that are regarded as fair by all concerned (Rapoport and Rapoport, 1974). What is important is that perceived equity is based on a full range of choices. For example, dual-earner couples often justify the woman's greater responsibility for family work by the man's greater earning power and hence economic contributions to the family (Brannen and Moss, 1987). However, if, for example, the woman's lower earnings are due to the lower valuing of the type of work women do, or to their broken career patterns, this is not based on a full range of options. The option for both partners to contribute equally to the breadwinner and caring roles is not available. Within a wider frame of options families would be able to make a genuine choice of how to distribute paid and unpaid work, and it is likely that diverse patterns would emerge.

To what extent can workplace change and/or social policy enhance gender equity in families? There is evidence that many men do wish to spend more time with their families, and in some cases are prepared to adapt their working lives considerably to do so (New Ways to Work, 1995), although others are constrained by organizational cultures, the demands of particular jobs and wider social expectations. Changes in the ways in which work is organized, based on an acceptance of the interdependence of work and family for all employees, have the potential to empower men and women to make time for family as well as other commitments. Will this be enough to bring about changes at the family level? Time alone may not be sufficient to bring about behavioural and attitudinal changes within all families. The impact of organizational change may be moderated by gender ideology and identity (Lee, 1983; Mederer, 1993), relative earnings and hence power and resources of family members (Hertz, 1992; Brannen and Moss, 1987) and the timing and compatibility of family members' work schedules (Brayfield, 1995). To date, most research examining the impact of organizational change processes and outcomes in relation to work and family has tended to focus on outcomes in only one of these interrelated social systems, the workplace. To some extent this may be due to a reluctance of researchers working in the public domain to move towards examining the private world of the family. Nevertheless, an understanding of the ways in which family members construct and reconstruct their roles and work towards gender equity is essential for a full understanding of the potential for work–family reconciliation.

Any wider attempts to engineer a shift in responsibilities in the family might be expected to provoke opposition from those who regard this as unethical and intrusive. While the state does take an interest in family matters where a genuine need is perceived (prevention of child abuse being an extreme example), clearly this is an area in which a sensitive approach is required in order to respect the boundaries of what is culturally acceptable. As with organizational interventions, it is essential to collaborate and consult with willing participants who want to find a way to solve perceived problems. The creation of the Child Support Agency in Britain in an attempt to ensure that absent fathers take financial responsibility for children has met with substantial opposition on all sides, illustrating the resistance that will be engendered by forms of intervention which do not take account of user perspectives. Examples do however exist of attempts to influence the balance of responsibilities in the home through approaches which respect individual choice. Sweden provides a good example of public initiatives to bring about change. Having provided opportunities for fathers to take leaves to be involved in childcare it is now recognized that this is not enough to bring about fundamental change in families, as men are often constrained by informal and gendered organizational cultures from taking these leaves (Haas and Hwang, 1995). New systems of non-transferable parental leave have been introduced to try to overcome this. Fathers can still decline to take leave, but if so, the overall amount of parental leave available to families is limited accordingly.

The Role of Research

Researchers also have a partnership role. Research can contribute to change in a number of ways. It can play a useful role in examining the impact of current workplace policies and practices and in exposing deep-seated biases as counterproductive. However, research findings are seldom translated into organizational change in a systematic way. In order to bridge the gap between research and practice a more proactive approach may be necessary, as illustrated in the action research project discussed in Chapter 11.

Research also has a role to play in contributing to change beyond the workplace. To the extent that there is to be a social role in encouraging particular ways of working and in encouraging shifts of responsibility in the family it is particularly important that research fully explores the impact on families of current and new ways of working. What is the impact of job insecurity, of time famine, of teleworking and other forms of work which intrude into the home, on children, elders and others? There is already some evidence that parents' cognitive preoccupation and unavailability can impact on parent–child relationships (Barling, 1994). We need to know what are the long term social costs. The costs for governments and for employers, are a vital part of the information needed to make decisions based on social ideology and on the business case. Research findings may influence processes of social change directly or indirectly. For example, research findings on business and social trends, including women's working patterns, have been taken into account in recent UK court decisions based on discrimination law. However, a more proactive approach may again be necessary to ensure that research is translated into practice. A major challenge for research is to consider how action research can be developed not only in but also beyond the workplace.

Conditions for Change

Several of the contributors to this book have pointed out that the workplace revolution to meet the work–family challenge is currently stalled. Some evidence has been presented to show that it can be moved forward in specific local contexts. To make further progress it is necessary to clarify the conditions under which productive partnerships can emerge or be created. One relevant factor for consideration appears to be timing – building on windows of opportunity and readiness, even in otherwise hostile contexts. For example, the demographic argument in the late 1980s provided an opportunity to develop the business case for policies to recruit and retain women employees. Similarly, current trends of restructuring and reengineering can be constructed as a window of opportunity for introducing work–family issues into a process which involves the deconstruction of organizational myths about traditional ways of working. Legislative milestones and the acceptance of certain basic rights can also create a window of opportunity for social policy development to support reconciliation. At the workplace level the question of readiness also emerges. We need to know what are the conditions under which organizations will be prepared to look at work–family issues as central to business goals. Does it require a certain level of awareness of work–family issues and motivation to find win–win solutions, or even the pre-existence of work–family 'benefits'? These are important questions for research, to indicate the route to developing partnerships and bringing about change.

Criteria of Success

While the process of reconstruction must be carried out with regard to specific contexts, the communication of case studies is essential to provide evidence of the effectiveness of the process. It is important to communicate the success stories. However, clear criteria of success are needed lest we communicate only limited changes. The labelling of companies as 'family-friendly' on the basis of policies, not practice or value change, and often in a business context which is inherently unfriendly to families, demonstrates the danger of uncritical assumptions of success based on low expectations. A challenge for researchers, managers and human resource professionals, as well as other partners, is to clarify the ultimate criteria we should be using to signal fundamental cultural change. As several authors in this book remind us, the process is likely to be an ongoing and dynamic one, with little opportunity for complacency. As the social and business environment evolves, so will the process of rethinking employment to sustain compatibility with the needs of all stakeholders.

References

Barling, J. (1994) 'Work and Family: In search of more effective workplace interventions', in C. Cooper and D. Rousseau (eds), *Trends in Organisational Behaviour*, vol. 1. Chichester: Wiley.

Brannen, J. and Moss, P. (1987) 'Dual earner households: Women's financial contributions after the birth of a first child', in J. Brannen and G. Wilson (eds), *Give and Take in Families: Studies in Resource Distribution*. London: Unwin Hyman.

Brayfield, A. (1995) 'Juggling jobs and kids: The impact of employment schedules on fathers' caring for children', *Journal of Marriage and the Family*, 57: 321–32.

Haas, L. and Hwang, P. (1995) 'Company culture and men's usage of family leave benefits in Sweden', *Family Relations*, 44: 28–36.

Hertz, R. (1992) 'Financial affairs: Money and authority in dual earner marriages', in S. Lewis, D.N. Izraeli and H. Hootsmans (eds), *Dual Earner Families: International Perspectives*. London: Sage.

Lee, R.A. (1983) 'Flexitime and conjugal roles', *Journal of Occupational Behaviour*, 4: 297–315.

Lewis, S. and Cooper, C.L. (1996) 'Balancing the work home interface: A European perspective', *Human Resource Management Review*, 5(4): 289–305.

Mederer, H. (1993) 'Division of labour in two earner homes: Task accomplishment versus household management as critical variables in perceptions about family work', *Journal of Marriage and the Family*, 55: 133–45.

New Ways to Work (1995) *Balanced Lives: Changing Work Patterns for Men*. London: New Ways to Work.

Pettigrew, A. (1973) *The Politics of Organisational Decision Making*. London: Tavistock.

Rapoport, R. and Rapoport, R. (1974) 'Men, women and equity', *Family Coordinator*, 171: 435–59.

Index